THE HR SCORECARD

Linking PEOPLE, STRATEGY, and PERFORMANCE

**BRIAN E. BECKER
MARK A. HUSELID
DAVE ULRICH**

HARVARD BUSINESS SCHOOL PRESS
BOSTON, MASSACHUSETTS

Library of Congress Cataloging-in-Publication Data

Becker, Brian E.
    The HR scorecard : linking people, strategy, and performance / Brian E. Becker,
Mark A. Huselid, David Ulrich.
      p. cm.
    Includes bibliographical references and index.
    ISBN 1-57851-136-4
    1. Organizational effectiveness—Evaluation. 2. Industrial management. 3.
Human capital. I. Huselid, Mark A., 1961- II. Ulrich, David, 1953- III. Title.
HD58.9.B43 2001
658.3—dc21

00-053945

The paper used in this publication meets the requirements of the American
National Standard for Permanence of Paper for Publications and Documents in
Libraries and Archives Z39.48-1992

To Mary, Emily, and Ethan

To Rebecca, Rachel, and Robert

To Wendy, Carrie, Monika, and Michael

Contents

Foreword

BOB KAPLAN AND I FIRST INTRODUCED the idea of a Balanced Scorecard in a 1992 *Harvard Business Review* article.[1] Since that time we, and our consulting organization, have had the opportunity to design Balanced Scorecards in more than 200 companies. These designs always start with the same simple question, What is your strategy? This experience has given us far reaching insights into the ways that executive teams think about strategy and their organizations. The typical executive team has a high degree of awareness and consensus around the financial strategy, as well as the priorities for operational process improvement. They typically have limited consensus around customer strategies (i.e., who are the target segments, what is the value proposition), although this has improved in recent years. But the worst grades are reserved for their understanding of strategies for developing human capital. There is little consensus, little creativity, and no real framework for thinking about the subject. Worse yet, we have seen little improvement in this over the past eight years.

The greatest concern here is that, in the New Economy, human capital is the foundation of value creation. (Various studies show that up to 85 percent of a corporation's value is based on intangible assets.) This presents an interesting dilemma: The asset that is most important is the least understood, least prone to measurement, and, hence, least susceptible to management. Clearly, we are at a watershed. As a new economic model ripples through the economy, a new science of management is needed. In an economy where value creation is dominated by human capital and other intangible assets, there can be no better starting point for this new science than with the measurement of human resource strategies. *The HR Scorecard* does just that and provides an important step forward in our ability to manage strategy.

Several facets of the book will make lasting contributions. First, the development of *causal models*, which show the relationship of HR value drivers with business outcomes, takes the Balanced Scorecard to the next level of sophistication. Second, the research into the drivers of high-performance HR organizations gives executives a framework with which to build strategies for human capital growth. And finally, their insights into the competencies required by HR professionals lay the groundwork for an organization that can deliver on the promise of its measurement systems.

We can't manage something that we can't describe. Measurement is the language used to describe organizations and strategy. Through the frameworks, research, and cases encompassed in this work, the authors have given us a new generation of tools to measure and manage the creation of human capital. *The HR Scorecard* should be essential reading for the New Economy manager.

DAVID NORTON
BOSTON, MASSACHUSETTS

Preface and Acknowledgments

PROFESSIONALS IN HUMAN RESOURCES are increasingly challenged to take a more strategic perspective regarding their role in the organization. We find that as HR professionals respond to this challenge, measuring HR's performance and its contribution to the firm's performance consistently emerges as a key theme. This should come as no surprise. The last decade has been highlighted by an ever-increasing appreciation for the value of intangible assets and the associated trend toward strategic performance measurement systems such as Robert Kaplan and David Norton's Balanced Scorecard. New opportunities for HR professionals, new demands for HR's accountability, and new perspectives on measuring organizational performance have all converged. This book is intended to guide HR managers through the challenge of these converging trends. It is based on more than a decade of academic research on the HR-firm performance relationship and grounded by our consulting work in a wide range of companies. The result is a new approach to managing a firm's "HR architecture" (the sum of the HR function, the broader HR system, and resulting employee behaviors) as a strategic asset, as well as measuring its contribution to the firm's performance.

Our work (some would call it an obsession) in measuring HR began with our efforts to try to understand whether, and if so by how much, this broader HR architecture contributes to firm success. Over the last decade we have collected data on HR management quality from nearly 3,000 firms and have matched these data with employee turnover, productivity, stock market, and accounting performance measures. We've visited these companies, followed their performance over time, written cases about them, and subjected them to detailed statistical analyses. All of these activities have led us to the same broad conclusion: Firms with more effective HR management systems consistently outperform their peers.

Yet, in our teaching and consulting work with executives we consistently confronted (and were confronted by) the same paradox: Evidence that HR *can* contribute to firm success doesn't mean that it is *now* effectively contributing to success in any given business. Managers (HR and line) have repeatedly challenged us with the question, Based on your research, how can I make HR a strategic asset in *my* firm?

We have come to believe that the capacity to design and implement a strategic HR measurement system—what we call in this book an *HR Scorecard*—represents an important lever that firms can use to design and deploy a more effective HR strategy. However, implementing effective measurement systems is not easy; if it were, we would see a lot more of them. In addition, being held accountable for results through measurement can be threatening. Many managers will avoid it if they can. But based on our experience, firms frequently underinvest in their people—and, just as important, invest in the wrong ways. Moreover, many firms seem to be unaware of the consequences of their investment decisions involving people. The most effective way we know to change the calculus is to develop a measurement system designed to link people, strategy, and performance. This is what this book is intended to do.

ACKNOWLEDGMENTS

This project draws inspiration and wisdom from the efforts and support of many individuals. We are especially indebted to Garrett Walker, director of HR Planning, Measurement and Analysis at GTE (now Verizon), and Steve Kirn, VP for Innovation and Organizational Development at Sears. Garrett and Steve were very generous with both their time and their patience, providing a window into the best current work on HR measurement systems. The reader will also quickly recognize the intellectual debt we owe to Bob Kaplan and Dave Norton. We have benefited not only from their work on "balanced" strategic performance measurement, but also from the passion and generosity with which they share those ideas. Brian Becker and Mark Huselid would also like to thank Reed Keller and Bob Lindgren of PriceWaterhouseCoopers, LLC for their vision and enthusiasm about measuring HR's impact on firm performance.

They displayed a confidence in these ideas, and in us, at a time when these ideas weren't very well accepted.

Our work has also benefited immensely from the influence of a wide variety of colleagues. We would particularly like to thank Jane Barnes, Dick Beatty, Wayne Brockbank, Susan Jackson, Steve Kerr, Jeffrey Pfeffer, and Randall Schuler for their ability to frame the issues about measurement and their willingness to debate these ideas and share their insights. Carol Tutzauer's familiarity with the Galileo program was an essential contribution to chapter 6. Wayne Cascio has also had an important influence on our thinking, especially evident in chapter 4.

This project would not have been possible without the financial support of the School of Management and Labor Relations at Rutgers University, the Human Resource Planning Society, and the SHRM Foundation. In addition to funding much of this research, Rutgers also provided Mark with a sabbatical to work on this project. Mark would also like to thank his graduate students in HR Strategy, HR Measurement, and Financial Analysis for HR Managers, who continually challenge him and help him to refine his thinking.

We also owe a special debt of gratitude to the editors at the Harvard Business School Press. The reader will benefit from the gentle, but firm, efforts of Nicola Sabin and Laurie Johnson to move us away from our natural tendencies to write like academics.

Finally, we are most grateful to our families, who provide love and support too valuable to measure.

BRIAN E. BECKER
MARK A. HUSELID
DAVE ULRICH

THE HR SCORECARD

1

HR AS A STRATEGIC PARTNER
The Measurement Challenge
How can we ensure that HR is *at* the table—
and not *on* the table?

A S YOU BEGIN TO READ THIS BOOK, take a moment to reflect on your firm's human resources "architecture"—the sum of the HR function, the broader HR system, and the resulting employee behaviors. Why are these three features important? How does the HR architecture help your company to excel in the marketplace?

If your organization is like most, you're probably finding it difficult to answer these questions. In our experience, many HR management teams have a well-developed vision of their department's strategic value (at least from the perspective of HR), but the CEO and senior line managers are at best skeptical of HR's role in the firm's success. Worse, in many firms, executives want to believe that "people are our most important asset," but they just can't understand how the HR function makes that vision a reality.

What explains this situation? We believe that these problems have the same root cause: HR's influence on firm performance is difficult to measure. Consider the elements and outcomes of your firm's human resources architecture that are tracked on a regular basis. You might have included total compensation, employee turnover, cost per hire, the percentage of employees who had a performance appraisal in the last twelve months, and employee attitudes such as job satisfaction. Now consider those HR attributes that you believe are crucial to the implementation of your firm's competitive strategy. Here you might mention a capable and committed workforce, development of essential employee competencies, or a training system that helps your employees learn faster than your competitors.

How well do your existing HR measures capture the "strategic HR drivers" that you identified in your second list? For most firms there won't be a very close match. More important, even in firms where HR professionals think there is a close match, frequently the senior executives do not agree that this second list actually describes how HR creates value. In either case, there is a disconnect between *what is measured* and *what is important*.

These questions are fundamental, because new economic realities are putting pressure on HR to widen its focus from the administrative role it has traditionally played to a broader, strategic role. As the primary source of production in our economy has shifted from physical to intellectual capital, senior HR managers have come under fire to demonstrate exactly *how* they create value for their organizations. More important, they have been challenged to serve increasingly as strategic partners in running the business.

But what does it mean to be a strategic asset? The literature defines the term as "the set of difficult to trade and imitate, scarce, appropriable, and specialized *resources* and *capabilities* that bestow the firm's competitive advantage."[1] Think about the difference between the ability to align every employee's efforts with the company's overall vision, and an innovative policy such as 360-degree performance appraisals. The first is a strategic capability whose cause is largely invisible to competitors; the second is a policy that, although initially innovative, is visible to competitors—and thus quickly copied. Simply put, strategic assets keep a firm's competitive edge sharp for the long haul—but by definition they are difficult to copy.

Thus HR's problem—that its impact on firm strategy is difficult to see—is the very quality that also makes it a prime source of *sustainable* competitive potential. But to realize this potential, human resource managers must understand the firm's strategy; that is, its plan for developing and sustaining an advantage in the marketplace. Then, they must grasp the implications of that strategy for HR. In short, they must move from a "bottom-up" perspective (emphasizing compliance and traditional HR) to a "top-down" perspective (emphasizing the implementation of strategy). Finally, they need innovative assessment systems that will let them demonstrate their influence on measures that matter to CEOs, namely, firm profitability and shareholder value.

THE EVOLVING PICTURE OF HR: FROM PROFESSIONAL TO STRATEGIC PARTNER

Recent decades have witnessed dramatic shifts in the role of HR. Traditionally, managers saw the human resource function as primarily administrative and professional. HR staff focused on administering benefits and other payroll and operational functions and didn't think of themselves as playing a part in the firm's overall strategy.

Efforts to measure HR's influence on the firm's performance reflected this mind-set. Specifically, theorists examined methodologies and practices that are focused at the level of the individual employee, the individual job, and the individual practice (such as employee selection, incentive compensation, and so forth). The idea was that improvements in individual employee performance would automatically enhance the organization's performance.

Although such research attempted to extend the range of HR's influence, it did little to advance HR as a new source of competitive advantage. It provided scant insight into the complexities of a strategic HR architecture. And simply put, it didn't encourage HR managers to think differently about their role.

In the 1990s, a new emphasis on strategy and the importance of HR *systems* emerged. Researchers and practitioners alike began to recognize the impact of aligning those systems with the company's larger strategy implementation effort—and assessing the quality of that fit. Indeed, although many kinds of HR models are in use today, we can think of them as representing the following evolution of human resources as a strategic asset:

The personnel perspective: The firm hires and pays people but doesn't focus on hiring the very best or developing exceptional employees.

The compensation perspective: The firm uses bonuses, incentive pay, and meaningful distinctions in pay to reward high and low performers.

This is a first step toward relying on people as a source of competitive advantage, but it doesn't fully exploit the benefits of HR as a strategic asset.

The alignment perspective: Senior managers see employees as strategic assets, but they don't invest in overhauling HR's capabilities. Therefore, the HR system can't leverage management's perspective.

The high-performance perspective: HR and other executives view HR as a system embedded within the larger system of the firm's strategy implementation. The firm manages and measures the relationship between these two systems and firm performance.

We're living in a time when a new economic paradigm—characterized by speed, innovation, short cycle times, quality, and customer satisfaction—is highlighting the importance of intangible assets, such as brand recognition, knowledge, innovation, and particularly human capital. This new paradigm can mark the beginning of a golden age for HR. Yet even when human resource professionals and senior line managers grasp this potential, many of them don't know how to take the first steps toward realizing it.

In our view, the most potent action HR managers can take to ensure their strategic contribution is to develop a measurement system that convincingly showcases HR's impact on business performance. To design such a measurement system, HR managers must adopt a dramatically different perspective, one that focuses on how human resources can play a central role in *implementing* the firm's strategy. With a properly developed strategic HR architecture, managers throughout the firm can understand exactly *how people create value* and *how to measure the value-creation process.*

Learning to serve as strategic partners isn't just a way for HR practitioners to justify their existence or defend their turf. It has implications for their very survival and for the survival of the firm as a whole. If the HR function can't show that it adds value, it risks being outsourced. In itself, this isn't necessarily a bad thing; outsourcing inefficient functions can actually enhance a firm's overall bottom line. However, it can waste much-needed potential. With the right mind-set and measurement tools, the HR architecture can mean the difference between a company that's just keeping pace with the competition and one that is surging ahead.

A recent experience of ours graphically illustrates this principle. In a company we visited, we asked the president what most worried him. He quickly responded that the financial market was valuing his firm's earnings at half that of his competitors'. In simple terms, his firm's $100 of cash flow had a market value of $2,000, while his largest competitor's $100 of cash flow had a market value of $4,000. He worried that unless he could change the market's perception of the long-term value of his organization's earnings, his firm would remain undervalued and possibly become a takeover target. He also had a large portion of his personal net worth in the firm, and he worried that it was not valued as highly as it could be.

When we asked him how he was involving his HR executive in grappling with this problem, he dismissed the question with a wave of his hand and said, "My head of HR is very talented. But this is business, not HR." He acknowledged that his HR department had launched innovative recruiting techniques, performance-based pay systems, and extensive employee communications. Nevertheless, he didn't see those functions' relevance to his problem of how to change investors' perceptions of his firm's market value.

Six months after our meeting, a competitor acquired the firm.

The sad truth is that the HR executive in this story missed a valuable opportunity. If he had understood and known how to measure the connection between investments in HR architecture and shareholder value, things might have turned out differently. Armed with an awareness of how investors value intangibles, he might have helped his president build the economic case for increased shareholder value.

The story of Sears, Roebuck and Co.'s recent transformation stands in stark contrast to this anecdote and shows what companies can achieve when they *do* align HR with the larger organization's strategy.[2] After struggling with lack of focus and losses in the billions in the early 1990s, Sears completely overhauled its strategy implementation process. Led by Arthur Martinez, a senior management team incorporated the full range of performance drivers into the process, from the employee through financial performance. Then, they articulated a new, inspiring vision: For Sears to be a compelling place for investors, they said, the company must first become a compelling place to shop. For it to be a compelling place to shop, it must become a compelling place to work.

But Sears didn't just leave this strategic vision in the executive suite or type it up on little cards for employees to put in their wallets. It actually *validated* the vision with hard data. Sears then designed a way to *manage* this strategy with a measurement system that reflected this vision in all its richness. Specifically, the team developed objective measures for each of the three "compellings." For example, "support for ideas and innovation" helped establish Sears as a "compelling place to work." Similarly, by focusing on being a "fun place to shop," Sears became a more "compelling place to shop."[3] The team extended this approach further by developing an associated series of required employee competencies and identifying behavioral objectives for each of the "3-Cs" at several levels through the organization. These competencies then became the foundation on which the firm built its job design, recruiting, selection, performance management, compensation, and promotion activities. Sears even created Sears University in order to train employees to achieve the newly defined competencies. The result was a significant financial turnaround that reflected not only a "strategic" influence for HR but one that could be measured directly.

Few firms have taken such a comprehensive approach to the measurement of strategy implementation as Sears has. Granted, retail service industries are characterized by a clear "line of sight" between employees and customers. Thus their value-creation story is easier to articulate. But that doesn't mean that other industries can't accomplish this feat. The challenges may be greater—but so are the rewards.

WHY HR? WHY NOW?

Consider the following:

> *In most industries, it is now possible to buy on the international marketplace machinery and equipment that is comparable to that in place by the leading global firms. Access to machinery and equipment is not the differentiating factor. Ability to use it effectively is. A company that lost all of its equipment but kept the skills and know-how of its workforce could be back in business relatively quickly. A company that lost its workforce, while keeping its equipment, would never recover.*[4]

This excerpt captures the difference between physical and intellectual capital—and reveals the unique advantages of the latter. The Coca-Cola Company's experience testifies to this reality. According to then-CFO

James Chestnut, after transferring the bulk of its tangible assets to its bottlers, Coke's $150 billion market value derived largely from its brand and management systems.[5]

The evidence is unmistakable: HR's emerging strategic potential hinges on the increasingly central role of intangible assets and intellectual capital in today's economy. Sustained, superior business performance requires a firm to continually hone its competitive edge. Traditionally, this effort took the form of industry-level barriers to entry, patent protections, and governmental regulations. But technological change, rapid innovation, and deregulation have largely eliminated those barriers. Because enduring, superior performance now requires flexibility, innovation, and speed to market, competitive advantage today stems primarily from the internal resources and capabilities of individual organizations—including a firm's ability to develop and retain a capable and committed workforce. As the key enabler of human capital, HR is in a prime position to leverage many other intangibles as well, such as goodwill, research and development, and advertising.

Table 1-1 takes a closer look at the major differences between tangible and intangible assets. It also suggests that managing HR requires vastly different skills from those needed to manage tangible assets. In particular, the benefits of HR as an asset are not always visible—they come to light only when the HR role is skillfully aligned with another intangible asset: the organization's strategy implementation system.

Table 1-1 Tangible versus Intangible Assets

Tangible Assets	Intangible Assets
Readily visible	Invisible
Rigorously quantified	Difficult to quantify
Part of the balance sheet	Not tracked through accounting
Investment produces known returns	Assessment based on assumptions
Can be easily duplicated	Cannot be bought or imitated
Depreciates with use	Appreciates with purposeful use
Has finite applications	Has multiple applications without value reduction
Best managed with "scarcity" mentality	Best managed with "abundance" mentality
Best leveraged through control	Best leveraged through alignment
Can be accumulated and stored	Dynamic, short shelf life when not in use

Source: Hubert Saint-Onge, Conference Board presentation, Boston, MA, October 17, 1996. Reprinted with permission.

INTANGIBLE ASSETS GENERATE TANGIBLE BENEFITS

The increasing importance of organizational capabilities and intangible assets is much more than academic speculation. Trends in U.S. equity markets also reflect this shift. Specifically, these markets have shown a consistent widening in the ratio of the *market* value of a firm (i.e., the shareholders' assessment of the firm's value) to its *book* value (the shareholders' initial investment). This ratio has more than doubled in the last ten years alone (see figure 1-1). This phenomenon is widespread, but it's particularly noteworthy in companies that rely heavily on intellectual capital as their source of competitive advantage. Some of these firms have invented entirely new business models based largely on intangible assets. For example, Dell and Amazon.com, which essentially deal in commodities, have reaped extraordinary gains in shareholder value through their management systems.

In addition, many financial analysts are now including intangibles in their valuation models. A recent study of financial analysts and portfolio managers reveals that, for the average analyst, 35 percent of his or her investment decision is determined by nonfinancial information (see table 1-2).

Figure 1-1   Market to Book Value of S&P 500

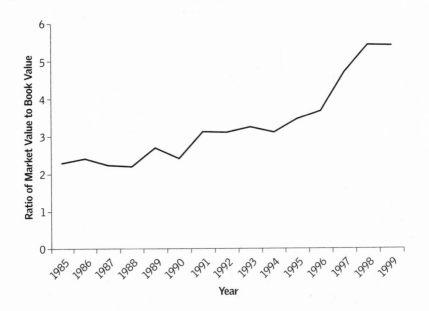

These results are striking for several reasons. First, notice that at least seven of these intangibles are affected by a strategically focused HR system, either directly or indirectly. Second, note that the most important intangible cited by financial analysts is the ability to implement strategy. This finding is consistent with one of the underlying themes in our book, namely, that the ability to execute strategy may be more important than the strategy itself. Indeed, a popular analogy compares the difference between strategic content and implementation to the difference between styles in a poker game. The former emphasizes what game you play; the latter, how you play your hand.

Yet despite the high ranking of strategy implementation in the table, financial analysts are often frustrated in their efforts to collect information on this form of organizational competency. Frequently, they resort to such unconventional sources as personal contacts throughout the firm and industry, contacts with customers, and rumor. Organizations that *do* link business performance measurement with strategy implementation thus position themselves well to communicate with analysts and thereby influence their perceptions of the market. By aligning the HR architecture with the firm's overall strategy, HR professionals could play a key role in shaping those perceptions.

Managers, too, are frustrated by the quality of nonfinancial information that they receive. Across a variety of data categories, including financial,

Table 1-2 Top Ten Nonfinancial Variables Considered by Financial Analysts

Variable	Rank
Execution of corporate strategy	1
Management credibility	2
Quality of corporate strategy	3
Innovation	4
Ability to attract and retain talented people	5
Market share	6
Management expertise	7
Alignment of compensation with shareholders' interests	8
Research leadership	9
Quality of major business processes	10

Source: J. Low and T. Siesfield, *Measures That Matter* (Boston: Ernst & Young, 1998).

operations, customer, and employees, J. Low and T. Siesfield, the authors of the study ranking nonfinancial variables, asked senior managers how much they valued this type of information and whether or not they would be willing to bet their jobs on the quality of this information within their own firms. Predictably, managers placed great value on financial data, and they also expressed a high degree of confidence in their own firm's financial information. Managers placed great value on information relevant to their firm's human capital as well. Yet they gave their own firms extremely low marks on the quality of employee-related data. The gap between the desired and actual data quality for people was more than fifty percentage points—substantially more than the gap found in any other category that they studied.

A CLOSER LOOK AT INTANGIBLES:
THE MEASUREMENT CHALLENGE

GTE (now part of Verizon) has been a leader in efforts to develop measures of intangible assets such as human capital. The firm has recognized both the limitations of traditional accounting measures for intangible assets, and the potential represented by more "balanced" performance measurement systems. According to Lawrence R. Whitman, deputy CFO at GTE:

> *A direct link between human capital and corporate financial results is not readily apparent in traditional accounting practices. Right now, we are only beginning to understand the potential of this tool, but it's the measurement process that's important. . . . Once we are able to measure intangible assets more accurately, I think investors and finance professionals will begin to look at human capital metrics as another indicator of a company's value.*[6]

Clearly, businesspeople everywhere recognize the importance of intangibles in today's marketplace. Yet managing these intangibles is challenging, for a number of reasons. For one thing, the accounting systems in use today evolved during a time when tangible capital, both financial and physical, constituted the principal source of profits. During this time, those organizations that had the most access to money and equipment enjoyed a huge competitive advantage. With the emphasis on knowledge and intangible assets in today's economy, conventional accounting systems actually create dangerous informational distortions. As just one example, these systems encourage short-term thinking with respect to the management of intangibles. Why? Because expenditures in these areas are treated as expenses rather than investments in assets. By contrast, investments in buildings and machinery are capitalized and depreciated over their useful lives. Consider the senior manager faced with the decision to invest $10 million in hard assets or $10 million in people. In practical terms, when a firm invests $10 million dollars in a building or other physical asset, this investment is depreciated over time, and earnings are reduced gradually over a twenty- or thirty-year period. In contrast, a $10 million dollar investment in people is expensed in its entirety (and therefore earnings are reduced by $10 million dollars) during the current year. For managers whose pay is tied to this year's earnings (as many are), the choice of investment is obvious.

As a result, companies under financial pressure tend to invest in physical capital at the expense of human capital—even though the latter may well generate more value. This kind of pressure can lead to poor decisions: for instance, to initiate a round of layoffs solely to garner short-term "cost savings." Research has repeatedly shown that after a layoff, the market may initially respond with a jump in share value. However, investors often eventually lose all of these gains, and sometimes more.[7] This pattern isn't surprising, given that people are a crucial source of competitive advantage rather than an expensive luxury that should be minimized.

The bottom line is this: If current accounting methods can't give HR professionals the measurement tools they need, then they will have to develop their own ways of demonstrating their contribution to firm performance. The first step is to discard the accounting mentality that says that HR is primarily a cost center in which cost minimization is the principal objective and measure of success. At the same time, HR managers must grasp the rare opportunity afforded them by this transitional period. Investors have made it clear that they value intangible assets. It's up to HR to develop a new measurement system that creates real value for the firm and secures human resources' legitimate place as a strategic partner.

THE HR ARCHITECTURE AS A STRATEGIC ASSET

If the focus of corporate strategy is to create sustained competitive advantage, the focus of HR strategy is equally straightforward. It is to maximize the contribution of HR toward that same goal, thereby creating value for shareholders. The foundation of a strategic HR role is the three dimensions of the "value chain" represented by the firm's HR architecture: the function, the system, and employee behaviors. Thinking about HR's influence on firm performance requires a focus on multiple levels of analysis. We use the term "HR architecture" to broadly describe the continuum from the HR professionals within the HR function, to the system of HR-related policies and practices, through the competencies, motivations, and associated behaviors of the firm's employees.[8] (See figure 1-2.)

The HR Function

The foundation of a value-creating HR strategy is a management infrastructure that understands and can implement the firm's strategy. Normally the professionals in the HR function would be expected to lead this effort. This implies a departure from the traditional functional orientation of many HR managers and a wider understanding of the strategic role that HR might play in the firm. For example, Mark Huselid, Susan Jackson, and Randall Schuler point out that human resources management (HRM) effectiveness has two essential dimensions. The first, *technical HRM*, includes the delivery of HR basics such as recruiting, compensation, and benefits. The second, *strategic HRM*, involves delivering those services in a way that directly supports the implementation of the firm's strategy.

Huselid and his colleagues found that most HR managers were very proficient in the delivery of traditional or technical HRM activities, but much less so in delivering strategic HRM capabilities. In a sample of

Figure 1-2 HR's Strategic Architecture

THE HR FUNCTION	THE HR SYSTEM	EMPLOYEE BEHAVIORS
HR professionals with strategic competencies	High-performance, strategically aligned policies and practices	Strategically focused competencies, motivations, and associated behaviors

nearly 300 large firms, the average level of technical proficiency was 35 percent higher than the average level of strategic HRM proficiency. HR managers were particularly limited in their ability to translate the firm's strategy and operational goals into actionable HR goals, and subsequently to implement those goals. Yet it was this ability to embed HR within the larger system of strategy implementation that turned out to have the most important influence on corporate financial performance. This was true whether firm performance was measured as sales per employee, cash flow per employee, or market value per employee. The authors conclude that most firms are already demonstrating acceptable levels of technical HRM competencies and effectiveness, noting that traditional HR skills have not diminished in value, but simply are no longer adequate to satisfy the wider strategic demands on the HR function.[9] The competencies that HR managers need to develop—and the ones that have the greatest impact on firm performance—are business and strategic HRM competencies.

The HR System

The HR system is the linchpin of HR's strategic influence. The model of this system advocated in this book is what we call a High-Performance Work System (HPWS). In an HPWS, each element of the HR system is designed to maximize the overall quality of human capital throughout the organization. To build and maintain a stock of talented human capital, an HPWS does the following:

- links its selection and promotion decisions to validated competency models;

- develops strategies that provide timely and effective support for the skills demanded by the firm's strategy implementation; and

- enacts compensation and performance management policies that attract, retain, and motivate high-performance employees.

The items on this list may seem obvious. However, they are vital steps in improving the quality of employee decision-making throughout the organization—something that makes good business sense as traditional command-and-control management models increasingly go out of fashion. In short, for HR to create value, a firm needs to structure each element of its HR system in a way that relentlessly emphasizes, supports, and reinforces a high-performance workforce.

But adopting a high-performance focus for individual HR policies and practices is not nearly enough. We use the term *system* intentionally here. Thinking systemically emphasizes the *interrelationships* of the HR system's components and the link between HR and the larger strategy implementation system. It is these linkages between a system's components—not any individual component itself—that make a system more than just the sum of its parts (see "The Laws of Systems Thinking").

THE LAWS OF SYSTEMS THINKING

Thinking systematically is a foundational competency for several steps in our model, because certain steps require understanding what happens when multiple systems intersect. While a comprehensive treatment of systems thinking is well beyond the scope of this book, we would like to revisit several pertinent "laws of systems thinking" described by management theorist Peter M. Senge.*

Today's Problems Come from Yesterday's "Solutions." HR managers operate within a larger organizational system, as well as within the HR system. Problems "solved" in one part of the business often crop up as new problems in another. For example, top managers face mounting pressure from investors to boost profits. They cut costs by laying off staff, particularly middle managers. This satisfies Wall Street, but in three or four years, the company finds itself faced with a leadership crisis. Moreover, HR is stuck with both a development and recruiting problem. Systems-savvy HR managers can point out the links between these problems and suggest ways to cut staff that protect the firm's cadre of future leaders.

The Easy Way Out Usually Leads Back In. One important benefit of systems thinking is that it helps us to adopt new perspectives on problems. Too often, we rely on comfortable and familiar solutions that have worked in the past. To truly serve as strategic partners, human resource professionals must view HR's value-creation role—particularly HR enablers—in a whole new light and resist the temptation to use "tried-and-true" but outdated ideas.

Cause and Effect Are Not Closely Related in Time and Space. This law speaks to the difference between leading and lagging indicators. HR's influence on firm performance is likely to be much less direct than that of other strategic drivers. This lag between cause and effect for HR performance drivers doesn't diminish their ultimate influence, but it does make it difficult to identify and measure that influence. Many senior managers rely primarily on conventional, financial performance measures—which are lagging indicators. They often try to solve financial problems by immediately cutting costs rather than identifying the fundamental sources of the problem. Pressured by the short-term demands of capital markets, they seek the quick fix—only to discover that such solutions either don't last or actually worsen the original problem.

The Highest Leverage Points Are Often the Least Obvious. Seasoned systems thinkers constantly look for the less obvious solution to a problem. Not surprisingly, for most CEOs, the obvious solutions to improved performance have rarely included HR.

This is the challenge facing human resource professionals. Problems in financial performance get everyone's attention, but no one thinks about how HR can help. Nevertheless, because HR drivers are so foundational, small changes in how they're managed gather momentum as they work their way through the strategy implementation process. For example, at Sears, a mere 4-percent increase in employee satisfaction reverberated through the profit chain, eventually lifting market capitalization by nearly $250 million.†

Cutting an Elephant in Half Doesn't Get You Two Smaller Elephants; It Gets You a Mess. In other words, if you try to dissect a system, expecting to be able to examine its parts in isolation, you may end up destroying it. Organizations are complex systems that involve interactions within and between many different subsystems. Thus, they are best understood from a systemwide perspective. Yet most managers think of their firm's subsystems as functions and limit their attention to their own "turf." Functional leaders might "see the firm's problems clearly, but none see how the policies of *their* department interact with [those of] others."‡ As Senge argues, it's the *interactions* between systems and among a system's parts that generate both problems and potential leverage points for change. Depending on the situation, different system interactions will be more or less important at various times. Skilled managers—including those HR professionals who want to be more than just administrators—know which interactions most require their attention, and when.

---

* Peter Senge, *The Fifth Discipline* (Doubleday: New York, 1990), 57–67.
† Anthony J. Rucci, Steven P. Kirn, and Richard T. Quinn, "The Employee-Customer-Profit Chain at Sears," *Harvard Business Review* 76, no. 1 (1998): 87.
‡ Senge, *The Fifth Discipline*, 66.

Our description of the HPWS raises the obvious question: What, exactly, are the specific policies and practices that lead to high performance? Since 1990, two of us have conducted a biannual survey of the HR management systems in U.S. publicly held companies. The foundation of this research effort has been a biannual survey of HR systems that targets a broad cross-section of publicly traded firms: firms with sales greater than $5 million and more than 100 employees. These data on HR systems are then matched with publicly available data on financial performance. This research program is ongoing and now includes more than 2,800 corporations.[10]

Each survey enabled us to construct an HPWS index that measures the extent to which a firm's HR system is consistent with the principles of a high-performance HR strategy. Table 1-3 compares firms in our 1998 sample at the two ends of the high-performance HR continuum. Based on our HPWS index, we calculated each firm's percentile ranking in our sample and then compared firms ranked in the top decile on the HPWS index with those in the bottom decile on several characteristics. The results in table 1-3 are based on the 429 firms in our 1998 sample. However, the results are very robust and highly similar for our 1992, 1994, and 1996 samples.[11]

Table 1-3   Comparison of High and Low HR Management Quality

	Bottom 10% HR Index (42 firms)	Top 10% HR Index (43 firms)
HR Practices		
Number of qualified applicants per position	8.24	36.55
Percentage hired based on a validated selection test	4.26	29.67
Percentage of jobs filled from within	34.90	61.46
Percentage in a formal HR plan including recruitment, development, and succession	4.79	46.72
Number of hours of training for new employees (less than 1 year)	35.02	116.87
Number of hours of training for experienced employees	13.40	72.00
Percentage of employees receiving a regular performance appraisal	41.31	95.17
Percentage of workforce whose merit increase or incentive pay is tied to performance	23.36	87.27
Percentage of workforce who received performance feedback from multiple sources (360)	3.90	51.67
Target percentile for total compensation (market rate = 50%)	43.03	58.67
Percentage of the workforce eligible for incentive pay	27.83	83.56
Percentage of difference in incentive pay between a low-performing and high-performing employee	3.62	6.21

	Bottom 10% HR Index (42 firms)	Top 10% HR Index (43 firms)
HR Practices (*continued*)		
Percentage of the workforce routinely working in a self-managed, cross-functional, or project team	10.64	42.28
Percentage of HR budget spent on outsourced activities (e.g., recruiting, benefits, payroll)	13.46	26.24
Number of employees per HR professional	253.88	139.51
Percentage of the eligible workforce covered by a union contract	30.00	8.98
HR Outcomes*		
Extent to which strategy is clearly articulated and well understood throughout the firm	3.40	4.21
Extent to which the average employee understands how his or her job contributes to the firm's success	2.80	4.00
Extent to which senior management sees employees as a source of value creation versus a cost to be minimized	3.31	4.21
Extent to which the executive leadership team is visionary	3.02	4.33
Extent to which the firm attempts to provide job security, even if confronted with declining financial performance	2.71	4.11
Extent to which the firm's decision-making style can be described as participative	3.02	3.81
Extent to which the firm's HR professionals are generally perceived to be administrative experts	3.76	4.56
Extent to which the firm's HR professionals are generally perceived to be employee champions	3.69	4.40
Extent to which the firm's HR professionals are generally perceived to be agents for change	3.31	4.12
Extent to which the firm's HR professionals are generally perceived to be business partners	3.19	4.30
Extent to which line managers generally believe that effective diversity management is a business imperative	2.45	3.65
Extent to which top management shows commitment to and leadership in knowledge sharing	2.99	4.05
Extent to which the firm has developed and communicated measures of financial performance	3.38	4.63
Extent to which the firm has developed and communicated measures of customer reactions	3.02	4.27
Extent to which the firm has developed and communicated measures of key business processes	3.09	4.13
Extent to which the firm has developed and communicated measures of learning and growth	2.26	3.12
Firm Performance		
Employee turnover	34.09	20.87
Sales per employee	$158,101	$617,576
Market value to book value	3.64	11.06

*Each of the variables in the "HR Outcomes" section is scaled from 1 to 6, where 1 = "not at all" and 6 = "to a very great extent."

The differences between these two groups of firms are very substantial, and these differences are not solely due to firm size, industry, or age. Firms with high-performance work systems adopt HR management practices very different from those adopted by firms with low-performance work systems: They devote considerably more resources to recruiting and selection, they train with much greater vigor, they do a lot more performance management and tie compensation to it, they use teams to a much greater extent, they have roughly double the number of HR professionals per employee, and they are much less likely to be unionized. Indeed, the most striking attribute of these comparisons is not any one HR management practice—it is not recruiting *or* training *or* compensation. Rather, the differences are much more comprehensive—and systemic.

The HR outcomes associated with this system are comprehensive as well. Compared with low-performing HR management systems, the very best firms in our sample are much more likely to have developed a clear strategic intent and communicated it effectively to employees. In addition, they are more likely to have their HR professionals rated positively in both their traditional and strategic roles. They are also more likely to have developed a comprehensive measurement system for communicating nonfinancial information to employees.

Finally, firms with the most effective HR management systems exhibited dramatically higher performance: Employee turnover was close to half, sales per employee were four times as great, and the ratio of firm market value to the book value of assets—a key indicator of management quality, as it indicates the extent to which management has increased shareholders' initial investment—was more than three times as large in high-performing companies.

An HPWS is itself a strategy implementation system, embedded within the firm's larger strategy implementation system. HR intersects with that larger system at many different points and perhaps with multiple elements of the HR system at the same point. Understanding how to identify those points of intersection in your own firm, and how to align the HR system accordingly, is the key to securing a strategic role for HR and knowing how to measure HR's impact on value creation. In addition, firms must constantly sharpen their awareness of how well the HR system's components are aligned, that is, how much they reinforce or conflict with one another. As an example of reinforcement, a firm might combine above-market pay policies with comprehensive performance management systems. This combination lets the firm cultivate a talented applicant and employee pool, and recognize and reward the best employees for superior performance. By contrast, when these components are in conflict, an organization might encourage employees to work together in teams, but then provide raises based on individual contributions.

In short, an HPWS directly generates unique customer value, or it leverages other related sources of such value. In certain service industries, the employee-customer relationship is so visible that its impact on value creation is unmistakable. But for most firms, value derives from operational processes or innovations that affect the customer in less obvious ways. It is these firms that most need to articulate the strategy implementation process and then align the HR system to support that process. And it is in these firms, where such alignments and strategies are not easily observed and thus imitated by competitors, that HR has the greatest potential.

In our view, this alignment process must begin with a clear understanding of the firm's value chain—a solid comprehension, throughout the firm, of what kind of value the organization generates and exactly how that value is created. For example, every firm should be able to describe how its ultimate financial goals are linked to key success factors at the level of its customers, operations, people, and IT systems. Robert Kaplan and David Norton have coined the term "strategy map" to describe these relationships.[12] With this shared understanding of the value-creation process, the organization can then design a strategy implementation model that specifies needed competencies and employee behaviors throughout the firm. The firm's system for managing people can then be geared toward the generation of these competencies and behaviors. In fact, a key distinguishing characteristic of a High-Performance Work System is not just the adoption of appropriate HR policies and practices such as employee acquisition, development, compensation, and performance management, but also the *way* in which these practices are deployed. In an HPWS, the firm's HR policies and practices show a strong alignment with the firm's competitive strategy and operational goals. Moreover, each HPWS will be different. No single best example exists; each organization must customize its system to meet its own unique strengths and needs. For example, table 1-3 shows that high-performing firms are characterized by greater use of incentive pay. However, the behaviors and outcomes that are being reinforced will differ substantially across firms and strategies.

Strategic Employee Behaviors

Ultimately any discussion of the strategic role of human resources or human capital will implicitly focus on the productive behaviors of the people in the organization. In one sense this is almost tautological since it is only through behaviors that human beings can influence their environment. We are interested, however, in certain types of employee behaviors and not others. In chapter 2 we describe our own research linking *employee strategic focus* to firm performance. This work emphasizes the importance of aligning organizational processes and support systems so that they encourage and motivate an understanding of "the big picture." Similarly, we define *strategic behaviors* as the subset of productive behaviors that directly serve to implement the firm's strategy. These strategic behaviors will fall into two general categories. The first would be the *core behaviors* that flow directly from behavioral core competencies defined by the firm. These are behaviors that are considered fundamental to the success of the firm, across all business units and levels. The second are *situation-specific behaviors* that are essential at key points in the firm's or business unit's value chain. An example of these latter behaviors might be the cross-selling skills required in the branch of a retail bank.

Integrating a focus on behaviors into an overall effort to influence and measure HR's contribution to firm performance is a challenge. Which ones are important? How should they be "managed"? We need to keep a few points in mind. First, the importance of the behaviors will be defined by their importance to the implementation of the firm's strategy. Understanding how people and processes within the firm actually create value is the first step. That analysis will reveal both the kinds of behaviors that are generally required throughout the firm and those with specific value at key points in the value chain. Second, it's essential to remember that we don't affect strategic behaviors directly. They are the end result of the larger HR architecture. Especially important is the influence of an HR system that is aligned with the firm's strategy.

ALIGNING PERFORMANCE MEASUREMENT AND STRATEGY IMPLEMENTATION

You are undoubtedly familiar with the assertion that "what gets measured gets managed—and what gets managed gets accomplished." But how true is this, really? Can measuring organizational processes provide competitive advantage? We believe that developing measurement competency *is* important, because it can add value at the level of the firm. But few managers (HR or otherwise) have strong competencies in this area. In recent years, HR managers have been asked to learn about finance and accounting. Now, they must hone their measurement skills as well.

We are not the first to emphasize the importance of measuring business performance from the perspective of strategy implementation, rather than relying simply on financial results. Robert Kaplan and David Norton's Balanced Scorecard approach pioneered this concept of moving beyond mere financial measurement.[13] To use this tool, a firm must specify not only the financial elements of its value chain but also the customer, business process, and learning and growth elements. Then, it must develop tangible ways to assess each.

The premise underlying the Balanced Scorecard approach is that senior managers have paid far too much attention to the financial dimensions of performance, and not enough attention to the forces that drive those results. After all, financial measures are inherently backward-looking. Because "performance drivers" are within management's control *now*, the entire Balanced Scorecard measurement system encourages managers to actively engage with the strategy implementation process, rather than simply monitor financial results. By specifying the vital process measures, assessing them, and regularly communicating the firm's performance on these criteria to employees, managers ensure that the entire organization participates in strategy implementation. The Balanced Scorecard approach thus makes strategy everyone's business.

THE PURPOSE OF THIS BOOK

In this book, we address the crucial question of how HR practitioners can measure their contribution to their firm's strategy implementation—and thus be *at* the table and not *on* the table. We believe that effective measurement systems serve two important purposes: They guide decision making throughout the organization, and they serve as a basis for evaluating performance. The measurement approach we describe addresses these two purposes in three ways. First, it encourages a clear, consistent, and shared view of how the firm can implement its strategy at each level in the organization. It won't guarantee that every employee can articulate the entire value-creation process, but it should ensure that each employee has a clear understanding of his or her own role in the process. Use of our model also builds consensus around how different elements within the organization contribute to value creation.

Second, our approach forces managers to focus on the "vital few" measures that really make a difference. Anyone could easily generate fifty or more measures of firm performance, across a variety of categories. Yet this exercise would probably be counterproductive because that many measures would be difficult to track. We argue that a truly effective measurement system contains no more than twenty-five measures.

Third, this approach lets practitioners express these vital few measures in terms that line managers and senior executives will understand— and value. In HR, conventional measures of cost control, such as hours of training, time to fill an opening position, and even turnover rates and employee satisfaction, will continue to lack credibility unless they are shown to influence key performance drivers in the business.

We've also organized the book around two central tenets. The first is that a firm's HR architecture—particularly the HR management system—can have a substantial impact on firm performance. This thesis will probably come as no surprise to most HR professionals. They believe that the field has always been important, even if many managers outside the HR function didn't recognize its true value. But for the first time, HR has the potential to boost the bottom line by a method other than simply by minimizing costs. To paraphrase C. K. Prahalad and Gary Hamel, HR professionals are now in a position to become numerator managers (contributing to top-line growth) rather than just denominator managers (cutting costs and reducing overhead).[14] However, to exert this influence on firm performance, the HR system has to be embedded in the organization's strategy implementation, that larger management system that is the key to sustained competitive advantage and financial success.

This strategic role also requires new competencies on the part of HR professionals. To be sure, the HR field has made huge technical strides in the last twenty years. Nevertheless, it has essentially been doing the same things, though better and more efficiently. The new economic paradigm requires that HR professionals do different things, in an entirely different role. This means more than just understanding the firm's articulated strategy. Being a strategic partner requires that HR professionals comprehend exactly what capabilities drive successful strategy implementation in their firms—and how HR affects those capabilities. This is a challenging task, for HR's traditional roles as administrative experts, employee champions, and agents of change are no less important in this new environment.

The second key tenet of this book follows directly from the first. It reflects the two most common questions we hear from HR practitioners:

- How can we measure the value of what we do in HR in terms that line and general managers will understand and respect? For example, how can we determine the return on investment (ROI) of a new training and development program?

- How can HR metrics be incorporated in my organization's measures of business performance?

To demonstrate its strategic contribution to senior line managers, HR needs a measurement system that focuses on two dimensions:

- cost control (driving out costs in the HR function and enhancing operational efficiency outside of HR), and

- value creation (ensuring that the HR architecture intersects with the strategy implementation process)

As we've seen, Kaplan and Norton's Balanced Scorecard framework has received enormous attention, in part because it incorporates measures that describe the actual value-creation process rather than focusing on just the financial *results* that traditional accounting methods assess. It is a framework that we will draw on heavily in this book. In addition, we seek to strengthen an aspect of the Balanced Scorecard approach that Norton and Kaplan themselves acknowledge to be its weakest feature— the question of how best to integrate HR's role into a firm's measurement of business performance. They note the following:

> *[W]hen it comes to specific measures concerning [HR and people-related issues] companies have devoted virtually no effort for measuring either outcomes or the drivers of these capabilities. This gap is disappointing, since one of the most important goals for adopting the scorecard measurement and management framework is to promote the growth of individual and organizational capabilities. . . . [This] reflects the limited progress that most organizations have made linking employees . . . and organizational alignment with their strategic objectives.*[15]

Our book is designed to close the gap that Kaplan and Norton have identified. The framework that we present here will help HR practitioners develop the conceptual and operational tools they need to structure their role in a way that adds unmistakable value. Moreover, it will show them how to demonstrate those gains in terms that senior HR managers and other leaders will find compelling.

OUR FOCUS ON HR MANAGERS

The reader will see that we have organized our work around the role of the HR professional rather than the general manager. By adopting such a focus, we do not mean to give the impression that line managers play an unimportant role in making HR a strategic asset. In fact, the appropriate values and behaviors of an organization's leadership team are key prerequisites for HR to realize the potential role we describe in this book. In addition, there are many general managers whose traditional view of HR's role would benefit from an introduction to these ideas. Nevertheless, HR managers have the greatest professional stake in the future role of HR in their organizations, and therefore we have chosen to orient the book to their particular challenge.

USING THIS BOOK

The next five chapters in this book show you how to actually create a measurement system for assessing HR's contribution to value creation in your firm. Chapter 2 describes a seven-step process that will lay the foundation for HR's strategic influence. We specifically highlight the importance of a strategically focused HR architecture as a prerequisite for a measurement system that can link HR with firm performance.

Chapter 3 then lays out a process for developing the HR Scorecard based on the concepts discussed in chapter 2. We specifically discuss how to incorporate concepts such as efficiency, value creation, and alignment in the HR measurement system.

HR measurement also means being able to evaluate HR programs and initiatives with the same rigor as decisions elsewhere in the organization. In chapter 4 we describe a process for cost-benefit analysis that will allow HR professionals to determine the return on investment for these decisions.

Chapter 5 offers a process for validating the quality of the measurement system you develop and the data it generates. Here we explore ways to determine when "enough is enough," define accountabilities for the measurement process, and present guidelines for developing measurement champions in your organization.

Chapter 6 focuses on one of the most difficult measurement challenges for a firm attempting to manage HR as a strategic asset—the problem of alignment. In this chapter we describe several ways to think about alignment and offer several alternative measurement approaches.

Chapter 7 discusses the prevailing competency models for HR professionals and how our view of what constitutes an appropriate set of HR competencies is influenced by the demands of a strategic measurement initiative.

In chapter 8 we conclude with a discussion of the challenges involved in implementing a strategically focused HR architecture and HR Scorecard. We develop a seven-step model for planning and evaluating the change management activities associated with the implementation efforts.

For those readers interested in the full extent of the theoretical underpinnings of our approach, we have also provided an appendix at the back of this book describing our research in more detail.

A FINAL NOTE OF ADVICE AND ENCOURAGEMENT

Clearly, designing any new measurement system for intangible assets isn't easy—if it were, most companies would have already done it. Embracing this challenge takes time and a lot of careful thought. We encourage you to progress through each chapter in this book in sequence and to actively engage with the concepts as much as possible. This means thinking about how your own HR architecture operates and identifying ways in which you can customize our approach to meet the unique needs and characteristics of your firm. We also fully expect you to involve your entire HR staff in mastering the tools described in this book. After all, real innovation comes only when people work together on the most pressing challenges of the workplace.

2

CLARIFYING AND MEASURING HR'S STRATEGIC INFLUENCE
Introduction to a Seven-Step Process

It was exciting stuff. We could see how employee attitudes drove not just customer service but also turnover and the likelihood that employees would recommend Sears and its merchandise to friends, family, and customers. We discovered that an employee's ability to see the connection between his or her work and the company's strategic objectives was a driver of positive behavior. . . . We were also able to establish fairly precise statistical relationships. We began to see exactly how a change in training or business literacy affected revenues.

ANTHONY J. RUCCI, STEVEN P. KIRN,
AND RICHARD T. QUINN[1]

THIS QUOTATION CAPTURES the energy that can be created when an organization aligns its HR architecture with its larger plan for strategy implementation—and devises a way to measure that alignment. If we take a closer look at Sears' transformational experience, we can see that the company's effort centered on telling the "story" of how value is created within the organization. Specifically, Sears executives clarified how their employees drive customer satisfaction and how that

satisfaction, in turn, fuels overall firm performance. They then reinforced
the story by involving a broad cross-section of senior managers, providing developmental opportunities for those supervisors who lacked the
leadership skills needed to implement the new strategy, and realigning
the HR system to support the strategy.

Equally important, they designed a measurement system that let them
test their hypotheses about how employee behaviors, customer satisfaction, and financial performance are all linked. In other words, Sears moved
beyond the hypothetical and devised ways to demonstrate objectively
HR's contribution to implementation of the company's new strategy.
Human resource managers could now cite hard evidence that "a 5-point
improvement in employee attitudes will drive a 1.3-point improvement in
customer satisfaction, which in turn will drive a .5% improvement in revenue growth."[2]

BALANCED PERFORMANCE MEASUREMENT

To achieve the kind of strategy alignment that Sears accomplished, a
company must engage in a two-step process. First, managers have to
understand fully the "story" of how value is created in their firm. Once
they achieve this understanding, they can then design a measurement
system based on that story. We can think of this process in terms of two
general questions:

First, how should strategy be implemented in our firm? This is another
way of asking how the firm generates value. Asking this question
focuses the organization on two dimensions of the strategy implementation story:

Breadth: The company must attend to more than financials,
which are just the outcomes of strategy implementation. To
truly grasp the value-creation story, the organization must also
focus on performance drivers (such as customer loyalty) that
it has identified as "key success factors."

Causal flow: This is the series of linkages among financial and
nonfinancial determinants of firm performance. All managers
need to have an understanding of this flow (though most lack
it). A comprehension of causal flow pushes managers to think

beyond the financials and appreciate the importance of other kinds of success indicators. It's not enough just to have a list of important nonfinancial measures of success. Managers also need to understand and incorporate the "causal logic" that gives these nonfinancials value in the organization. Figure 2-1 shows the kind of basic framework that a firm can conceptualize by asking itself how strategy should be implemented.

Second, what performance measures capture this broadly defined strategy implementation process? This question encourages managers to attach metrics to the conceptual foundation that they envisioned after understanding their firm's value-creation story.

Once high-level managers have addressed these two questions, they must then communicate it to middle managers and front-line employees. That way, every member of the organization knows how to support the firm's success. These questions also help the organization decide how to allocate resources so as to breathe life into the value-creation story. Finally, and most important, the insights generated by the questions guide the decisions that every employee makes, every day.

Figure 2-1   A Simple Illustration of Value Creation

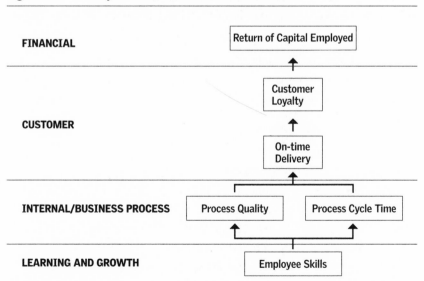

Source: Robert S. Kaplan and David P. Norton, *The Balanced Scorecard* (Boston, MA: Harvard Business School Press, 1996), 31.

Balanced performance-measurement models, such as the one we present in this book, pull the answers to these two questions together in a powerful assessment tool. The model recognizes the importance of both intangible and tangible assets, and of financial and nonfinancial measures. It also acknowledges the complex, value-generating connections among the firm's customers, operations, employees, and technology,[3] and integrates HR's role in an unprecedented way. Finally, the model highlights the important distinction between lagging and leading indicators. *Lagging indicators*, such as financial metrics, typically reflect only what has happened in the past. Such metrics may accurately measure the impact of prior decisions, but they won't help you to make today's decisions, nor do they guarantee future outcomes. The popular analogy compares using them to guide decisions about the future to driving your car by looking in the rearview mirror! Therefore, you also need a set of metrics called *leading indicators*. This will be different for each firm, but examples might include R&D cycle time, customer satisfaction, or employee strategic focus. These indicators assess the status of the key success factors that drive implementation of the firm's strategy. And by their very nature, they emphasize the future rather than the past.

INTEGRATING HR INTO BUSINESS PERFORMANCE MEASUREMENT: UNDERSTANDING HR DELIVERABLES

Grasping the relationships among key success factors is essential for measuring HR's traditionally elusive role in driving organizational performance. Once a company firmly anchors HR in its strategy implementation system, it can then see the connections between HR and the company's success drivers. By measuring HR's effect on these drivers, the firm can quantify HR's overall strategic impact.

To integrate HR into a business-performance measurement system, managers must identify the points of intersection between HR and the organization's strategy implementation plan. We can think of these points as *strategic HR deliverables*, namely, those outcomes of the HR architecture that serve to execute the firm's strategy. This is in contrast to HR "doables" that focus on HR efficiency and activity counts. These deliverables come in two categories: performance drivers and enablers. HR *performance drivers* are core people-related capabilities or assets, such as employee productivity or employee satisfaction. Even though these may seem so important as to be generic, there is actually no single correct set of performance drivers. Each firm custom-identifies its own set based on its unique characteristics and the requirements of its strategy implementation process.

Enablers reinforce performance drivers. For example, a particular change in a company's reward structure might encourage preventive maintenance rather than reactive maintenance. An emphasis on preventive maintenance might in turn "enable" a performance driver called "on-time delivery." Any performance driver may have several enablers. The enablers themselves, in isolation, may seem mundane, but—as we'll see—their cumulative effect can have strategic importance.

Let's look at these two categories of HR deliverables in greater detail.

HR Performance Drivers

Perhaps not surprisingly, human resource managers tend to focus on HR performance drivers in attempting to demonstrate their strategic influence. But all too often, they merely assert the importance of a particular driver, such as employee satisfaction, without being able to make the business case for its primacy. This predicament stems from the difficulties inherent in discerning HR's actual contribution to overall mission and strategy. Because of this difficulty, companies often experience a disconnect between the metrics they use and the HR policies they institute. For example, one firm we know of incorporates various sophisticated measures into its bonus compensation system, but HR's measures consist of simple hurdles that any manager can achieve (for instance, "100 percent of direct reports have filed a career development plan"). Such simplistic measures undermine HR's credibility in the wider organization.

The credibility of HR measures is particularly important when financial and nonfinancial performance measures conflict. Inevitably, there comes a time when people measures are up, but financials are down. Naturally, the CFO objects to paying bonuses when "performance" doesn't warrant it. However, such reactions miss an essential point: Balanced performance measurement means paying attention to *both* lagging and leading indicators. And, it's the *leading* indicators—such as HR measures—that really drive value creation in the organization. The hesitation to reward managers when people measures are up and financial measures are down reflects a lack of agreement among executives that HR measures in fact drive the entire company's performance. In this example, the reward system has been "balanced" to address some vague concern about "people issues," but no one can articulate how these measures reflect value creation in the firm.

Moreover, managers often don't understand the delays inherent in leading indicators. High HR scores in the face of low financials actually signal improved financials in the future, assuming that other leading indicators are also positive. The reverse is equally true, of course. Strong financials in the face of weak HR drivers and other leading indicators should raise concerns about future financial performance. The lesson? Because truly balanced performance measurement systems reflect both current and future financial performance, managers must interpret them differently from the way they do traditional performance measures.

Identifying key HR performance drivers can be challenging, because they are unique to each firm. The experience at Quantum Corporation offers an apt example. At Quantum, a leading manufacturer of hard disks and computer peripherals, executives emphasize something they call "time-to-volume." In Quantum's view, being first to market does not mean being first to announce or demonstrate a new product.[4] Rather, it means that customers actually get the new products they want, when they want them, and in the quantities they require. Time-to-volume hinges on rapid product development—without the sacrifice of quality—plus the ability to ramp up production fast enough to meet customers' needs. Quantum identified a set of *value behaviors*, such as staying flexible and adaptable, taking initiative for one's own development, and resolving issues in an objective manner, as one time-to-volume driver. There is nothing ad hoc or symbolic about the importance of these behaviors to the success of the company. Quantum integrates them directly into its performance criteria and gives them equal weight with more traditional performance measures. Indeed, one-half of bonus and merit pay is based on financial results, and one-half on an employee's adherence to the value behaviors. As one senior executive observed, "You can't simply 'get results' too often while leaving a pile of dead bodies behind you."

HR Enablers

As we mentioned, HR enablers reinforce core performance drivers. To provide another example, if a firm identifies employee productivity as a core performance driver, then "re-skilling" might be an enabler. We encourage human resource managers to focus as much on HR enablers as they do on HR performance drivers, but to dramatically expand the concept. For instance, rather than thinking just in terms of *HR-focused* enablers in your organization (those enablers that influence the more central HR performance drivers), try thinking about how *specific* HR enablers also reinforce performance drivers in the operations, customer, and financial segments of the organization.

Our experience with a major money-center bank illustrates what can happen when managers *don't* connect HR enablers with various performance drivers in the broader organization. This particular bank had decided to shift the focus of its retail business from service to sales. The bank identified a set of performance drivers that included increased cross-selling to existing customers, teller product knowledge, and sales skills. However, its HR enablers still emphasized service. For instance, the organization still had the following:

- training programs that focused on service rather than sales;

- performance appraisal and merit pay that rewarded service rather than sales;

- hiring practices based on service competencies rather than sales competencies;

- turnover rates that undermined relationship building between tellers and retail customers; and

- low pay and benefits for tellers, who were considered overhead rather than a source of revenue growth.

Because of the disconnect between its new goals and outdated HR enablers, the bank failed to achieve its sales and profitability targets. Without the properly aligned enablers, it was simply unable to implement its new sales strategy. The lesson here is that the entire HR *system* influences employee behavior from many points. Thus HR has that many more opportunities to enable—or impede—the firm's key performance drivers.

Another example from the banking industry illustrates how easy it is to overlook the power of HR enablers. When the Wells Fargo Online Financial Services (OFS) group implemented a Balanced Scorecard to measure the firm's overall progress toward its goals of growing revenue and maximizing profits, it identified three key strategic drivers[5]:

- add and retain high-value and high-potential-value customers;

- increase revenue per customer; and

- reduce cost per customer.

Figure 2-2 articulates the "story" of how OFS expected to achieve those goals. OFS also identified several HR performance drivers that it felt would play an important part in the success of its strategy, shown in the Learning and Growth section of the figure:

- attract and retain key OFS players and staff;

- enhance OFS bench strength and succession planning;

- increase managerial competency and functional competency at all levels;

- continue development of the OFS organization and culture; and

- deploy the Scorecard and embed it in OFS.

According to Mary D'Agostino, VP of strategy at OFS, acknowledging these HR drivers signaled an important step for Wells Fargo, in which the culture "embraces financial measures." But OFS managers never achieved consensus on *how* these HR drivers directly affected the three strategic goals. As a result, while the company agreed to monitor these drivers yearly, it neglected to formally build them into its Scorecard.

In short, human resources managers should evaluate the degree to which their firm's entire *system* of enablers—from employee selection to development and rewards—supports the *non*-HR drivers outlined in the firm's Scorecard. For example, one common performance driver is to "develop superior service quality." But if line managers are struggling with high staff turnover and insufficient rewards for service quality, how can they achieve their targeted service quality levels? As another example, suppose an organization's R&D function had identified timeliness of marketable new product innovations as a key performance driver. By understanding how the R&D unit contributes to the firm's larger strategy implementation process, this organization's HR manager could readily generate ideas for enabling the R&D unit's success. Specifically, she might suggest a reward system that encourages marketable innovations, a timely sourcing function that provides technological expertise, and incentives to

Figure 2-2 Preliminary Linkage Map

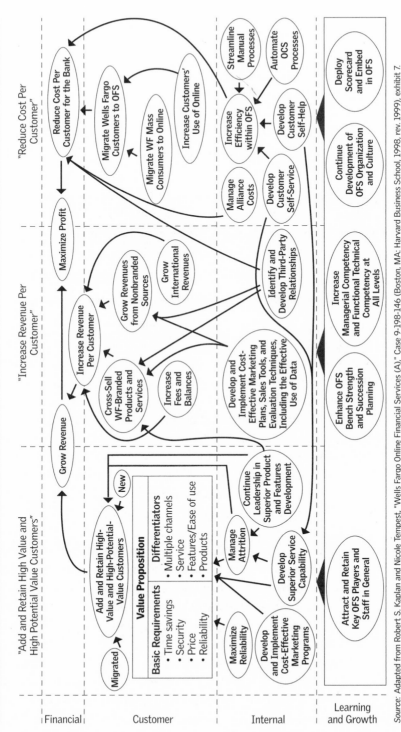

Source: Adapted from Robert S. Kaplan and Nicole Tempest, "Wells Fargo Online Financial Services (A)," Case 9-198-146 (Boston, MA: Harvard Business School, 1998, rev. 1999), exhibit 7.

encourage a low level of employee turnover among key R&D talent. This kind of synergy makes for true business partnering between HR and the rest of the organization.

A SEVEN-STEP MODEL FOR IMPLEMENTING HR'S STRATEGIC ROLE

How can HR formalize this kind of strategic role? Figure 2-3 illustrates how HR can link its deliverables to the firm's strategy implementation process. While we elaborate on various components of this model in subsequent chapters, we summarize it for you in the following seven steps:

Step 1: Clearly Define Business Strategy

At the strategy-development "table," senior HR leaders provide an essential perspective. By focusing on how to *implement* the strategy rather than solely on what the strategy consists of, they can facilitate a discussion about how to communicate the firm's goals throughout the organization. When strategic goals are *not* developed with an eye toward how they will be implemented and communicated throughout the organization, they tend to become very generic—for example, "maximize operating efficiency," or "increase presence in international markets," or "improve productivity." These goals are so vague that individual employees simply can't know how to take action to achieve them. Worse, employees can't recognize them as unique to their firm. To illustrate, we often run a simple experiment in our executive education classes. We ask participants to write down their firm's mission or vision statement, which we then retype (removing any mention of the firm's name) and redistribute among the group. Next we ask participants to pick out their own mission and vision statements from this collection. These statements are so vague—and so similar—that most find it very difficult to do so.

Clarifying your organization's strategy in precise terms can take practice. The key thing is to state the firm's goals in such a way that employees understand their role and the organization knows how to measure its success in achieving them.

Step 2: Build a Business Case for HR as a Strategic Asset

Once a firm clarifies its strategy, human resource professionals need to build a clear business case for *why* and *how* HR can support that strategy. In making this business case, you have the benefit of a decade of systematic research to support your recommendations. While a comprehensive review of this research is beyond the scope of this book, we can highlight the key results. First, evidence gathered from four national surveys and more than 2,800 firms strongly suggests that a high-performance work

Figure 2-3 Transforming the HR Architecture into a Strategic Asset

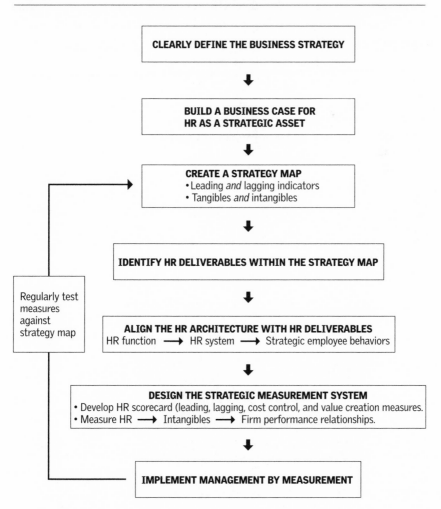

system has a distinct, positive influence on a firm's financial performance. Figure 2-4 illustrates those results.

The x-axis in figure 2-4 reflects the extent to which a firm's HR system is consistent with our principles of a High-Performance Work System, ranging from 0 for the lowest-rated firms in our survey to 100 for the
highest-rated firms. The y-axis represents the market value per employee
associated with different points on our 1996 HR index. Once again, the
results demonstrate that better HR management matters—and it does so
in terms that matter *outside* HR.

Figure 2-4 also indicates that the returns from investments in a high-
performance HR strategy are not linear. Firms in this sample appear to have
three distinct experiences as their HR systems become more focused on
performance. First, firms moving from the lowest percentile rankings to the
twentieth percentile enjoy a significant improvement in firm performance.
At this point, HR functions move from being an impediment to strategy
implementation to having a neutral strategic influence. Said differently, by

Figure 2-4   HR as a Source of Value Creation

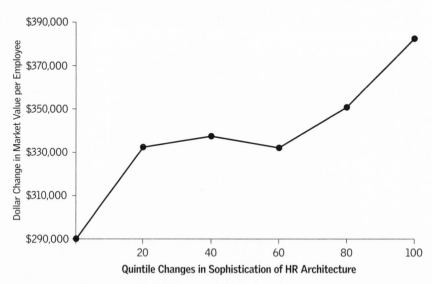

Note: The relationship between the HPWS index and market/book value in this figure is adjusted for company differences in research and development, industry, sales growth, employment level, and unionization. Note also that the
market values per employee reflect 1996 levels and will have increased over time.

Source: Mark A. Huselid and Brian E. Becker, "High Performance Work Systems and Organizational Performance,"
paper presented at 1995 Academy of Management annual meeting, Vancouver, B.C., August 1995.

improving to the twentieth percentile, the HRM system creates value simply by getting out of the way.

Second, for the broad middle range (twentieth to sixtieth percentile firms), improving the quality of a firm's HRM system has little marginal impact on firm performance. This marks the consolidation of the transformation from a personnel to a professional focus in human resources. This approach does no damage, but HRM is still not really a strategic partner.

Finally, firms above the sixtieth percentile not only have adopted the appropriate HRM practices and implemented them effectively throughout the firm but also have begun to integrate the HRM system into the strategic "fabric" of the firm. As a practical matter, above the sixtieth percentile, the marginal impact of HRM on firm performance is the same as it is for those firms below the twentieth percentile, but for different reasons. The very best firms in our sample enjoy the payoffs from combining the appropriate HRM policies and practices into an internally coherent system that is directly aligned with business priorities and operating initiatives most likely to create economic value. In essence, our findings point to the significant financial returns available to firms that dramatically increase the quality of their HRM systems.

While these effects are financially significant, keep in mind that they do not represent a magic bullet. That is, simple changes in an HR practice will not immediately send a firm's stock price soaring. Remember that our HR measure describes an entire human resource *system*. Changing this system by the magnitude required to enjoy these gains takes time, insight, and considerable effort. It's fair to say that it requires a *transformation* of the HR function and system. If it could be done overnight, human resource systems would be easily imitated and would quickly lose much of their strategic character.

The business case for a strategic HR role must also incorporate HR's key influence on strategy implementation and the role of strategically focused measurement systems. Figure 2-5 describes the model for such a business case based on our most recent survey of more than 400 firms.[6] These results tell a simple but powerful story. Consistent with the premise of this book, our research suggests that strategy *implementation*, rather than strategy *content*, differentiates successful from unsuccessful firms. It is simply much easier to choose an appropriate strategy than it is to implement it effectively. Moreover, successful strategy implementation is driven by employee strategic focus, HR strategic alignment, and a balanced performance measurement system. The linchpin of successful strategy implementation is a strategically focused workforce, which we could consider the ultimate HR performance driver. Finally, a balanced performance measurement system, in tandem with an aligned HR system and effective knowledge management, is the foundation for a strategically focused organization.[7]

Step 3: Create a Strategy Map

Clarifying your firm's strategy sets the stage for implementing that strategy. But it is just the first step. In most organizations, the customer value embodied in the firm's products and services is the result of a complex, cumulative process—what Michael Porter refers to as the firm's *value chain*.[8] All firms have a value chain—even those that haven't articulated it—and the company's performance measurement system must account for every link in that chain.

To define the value-creation process in your organization, we recommend that the top- and mid-level managers who will be implementing the firm's strategy develop what Bob Kaplan and Dave Norton call a strategy map to represent the firm's value chain.[9] These are diagrams of the value chain, such as those shown in figures 2-1 and 2-2. Such graphic representations of the company's value chain reveal *how* the firm creates

Figure 2-5 HR and Strategy Implementation

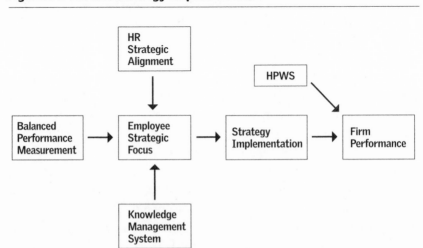

value in terms that managers and employees alike can grasp and act on. The value-chain mapping process should involve managers from all functions across the organization. This broad participation not only improves the quality of the strategy map but also increases buy-in among critical players. To begin the mapping process in your own organization, take a close look at your company's strategic objectives and ask yourself the following questions:

- Which strategic goals/objectives/outcomes are critical rather than nice to have?

- What are the performance drivers for each goal?

- How would we measure progress toward these goals?

- What are the barriers to the achievement of each goal?

- How would employees need to behave to ensure that the company achieves these goals?

- Is the HR function providing the company with the employee competencies and behaviors necessary to achieve these objectives?

- If not, what needs to change?

These simple questions can generate a wealth of information about how well a firm's HR function has been contributing to the organization's success. We also suggest supplementing these discussions with a variety of other information-gathering tools, including questionnaires to test employees' understanding of the firm's goals, and surveys to generate additional data about the firm's performance drivers and organizational capabilities. Once you think you have a full picture of your firm's value chain, translate the information that you have gathered into a conceptual model using language and graphics that make sense in your organization. Then test for understanding and acceptance in small groups of opinion leaders and thought leaders throughout the firm.

A strategy map of the value-creation process contains *hypotheses*, or predictions, about which organizational processes drive firm performance. Normally, a company validates these hypotheses only after achieving targets on performance drivers and observing the impact of these results on firm performance. However, if the organization can graphically depict the relationships among performance drivers while mapping the firm's value chain, it can have that much more confidence in its strategy implementation plan.

Sears is a good example of an organization that had a chance to test its hypotheses and further refine its strategy map based on actual experience. Beginning with the work-shop-invest model described in chapter 1, Sears dramatically enhanced its understanding of these constructs as it gained more experience with the model—which it subsequently used to enhance the quality of its measurement system. Figure 2-6 describes the more comprehensive ("total performance indicator") strategy map that Sears developed at the level of the full-line retail store.

Step 4: Identify HR Deliverables within the Strategy Map

We mentioned earlier that HR creates much of its value at the points of intersection between the HR system and the strategy implementation system. Maximizing that value requires an understanding of both sides of that intersection. Historically, HR managers lacked the requisite knowledge of the business side of the intersection, and general managers did not fully appreciate the HR side. While this gap has narrowed in recent decades, human resource managers should take primary responsibility for depicting both HR performance drivers *and* HR enablers on the strategy map.

This process can be difficult. On the one hand, human resource performance drivers such as employee competence, motivation, and availability are so fundamental that it may be virtually impossible to know where to locate them on the map. To perform this step, we recommend asking yourself which *HR* deliverables (again, both performance drivers and enablers) support the *firm*-level performance drivers depicted in the strategy map. Try to focus on the kinds of strategic behaviors that are broadly a function of competencies, rewards, and work organization. For example, your firm may decide that employee stability (i.e., low turnover) improves R&D cycle time (a firm-level performance driver). Employee stability is thus a key HR enabler. Seeing this connection would prompt you to design policies—such as above-market-rate salaries or bonuses—that would encourage lengthy tenure among experienced R&D staff.

Figure 2-6 Sears "Total Performance Indicator" Model for Full-Line Retail Stores

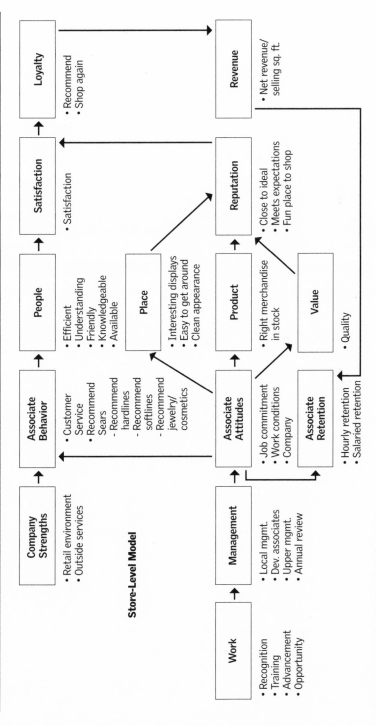

Source: Sears, Roebuck and Co. Reprinted with permission.

LINKING HR TO STRATEGY AT GTE

Steps 1 through 3 in the model described in this chapter are much more straightforward if the company has implemented, or is in the process of implementing, a wider Balanced Scorecard. In some cases, however, HR managers have to approximate Steps 1 through 3 without the benefit of the more systematic analysis that would have been part of a larger Balanced Scorecard effort. The experience at GTE is a good illustration of how, when the larger organization has not participated in the creation of a "strategy map" linking leading and lagging indicators of strategic performance, HR can begin to link its measurement system to the enterprise strategy.

At GTE, HR initially developed the firm's "people imperatives" as part of a top leadership planning process called "Leadership 2000." These imperatives focused on the new behaviors and capabilities required to drive business results over the next five to ten years. This in turn was the foundation for a new HR strategy that was organized around five strategic thrusts, as follows:

- talent;
- leadership;
- customer service and support;
- organizational integration; and
- HR capability.

Most important, GTE HR didn't stop with these very high level strategic thrusts. Instead, they met with GTE business leaders and found out what it was about each of the five strategic thrusts that kept the business leadership "awake at night." This alignment process resulted in seventeen specific questions that became the organizing focus for the metrics in HR's own Balanced Scorecard. Some examples of these questions include the following:

- Do we have the talent we need to be successful in the future?
- How is HR helping GTE position itself to meet the needs of external customers?
- Is HR viewed as an enabler to attracting and retaining top talent at GTE?
- Are we managing the cost of turnover/churn?
- Are we managing financial risk?
- What is GTE's return on investment in people?

Source: Garrett Walker, HR director at GTE, interview with author (Mark Huselid), August 2000; and *Measure What Matters: Aligning Performance Measures with Business Strategy* (American Productivity and Quality Center, 1999).

Step 5: Align the HR Architecture with HR Deliverables

Up until now, you've been thinking "top down," whereby strategy tells you which HR deliverables you should focus on (Step 4). Now the question is, How can the HR system (rewards, competencies, work organization, etc.) be structured so as to provide those deliverables? Figure 2-7 illustrates how a properly aligned HR system creates the HR deliverable (low turnover among senior R&D employees) that enables a key performance driver (cycle time) in the strategy map. The experience at GTE illustrates these same concepts. As described in the sidebar "Linking HR to Strategy at GTE," GTE has developed a Scorecard for the HR function (see chapter 3) that focuses on five enterprise-wide HR performance drivers, which it calls strategic "thrusts." These are human-capital-related areas that are important to successful strategy implementation overall, but are not specifically linked to a particular business problem.

However, GTE has also used these strategic "thrusts" to guide its analysis of unique HR problems facing its respective business units. This is very similar to our notion of the HR enabler, which is a highly focused point of impact for the HR architecture. For example, in one SBU, a strategic performance driver is making service a key market differentiator. Based on an analysis by GTE HR, the HR deliverable, to use our terms, is a "stable and engaged workforce." We would differentiate this deliverable as an HR enabler because it would not rise to the level of an enterprise-wide HR performance driver. Finally, GTE HR aligns the HR system to provide the necessary talent acquisition, incentive plans, culture initiatives, and "brain drain" initiatives to provide the required HR deliverable.

GTE HR has also worked with individual business units to develop SBU-specific strategy maps that more systematically describe and guide HR's contribution to the unit's strategy. For example, GTE's Wireless

Figure 2-7   Intersection of HR with Strategy Map

group decided to focus on a key market to increase sales and revenue. HR worked with business leaders in Wireless to develop the unique competencies needed to implement that strategy. Figure 2-8 describes the relationship between HR's initiatives and financial performance. Here the HR deliverable is a set of sales skill competencies.

Figure 2-8 represents results one might expect from following Steps 1 through 4 at the SBU level. Implementing Step 5 means developing a competency model and development program to provide the HR deliverable specifically required by this strategy.

Step 5 brings your firm's value-creation story to life by aligning the HR system with the firm's larger strategy-implementation system. But to do this, you need to think about how the components *within* your HR

Figure 2-8   Strategy Map: Competency Skill Attainment Focus

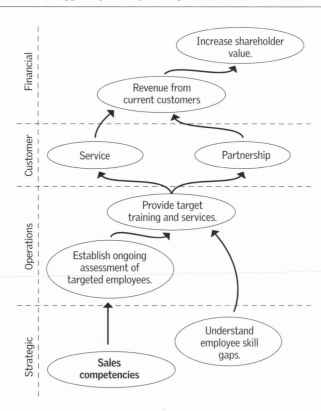

Source: Reprinted with permission of GTE Corporation.

system fit together (internal alignment) as well as how the HR system aligns with (that is, supports) the other elements in the firm's value chain (external alignment). These concepts of internal and external alignment are closely interrelated. Specifically, internal alignment is necessary but not sufficient in itself for external alignment to occur. For example, in the 1980s, IBM was characterized by high levels of internal HR alignment. Led by one of the largest and most competent cadre of human resource professionals in business history, the company designed a remarkably cohesive HR management system and then linked it tightly with its competitive strategy. This HR system was so cohesive that when IBM changed its strategy, many established human resource structures became irrelevant and even inappropriate. A highly cohesive HR strategy will fail if it is not periodically reshaped so as to align with the firm's larger (and often changing) business strategy. Yet all firms need an internally aligned HR strategy in order to achieve their overall goals.

*Mis*alignment between the HR system and the strategy implementation system can actually destroy value, as our experience with a large money center demonstrated. Like many other banks in this industry, the firm in question switched from full-time to part-time front-line tellers to save payroll costs. In many of its locations, the company outsourced entire cadres of tellers and then leased the employees back from a contractor. In the short run, this strategy did lower labor costs. However, about a year later, the bank faced a shortage of candidates for the head teller and junior loan officer positions. Not only had the organization dismantled the training and development opportunities that had historically prepared tellers for promotion, but in its shift to part-time employment, it had attracted workers who weren't particularly interested in full-time positions, as well as some individuals who were not necessarily "promotable." As an unintended consequence of the shift toward part-time employment, recruiting and compensation costs shot up for positions two to three levels above the entry-level teller positions. The bank was now forced to hire from the outside, but it no longer had the selection and training systems in place to do so. In the long run, total compensation costs thus *increased* significantly, including considerable time lost and discontent among other employees. The lesson is that the measurement system adopted by the firm (short-term payroll costs) eventually harmed the business's overall performance and had exactly the opposite effect of what the problem fixers intended.

UNINTENDED CONSEQUENCES AT GTE

The systemic thinking encouraged by a "balanced" performance measurement model is illustrated by the experience of GTE. Prior to the development of their Scorecard, GTE HR had been under strong pressure by line managers to focus largely on efficiency and cost control. In response, HR in one region reduced cycle time to fill jobs by 50 percent below the company average and generally achieved very low staffing costs. However, the GTE call centers in this region were not seeing the benefits of this HR efficiency in their business results. Instead they had a turnover rate twice the company average and falling customer service levels.

What happened? Both line managers and GTE HR had been thinking too narrowly about HR's influence on the business and didn't anticipate the indirect influence of those decisions. As it turned out, GTE HR had started recruiting from a different talent pool to reduce their cycle time. They shifted from a pool of graduating students and experienced professionals to temporary agencies and job bank applicants. Cycle time and staffing costs fell, but with the result that the sourcing process was less selective and new hires did not have the same "fit" as past hires. The result was higher turnover rates and higher training costs, as these hires lacked many of the foundational skills of the earlier pool. Customer service levels fell as turnover increased the percentage of inexperienced employees and further diverted more experienced staff from customers to support these new employees.

The new partnership with business leaders encouraged by the HR Scorecard resulted in a more complete understanding of these systemic relationships. The result was an acceptance that longer cycle times and higher staffing costs are actually investments with substantial positive business results.

Step 6: Design the Strategic HR Measurement System

Steps 1 through 5 guide the development of the HR architecture and lay the groundwork necessary to measure the HR-firm performance relationship. In Step 6, you actually design that HR measurement system. This requires not only a new perspective on measuring HR performance, but also the resolution of some technical issues that many HR professionals may not be familiar with.

To measure the HR-firm performance relationship with precision, you need to develop valid measures of HR deliverables. This task has two dimensions. First, you have to be confident that you have chosen the correct HR performance drivers and enablers. This requires that you clearly comprehend the causal chain for effective strategy implementation in your organization. Second, you have to choose the correct *measures* for those deliverables. For example, in figure 2-7 the HR deliverable is senior staff employment stability, but there are several ways this concept could be measured. Developing the actual measure would require that you precisely define who constitutes the senior staff (for example, those with five to fifteen years of professional experience) and what you mean by employment stability. Does the latter include all turnover or just voluntary? Does it include individuals who have been promoted to management responsibilities? Finally, you need to measure those variables accurately.

In our experience, most firms go through several stages of increasing sophistication when they develop an HR Scorecard. Figure 2-9 illustrates the measurement choices facing HR professionals. Most HR measurement systems fall in the Traditional category, or Stage 1. These include operational metrics such as cost per hire and activity counts. The gap between Stages 1 and 2 in the diagram symbolizes the substantial divide between a strategically and operationally focused HR measurement system.

Figure 2-9   The Creation of Employee Strategic Focus Through Increasing Measurement Sophistication

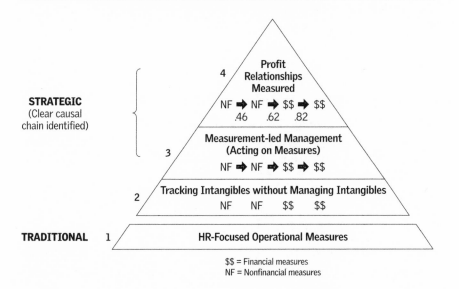

$$\$\$ = \text{Financial measures}$$
$$\text{NF} = \text{Nonfinancial measures}$$

In the second stage, HR measures have the aura of strategic import, but they do little to validate HR's role as a strategic asset. Firms may declare several "people" measures, such as employee satisfaction, as having strategic value, and these metrics might even make their way into the reward system in some fashion. In such cases, there is a "balance" between financial ($$) and nonfinancial (NF) measures, but there is no consensus about how these variables serve to implement strategy. There is therefore no strategic logic linking these measures together. Such firms have skipped Steps 2 through 5 in our model.

Stage 3 in figure 2-9 is a key transition point. The firm includes non-financial measures (among them HR measures) in its strategic performance measurement system. In addition, it locates each measure within a strategy map. For the first time, human resource measures are legitimately tracking HR's contribution to firm performance.

In Stage 4, HR measurement systems let the firm estimate the impact of HR policies on firm performance. If the firm's value chain is short, as it is at Sears, the company can gauge the full impact of HR on overall performance. In organizations with more complex value chains, estimates of HR's influence may be limited to segments within the chain. Just because you can't capture the full impact of HR on firm performance, that doesn't mean that you shouldn't measure part of the impact. For example, consider the example of an imaginary company called Petro Pipeline in figure 2-10. This describes a very small portion of a larger strategy map depicting Petro's strategy implementation system. It would be reasonably straightforward to measure the influence of the HR deliverables (improved employee focus on preventive maintenance) on "repair down time" and subsequent effects on customer perceptions of Petro as a reliable provider.

Clearly, measuring the HR-firm performance relationship is not an all-or-nothing proposition. Any progress beyond traditional measurement approaches is likely to yield substantial improvement later in the value chain. The more sophisticated the measurement system, the greater the eventual benefits.

Step 7: Implement Management by Measurement

Once the HR Scorecard is developed along the principles described in our model, the result is a powerful new management tool. Actually implementing this tool is much more than just "keeping score" of HR's impact on firm performance. If the Scorecard is aligned with the imperatives of the firm's strategy, HR professionals will have new insight into what it takes to actually manage HR as a strategic asset.

For example, GTE HR had always measured the turnover rates in its businesses, but prior to the development of its HR Scorecard, there had been little effort to understand the underlying dimensions of the turnover rates and their consequences for organizational profitability. In other words, although GTE HR measured turnover in the past, it really didn't manage it as a business problem in its respective business units. As the HR Scorecard was implemented, these turnover rates were more closely analyzed indicating substantial increases among new hires and the most experienced employees. The result was new HR interventions for both groups that addressed these problems with associated benefits for the performance of the business units involved.[10]

Figure 2-10   Influence of HR Enablers at Petro Pipeline

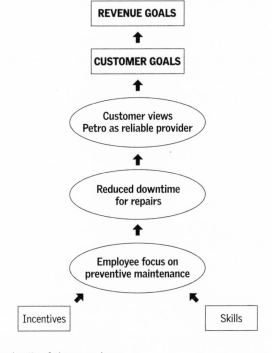

Note: This figure is a subsection of a larger causal map.

Implementing a new management process based on the work done in Steps 1 through 6 requires considerable change and flexibility. Moreover, the process is not just a one-time event. Human resource leaders must regularly review the HR deliverables they've defined in order to be sure that these drivers and enablers remain strategically significant. This is particularly true for HR enablers that have direct links to specific business objectives. Skilled HR managers understand when an enabler is no longer playing a strategic role and needs to be replaced.

SUMMARY: DEVELOPING WORLD-CLASS PERFORMANCE MEASUREMENT

Developing a world-class performance measurement system hinges on a clear understanding of the firm's competitive strategy and operational goals—and a definitive statement of the employee competencies and behaviors required to achieve the firm's objectives. Moreover, a systems perspective is a prerequisite for cultivating internal and external alignment of the HR system and thus for generating true competitive advantage. Measurement systems—for the firm as a whole or for the HR function—can create value only when they are carefully matched with the firm's unique competitive strategy and operational goals. Thus, firms should benchmark other organizations' measurement systems with caution. In the case of measurement systems, "best practices" may not be portable across firms. Therein lies their competitive value!

3

CREATING AN
HR SCORECARD

A
S WE'VE SEEN, an HR Scorecard lets you do two important things: (1) manage HR as a strategic asset and (2) demonstrate HR's contribution to your firm's financial success. Although each firm will depict its Scorecard in its own way, a well-thought-out Scorecard should get you thinking about four major themes: the key human resource deliverables that will leverage HR's role in your firm's overall strategy, the High-Performance Work System, the extent to which that system is aligned with firm strategy, and the efficiency with which those deliverables are generated.

We discuss these dimensions of the HR Scorecard in more detail later in this chapter. However, to begin to understand what building an HR Scorecard requires, let's look at that process in a company we'll call HiTech. For the sake of illustration, we'll focus on HiTech's R&D function and explore HR's potential role in this unit's strategy implementation model. As in many business units, R&D at HiTech has profitability goals that hinge on both *revenue growth* and *productivity improvement*—two important performance drivers. To build an HR Scorecard for just this unit, we need to understand the role that HR plays in these two dimensions of the R&D strategy map. We could describe this role as follows:

- *Revenue growth* ultimately derives from increased customer satisfaction, which in turn is boosted by product innovation and reliable delivery schedules, among other things.

  - Product innovation strongly depends on the presence of talented staff with significant company experience. Through competency-based selection methods and retention programs, HR contributes to stable, high-talent staffing in R&D.

  - Reliable delivery schedules in part hinge on the maintenance of optimal staffing levels in manufacturing. Even if turnover in manufacturing is low, the company must fill vacancies quickly. By reducing recruiting cycle time, HR supports optimal staffing levels.

- *Productivity improvement* has links to the maintenance of optimal production schedules, which in turn depends on the maintenance of appropriate staffing levels. Again, HR recruiting cycle time drives staffing levels.

DEVELOPING AN HR MEASUREMENT SYSTEM

Now let's "walk through" a few steps in the HR Scorecard approach in order to illustrate how HiTech might begin developing its human resource measurement system.

Identifying HR Deliverables

There are two HR deliverables in this example. The first is *stable, high-talent staffing in the R&D function*. This deliverable has several dimensions. For one thing, the R&D staff must have the unique competencies defined by HiTech and must demonstrate those competencies at the highest levels. These competencies combine cutting-edge technical knowledge with the specialized product demands found in HiTech. Thus they are not influenced by in-house professional-development efforts. Moreover, because these competencies are specific to HiTech and require several years of firm experience to develop, the company must keep its R&D staffing turnover very low.

The second HR deliverable is *optimal staffing levels in the manufacturing unit*.

Both of these deliverables have clear implications for HiTech's overall performance. One contributes to revenue growth, while the other influences productivity growth.

High-Performance Work System

Once the HR deliverables have been clearly defined, we can begin to identify and measure the foundational High-Performance Work System elements that help to generate those deliverables. We term these elements a High-Performance Work System to represent the fact that they have been selected specifically with the intent of implementing strategy through the HR deliverables. In the case of HiTech, this means designing and implementing a validated competency model linked to every element in the HR system, and providing regular performance appraisals to all employees. As with all of the other elements of the HR scorecard, there are a variety of ways that these data can be represented. The most common approach is to present the proportion of achievement on each element, although it is also possible to indicate whether or not each element is either up to standard or below standard with a toggle indicating red (below standard), yellow (marginal), or green (meets standard).

Identifying HR System Alignment

What HR system elements need to reinforce one another so as to produce the two HR deliverables? In the case of stable, high-talent staffing in R&D, we can assume that the firm has developed a validated competency model. At HiTech, selection into these positions must correspond to the existing competency model, and the quality of the hires should be at the highest levels. These alignment goals would strongly influence the particular sourcing decisions needed to produce those results. However, the sourcing decisions do not have to be part of the HR Scorecard. The assumption is that since you are measuring the outcomes of those sourcing decisions and since "what gets measured gets managed," then sourcing decisions will be guided by the need to achieve these outcome goals.

HiTech also needs to enact the kinds of retention policies that build experience in the R&D unit. Note, though, that *understanding* that retention policies are a key leading indicator is more important than the actual selection of policies, which are unique to each firm. At HiTech, a carefully chosen range of HR activities and policies, from supervisory training to unique benefit packages, might be in order. The key thing is that seemingly irrelevant HR "doables" have a clear strategic rationale.

To achieve optimal staffing in manufacturing, HR must keep its recruiting cycle time short. The appropriate alignment measure—for example, a fourteen-day recruiting cycle time—would reflect progress toward that objective.

Identifying HR Efficiency Measures

In this simple example, HiTech could identify cost per hire as a strategic efficiency measure. For both deliverables, cost per hire will probably be higher than average. But, the benefits of those hiring processes will also be well above average. The HR Scorecard that HiTech develops should highlight these links between important costs and benefits.

Figure 3-1 gives you a basic idea of how HiTech's R&D HR Scorecard might look. Of course, an HR Scorecard for the entire company would include many more entries. This diagram represents a concise but comprehensive measurement system that will both guide HR strategic decision making and assess HR's contribution to R&D's performance. More important, the scorecard is presented in such a way that it reinforces the "causal logic" or strategy map of how HR creates value at HiTech.

THE THINKING BEHIND THE HR SCORECARD

Why have we chosen the identification of HR deliverables, the use of the High-Performance Work System, HR system alignment, and HR efficiency measure as essential elements of the HR Scorecard? We believe that this arrangement reflects a balance between the twin HR imperatives of cost control and value creation. Cost control comes through measuring HR efficiency. Value creation comes through measuring HR deliverables, external HR system alignment, and the High-Performance Work System. These last three essential elements of the HR architecture trace a value chain from function to systems to employee behaviors.

In the following two sections, we outline a way of thinking about cost control and value creation. Again, it is more important that managers understand the reasoning behind the Scorecard than narrowly follow the particular format we have selected. The value of the Scorecard diagram itself lies in the thinking that goes into it and its power as a decision-making tool once it's constructed.

The Bottom-Line Emphasis: Balancing Cost Control and Value Creation

Like most HR managers, you are probably under constant pressure to help your organization "drive out costs." Indeed, many line managers consider much of what HR does as overhead. In many instances, these managers are correct, which puts even more responsibility on HR to find efficiencies wherever possible. We acknowledge these demands and believe that every HR Scorecard should include a dimension that captures the efficiency of the HR function. The problem is that, in organizations that view HR as nothing more than a cost center, efficiency of the HR function tends to be the only bottom-line metric in the HR measurement system.

Yet despite this imperative to measure HR efficiency, the HR function does not have a strategic significance for the organization. HR efficiency

Figure 3-1 HR Scorecard for HiTech's R&D Function

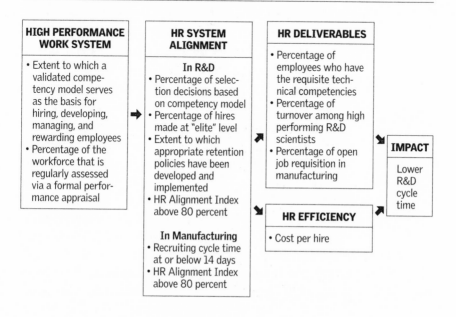

HIGH PERFORMANCE WORK SYSTEM	HR SYSTEM ALIGNMENT	HR DELIVERABLES
• Extent to which a validated competency model serves as the basis for hiring, developing, managing, and rewarding employees • Percentage of the workforce that is regularly assessed via a formal performance appraisal	**In R&D** • Percentage of selection decisions based on competency model • Percentage of hires made at "elite" level • Extent to which appropriate retention policies have been developed and implemented • HR Alignment Index above 80 percent **In Manufacturing** • Recruiting cycle time at or below 14 days • HR Alignment Index above 80 percent	• Percentage of employees who have the requisite technical competencies • Percentage of turnover among high performing R&D scientists • Percentage of open job requisition in manufacturing

IMPACT

Lower R&D cycle time

HR EFFICIENCY

• Cost per hire

has the same value as any other accounting-focused form of cost control, but it doesn't generate unique, intangible assets over the long run. Recall our analysis in chapter 1 of how the structure and alignment of the HR system contribute to shareholder value. We made no mention of HR efficiency in that discussion, because it is not typically a source of value creation. And in chapter 2, where we discuss the research behind making the business case for strategic management of HR, we did not mention efficiency.

Why have we put so little emphasis on this theme? First, efficiency in the HR function simply can't generate enough cost savings to substantially affect shareholder value. Second, whatever competitive advantage such efficiencies might offer is very likely lost as other firms adopt such practices. In other words, most HR functions are fairly adept at providing efficient HR processes; this capability doesn't distinguish the successful from the unsuccessful firm. Therefore, these sorts of measures will play a limited role in determining HR's strategic influence.

There's a crucial difference, however, between cost control and efficiency within the HR function and HR's contribution to cost saving and efficiency in line operations. For example, most balanced performance measurement systems contain metrics assessing both revenue growth and productivity or efficiency. "Efficiency" will often be represented by a financial lagging indicator, such as "reduce unit costs." A number of performance drivers will map onto that indicator (the arrows in your strategy map), but many won't. When HR enablers affect the "efficiency" component of those drivers, they are actually influencing the efficiency of line operations. In the HiTech example, there is a clear line of sight between efficient HR recruiting processes and the firm's bottom line through HR's contribution to improved operating efficiency. This point was also illustrated by our example in chapter 2 of GTE's traditional narrow focus on HR efficiency. Their efforts to reduce hiring cycle as an efficiency measure ultimately resulted in business problems that were much more significant than the original efficiency gains.

Still, the HR Scorecard needs to emphasize HR's value creation, tempered by attention to efficiency. Only in this way can the human resource management system strengthen HR's strategic influence in the organization overall. That is why most of the Scorecard should focus on the value created through HR's contribution to strategy implementation. Figure 3-2 illustrates this perspective.

As this figure suggests, if HR managers are measuring what matters, they are measuring those HR decisions and outcomes that get the highest rate of return. For example, the operational side (the traditional focus of HR) focuses largely on doables (HR efficiency) and generates a limited rate of return. Though exceptions exist, we consider the operational-high-return outcome an "empty set." There are so few high-return opportunities on this side of HR that they probably are not worth exploring at length here. At the same time, blindly focusing on "strategy" doesn't guarantee high returns either. In fact, this "tunnel vision" led to much of the frustration in the early years of "strategic" HR. During that time, human resource managers devoted too much effort to getting a seat at the strategic planning table and overlooked the greater opportunities available in strategy execution. They weren't developing a strategically focused HR architecture that is the key to HR's value as a strategic asset. These HR managers were operating in that lower-right-hand corner, exchanging one low-return philosophy for another.

Balancing cost control and value creation measures helps HR managers to avoid another mistake as well: the tendency to focus on the benefits of HR's strategic efforts while ignoring the costs of those benefits. The highest rates of return for HR come from a disciplined strategic focus. HR deliverables, rather than doables, are the source of these benefits, but only if the HR system is managed efficiently. Remember doables tend to be cost-focused; deliverables, benefits-focused. In practice, many

Figure 3-2   Balancing Cost Control and Value Creation

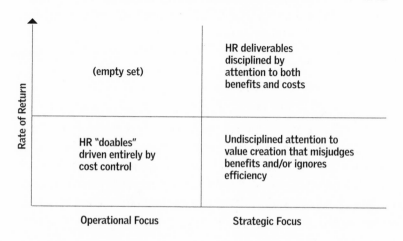

HR processes that comprise the doables are the costs associated with generating the deliverables. It's not that doables are unimportant; it's just that you need to gauge how well they translate into deliverables with value. You must keep both in mind when evaluating HR's *overall* rate of return.

Let's revisit the HiTech example to see how this works. In that scenario, HR's ability to reduce recruiting cycle time improved operational efficiency in the R&D unit and would ultimately boost financial performance for the entire firm. But reducing recruiting cycle time from, say, fifty-two to fourteen days might well have required special investment in staff or technology. Managers focused only on efficiency may have recoiled at the additional cost and rejected the decision to invest. Even HR managers who understood that this was the right decision may have had only a vague sense of whether the benefits would truly justify the cost. An appropriate measurement system would have shown them in concrete terms that the decision to invest in reduced recruiting cycle time could pay off.

This example illustrates another advantage of understanding the balance between cost control and value creation. Many HR managers work for firms that pride themselves on being "lean and mean." Such organizations keep HR thinly staffed, so as to control overhead as much as possible. This policy can be shortsighted if HR is truly to serve as an intangible asset. As we saw in chapter 1, high-performing firms had more than twice as many HR professionals per employee as did low-performing firms. Even more frustrating, many organizations now expect HR managers to play a strategic role—but with no increase in resources. Under these circumstances, most managers are almost doomed to fail. The only way they can pass this test is to demonstrate, through their measurement system, how resources allocated to HR might actually create value.

The Architectural Emphasis:
Which HR Value Chain Elements Go into the Scorecard?

Since the primary focus of HR's strategic role is value creation, thinking about HR architecture means taking the broad view of HR's value chain. Just as a corporate scorecard contains both leading and lagging indicators, the HR Scorecard must do the same. Of the four HR architecture elements that we recommend including in the Scorecard—High-Performance Work System, HR system alignment, HR efficiency, and HR deliverables—the first two are leading indicators and the second two are lagging indicators for HR's performance.

Measuring the High-Performance Work System lays the foundation for building HR into a strategic asset. A High-Performance Work System maximizes the performance of the firm's employees. The problem is that the performance dimension tends to get lost in the attention most firms give to issues of efficiency, compliance constraints, employee relations, etc.—none of which is part of HR's strategic role. This is a mistake. The performance dimension needs to have prominence if a firm wants to enjoy the financial benefits that the Scorecard approach makes possible. Therefore, every firm's HR measurement system should include a collection of indicators that reflects the "performance focus" of each element in the HR system.

As we've seen, measuring HR system alignment means assessing how well the HR system meets the requirements of the firm's strategy implementation system, or what we have called "external" alignment. We have also mentioned "internal" alignment, defined as the extent to which each of the elements worked together rather than in conflict with one another. We do not give equal emphasis to internal alignment in our measurement system because, if the HR system is uniformly focused on strategy implementation, the elements should tend toward internal alignment. In other words, if HR managers can manage external alignment, then internal misalignments will tend to disappear. A focus on internal alignment becomes more appropriate as an initial diagnostic for those firms that have not adopted a strategic HR perspective. Internal misalignment, therefore, is much more likely to be a symptom of an operationally focused HR system.

HR efficiency reflects the extent to which the HR function can help the rest of the firm to generate the needed competencies in a cost-effective manner. This does not mean that HR should try to simply minimize costs without attention to outcomes, but neither should they "throw money off the balcony." The metrics included in this category should reflect that balance.

And finally, HR deliverables are the key human-capital contributors to implementation of the firm's strategy. They tend to be strategically focused employee behaviors, such as the low turnover rates in the HiTech example.

How does this simple illustration in figure 3-3 help us in understanding the appropriate structure of an HR Scorecard? While we will develop these ideas in more detail later in the chapter, there are some organizing principles to keep in mind. The structure of a strategic HR measurement system depends on striking the correct balance between efficiency and value creation, while being guided by a broad strategic rather than a narrow operational perspective on HR.

It is important to understand that proper positioning on both dimensions (see figure 3-3) provides the basis for synergies between HR management and the measurement system. In other words, for HR to be able to demonstrate a significant impact on firm performance, the HR architecture must be designed as a strategic asset and the HR measurement system must be designed to guide the management of that strategic asset.

CONSTRUCTING THE HR SCORECARD

Now that we've talked about the four dimensions—HR deliverables, the High-Performance Work System, external HR system alignment, and HR efficiency—that should go into the HR Scorecard and the reasoning behind including them, let's move on to how you might actually use them to construct your Scorecard. First, we will take a closer look at each dimension.

The High-Performance Work System

HR's strategic influence rests on a foundation of high-performing HR policies, processes, and practices. However, given the conflicting demands that HR managers typically confront, these professionals need a set of measures that keep the performance dimension of those HR activities at the forefront of their attention. Such measures don't reflect *what is* as much

Figure 3-3 The Synergy of Measurement Structure

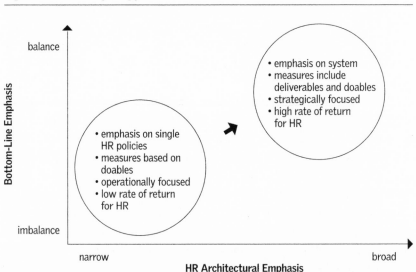

as they remind managers of *what should be*. Therefore, they can be represented on the HR Scorecard as simple toggles, indicating "unsatisfactory" or "satisfactory." Or, they can be included as metrics along a continuum.

For an illustration of the kinds of broad questions we include in our HPWS survey, see the sidebar "Examples of High-Performance Work System Measures." As you can see, these questions are not designed to test whether an organization is current on the very latest HR fad or has added another ten degrees to its performance-appraisal system. Rather, they work through each HR function from a "macro" level and highlight the performance orientation of each activity.

EXAMPLES OF HIGH-PERFORMANCE WORK SYSTEM MEASURES

- How many *exceptional* candidates do we recruit for each *strategic* job opening?

- What proportion of all new hires have been selected based primarily on *validated* selection methods?

- To what extent has your firm adopted a professionally developed and validated competency model as the basis for hiring, developing, managing, and rewarding employees?

- How many hours of training does a new employee receive each year?

- What percentage of the workforce is regularly assessed via a formal performance appraisal?

- What proportion of the workforce receives formal feedback on job performance from multiple sources?

- What proportion of merit pay is determined by a formal performance appraisal?

- If the market rate for total compensation would be the fiftieth percentile, what is your firm's current percentile ranking on total compensation?

- What percentage of your exempt and nonexempt employees is eligible for annual cash or deferred incentive plans, or for profit sharing?

- What percentage of the total compensation for your exempt and nonexempt employees is represented by variable pay?

- What is the likely *differential* in merit pay awards between high-performing and low-performing employees?

Jeffrey Pfeffer has developed a similar set of high-performance characteristics that he associates with a firm's ability to transform people into a source of competitive advantage.[1] He includes selective hiring, high pay, incentive pay, employee ownership, information sharing, and an emphasis on training and development. But in addition, he cites several dimensions designed to provide more employee equity in organizational processes and outcomes. Among the latter, he mentions employee participation and empowerment, narrower pay differentials across the firm, symbolic egalitarianism, and greater employment security. For your reference, we've listed more High-Performance Work System metrics in table 3-1.

HR System Alignment

The next component in the HR Scorecard encourages you to gauge the alignment of the HR system with drivers of the firm's strategy implementation process. To transform a generic High-Performance Work System into a strategic asset, you need to focus that system directly on the human-capital aspects of those drivers.

Choosing the correct alignment measures is relatively straightforward, if you begin with the process discussed in chapter 2. This process helps you understand the exact HR deliverables required to create value in the organization, which in turn indicates specific elements of the HR system (leading indicators) that must reinforce one another in order to produce those deliverables. Therefore, specific alignment measures will

Table 3-1   High-Performance Work System Measures

Average merit increase granted by job classification and job performance	Percentage of employees whose pay is performance-contingent
Backup talent ratio	Percentage of employees with development plans
Competency development expense per employee	
Firm salary/competitor salary ratio	Percentage of total salary at risk
Incentive compensation differential (low versus high performers)	Quality of employee feedback systems
	Range (distribution) of performance-appraisal ratings
Number and quality of cross-functional teams	Range in merit increase granted by classification
Number and type of "special projects" to develop high-potential employees	
Number of suggestions generated and/or implemented	

be linked directly to specific deliverables in the Scorecard. Connecting them in this way highlights the cause-and-effect relationships needed to support HR's contribution to firm performance.

To select the appropriate alignment measures, focus on those elements of your HR system that make a definable and significant contribution to a particular HR deliverable. These differ for each firm, but the experience at Sears described in chapter 1 is a good example. Identifying these measures requires you to combine a professional understanding of HR with a thorough knowledge of the value-creation process in your own firm. Remember that the alignment measures will follow directly from the "top-down" process. Based on the larger "strategy map" (Step 3 in our seven-step model), you will identify your HR deliverables, which in turn will point to certain elements of the HR system that require alignment. Therefore, there are no standard alignment measures that can be provided as examples. Instead, we emphasize the need for a standard process by which each firm will develops its own set of alignment measures.

Much like the High-Performance Work System measures, the external HR system alignment measures are designed largely for use within a firm's HR department. They too can be represented as toggles on the Scorecard, indicating alignment or nonalignment. The key issue is that they prompt HR managers to routinely think about alignment issues and highlight areas requiring action.

HR Efficiency: Core versus Strategic Metrics

As an HR professional, you doubtless have access to a wide range of benchmarks and cost standards by which you can measure HR's efficiency. We show a number of these in table 3-2.[2] All of these metrics encourage cost savings and are the kinds of measures you would find in the first level of our measurement pyramid (figure 2-9 in chapter 2). But unless you want HR to be treated like a commodity in your organization, you should beware of building your measurement system unthinkingly on these generic benchmarks. Instead, separate out the costs associated with HR commodities such as employee benefits transactions and policy compliance, and the unique investments required to create HR's strategic value in your organization. (These choices will differ for each organization. Part of our rationale for including such a long list of potential metrics is to highlight the importance of choosing key metrics carefully using the process we have described. Otherwise, it is possible to become over-whelmed by the potential choices). Benchmarking is fine for the HR commodity activities, but it has no significant influence on your firm's ability to implement its strategy.

Table 3-2 HR Efficiency Measures (Doables)

Absenteeism rate by job category and job performance	Number of stress-related illnesses
Accident costs	Number of training days and programs per year
Accident safety ratings	Offer-to-acceptance ratio
Average employee tenure (by performance level)	OSHA audits
Average time for dispute resolution	Percentage of and number of employees involved in training
Benefits costs as a percentage of payroll or revenue	Percentage of correct data in HR information system
Benefits costs/competitors' benefits costs ratio	
Compliance with federal and state fair employment practices	Percentage of employee development plans completed
Compliance with technical requirements of affirmative action	Percentage of employees with access to appropriate training and development opportunities
Comprehensiveness of safety monitoring	
Cost of HR-related litigation	Percentage of new material in training programs each year
Cost of injuries	Percentage of payroll spent on training
Cost per grievance	Percentage of performance appraisals completed on time
Cost per hire	
Cost per trainee hour	Response time per information request
HR department budget as a percentage of sales	Sick days per full-time equivalent per year
HR expense per employee	Speed of salary action processing
HR expense/total expense	Time needed to orient new employees
Incidence of injuries	Time to fill an open position
Interviews-per-offer ratio (selection ratio)	Total compensation expense per employee
Lost time due to accidents	Total HR investment/earnings
Measures of cycle time for key HR processes	Total HR investment/revenues
Number of applicants per recruiting source (by quality)	Turnover by recruiting source
	Turnover costs
Number of hires per recruiting source (by quality)	Turnover rate by job category and job performance
Number of courses taught by subject	Variable labor costs as percentage of variable revenue
Number of recruiting advertising programs in place	
	Workers' compensation costs
Number of safety training and awareness activities	Workers' compensation experience rating

Source: Adapted from Dave Ulrich, "Measuring Human Resources: An Overview of Practice and a Prescription for Results," *Human Resources Management* 36 (Fall 1997): 303–320.

We thus recommend that HR managers divide their key efficiency metrics into two categories: core and strategic. *Core* efficiency measures represent significant HR expenditures that make no direct contribution to the firm's strategy implementation. *Strategic* efficiency measures assess the efficiency of HR activities and processes designed to produce *HR deliverables*. Separating these two helps you evaluate the net benefits of strategic deliverables and guides resource-allocation decisions. To see how this works, consider the following HR efficiency measures:

- benefit costs as a percentage of payroll

- workers' compensation cost per employee

- percentage of correct entries on HR information system

- cost per hire

- cost per trainee hour

- HR expense per employee

The first three measures on the list would typically go in the core efficiency category. While certain benefit costs might give a firm an edge in recruiting high-talent employees, above-average benefit costs or workers' compensation payments are legitimately considered expenses rather than human-capital investments. Likewise, transactional accuracy marginally improves employees' work experience, but it has little strategic significance.

Now look at the last three measures. Notice that these expenditures can each be thought of as investments that would yield considerable strategic value. To determine their value, you would go through the seven-step process described in chapter 2, tracing the links between a strategic efficiency measure and the subsequent elements in the HR value chain. Again, the HiTech example of reducing recruiting cycle time applies. Tightening this cycle may well raise "cost per hire," but in fact this practice is the first step in producing an HR enabler (stable staffing in R&D) that is essential to a key performance driver (R&D cycle time) in the firm's strategy implementation process. This is a good illustration of how a firm might attend to both the benefits and costs of an HR deliverable (see the upper-right box in figure 3-2).

HR Deliverables

HR deliverable measures help you identify the unique causal linkages by which the HR system generates value in your firm. They are not necessarily expressed in terms of firm performance or dollars, but they should be understood broadly to influence firm performance. The test of their importance is that senior line managers understand their significance and are willing to pay for them.

One challenge in measuring the impact of such "upstream" drivers is to avoid measure proliferation. It is easy to think that everything is important, but if you do this, soon nothing is important. For measurement to matter, you have to measure only what matters. HR deliverable metrics that cannot be tied directly to your firm's strategy map should not be included in the HR Scorecard. Once again, the process outlined in chapter 2 ensures that your HR measurement process has the proper foundation.

Choosing the appropriate HR deliverable measures depends on the role that HR will play in strategy implementation. At one extreme, HR deliverables could be characterized as *organizational capabilities*.[3] Such capabilities would combine individual competencies with organizational systems that add value *throughout* the firm's value chain.

Note, though, that a capability is so central to successful strategy implementation that it cannot be linked to just one performance driver. We know of a major international consumer-products firm that wanted to dramatically restructure its leadership capabilities. In management's view, the firm with the best leadership talent would win in the marketplace, and this company intended to cultivate the best leadership talent in its industry. To achieve this goal, the management team developed its own competency model, which it considered proprietary. Next, it brought the executive search function in-house so that executive sourcing would reflect the proprietary competency model. Finally, the team added a powerful staffing-information system that would enable managers throughout the world to rapidly and effectively identify available managerial talent. No single element of this effort would constitute a strategic asset by itself, but taken together, these elements helped the firm develop a new organizational capability that senior line managers consider a key to the organization's future success.

Thinking about HR deliverables in terms of organizational capabilities has a distinct appeal for human resources managers interested in underscoring HR's strategic value. This is because such capabilities seem to offer a competitive advantage so compelling that other managers can't help but acknowledge their strategic value. The problem is that without clear validation of that strategic value from the senior executive team, HR managers will have a difficult time making the case post hoc. Viewing HR deliverables as organizational capabilities is thus an appropriate but limited measure of HR's strategic value. Identify this potential where possible, but also recognize that much of HR's strategic value lies elsewhere. Most important, don't try to puff up every HR initiative as a potential organizational capability. This kind of posturing will only undermine HR's legitimate strategic contribution.

In short, we are talking about taking a different perspective on HR's influence on firm performance. One approach is to focus on comprehensive people-related capabilities (such as leadership and organizational flexibility). It's easy to imagine how such capabilities contribute to organizational success in general, and perhaps even in your own organization. They are also appealing because they immediately allow HR managers to recast what they are doing in "strategic" terms. While we don't dismiss this approach out of hand, we encourage HR managers to understand its limitations as well. Most important, an approach that thinks only of HR deliverables in terms of organizational capabilities tends not to link those deliverables concretely to the strategy implementation process. In other words, the valuation of those deliverables requires much the same leap of faith that has historically undermined HR's link to firm performance.

In contrast, with our seven-step model, measuring HR's contribution does not require a direct leap from HR deliverable to firm performance. Instead there is a "causal logic" between HR and other non-HR business outcomes (such as R&D cycle time in HiTech), which line managers consider credible.

For this reason, as you structure the "HR deliverables" section of your Scorecard, you should focus more on HR performance drivers and HR enablers than on potential organizational capabilities. These measures represent the human-capital dimensions of discrete performance drivers in the firm's strategy map. Their individual effects on firm performance are much smaller than that of an HR capability, but there are so many of them that, cumulatively, they represent a significant source of value creation. Table 3-3 shows a list of potential HR performance-driver measures for purposes of illustration.[4] However, we would never recommend selecting a measure without following the earlier steps in our model.

Ideally, the "HR deliverables" section of your Scorecard will include some measure of the strategic *impact* of the deliverables you've identified. This could include estimates of the relationships between each deliverable and individual firm-level performance drivers in the strategy map. Or, in a more elaborate system, you could link the effects of the deliverables through the performance drivers and ultimately to firm performance. We saw this approach in the Sears story.

At this point, you will have defined the constituent elements of HR's strategic impact on your organization. Yet even the HR deliverables represent just the *hypothetical* strategic influence of HR. Where possible, we encourage human resource managers to try to establish the *actual* impact of these deliverables on firm performance. This is the last piece of the sophisticated HR measurement system described in chapter 2. It allows you to confidently make precise statements such as "HR deliverable *a* increased *x* by 20 percent, which reduced *y* by 10 percent, which in turn increased shareholder value by 3 percent." We discuss this aspect of designing your HR measurement system in more detail in chapter 5.

BASING THE HR SCORECARD ON THE HR FUNCTION

Our approach to HR performance measurement has been to adopt as comprehensive a definition of HR as possible, hence our emphasis on what we call the HR architecture. This has involved both a somewhat different perspective on "HR" in the firm and some new ideas about the important dimensions of HR's performance. Making the leap from little or no performance measurement for HR to the concept of measuring the performance of the HR architecture can be daunting. Some firms may be more comfortable developing a Scorecard for the HR function as an interim step in this process. While we believe that the benefits of a more broadly focused Scorecard are compelling, some very good examples of HR Scorecards in practice have been organized around the HR function.

Figure 3-4 illustrates a graphical depiction of GTE's HR Scorecard. Here the HR function is viewed as an organizational unit that can be analyzed in terms of the leading and lagging indicators associated with a Balanced Scorecard. In this approach the "Operations" and "Customers" are not the larger operations or customers of GTE, but rather the operations or customers of GTE's HR function. This choice makes it more difficult to explicitly link HR to strategy implementation through the Scorecard, but it is a reasonable decision given that, at the time, the larger organization

Table 3-3   HR Performance-Driver Measures

Access to business information to facilitate decision making

Adherence by the workforce to core values, such as cost consciousness

Average change in performance-appraisal rating over time

Change in employee mind-set

Climate surveys

Consistency and clarity of messages from top management and from HR

Customer complaints/praise

Customer satisfaction with hiring process

Degree of financial literacy among employees

Degree to which a "shared mind-set" exists

Diversity of race and gender by job category

Effectiveness of information sharing among departments

Effectiveness of performance appraisal processes for dealing with poor performers

Employee commitment survey scores

Employee competency growth

Employee development/advancement opportunities

Employee job involvement survey scores

Employee satisfaction with advancement opportunites, compensation, etc.

Employee turnover by performance level and by controllability

Extent of cross-functional teamwork

Extent of organizational learning

Extent of understanding of the firm's competitive strategy and operational goals

Extent to which employees have ready access to the information and knowledge that they need

Extent to which required employee competencies are reflected in recruiting, staffing, and performance management

Extent to which employees are clear about the firm's goals and objectives

Extent to which employees are clear about their own goals

Extent to which hiring, evaluation, and compensation practices seek out and reward knowledge creation and sharing

Extent to which HR is helping to develop necessary leadership competencies

Extent to which HR does a thorough job of pre-acquisition soft-asset due diligence

Extent to which HR leadership is involved early in selection of potential acquisition candidates

Extent to which HR measurement systems are seen as credible

Extent to which information is communicated effectively to employees

Extent to which the average employee can describe the firm's HR strategy

Extent to which the average employee can describe the firm's strategic intent

Extent to which the firm shares large amounts of relevant business information widely and freely with employees

Extent to which the firm has turned its strategy into specific goals/objectives that employees can act on in the short and long run

Extent to which top management shows commitment and leadership around knowledge-sharing issues throughout the firm

Percentage of employees making suggestions

Percentage of female and minority promotions

Percentage of intern conversion to hires

Percentage of workforce that is promotable

Percentage of repatriate retention after one year

Percentage of employees with experience outside their current job responsibility or function

Percentage of retention of high-performing key employees

Perception of consistent and equitable treatment of all employees

Performance of newly hired applicants

Planned development opportunities accomplished

The ratio of HR employees to total employment

Requests for transfer per supervisor

Retention rates of critical human capital

Success rate of external hires

Survey results on becoming "the" employer of choice in selected, critical positions

Source: Adapted from Dave Ulrich, "Measuring Human Resources: An Overview of Practice and a Prescription for Results," *Human Resources Management* 36 (Fall 1997): 303–320.

had not developed a strategy map as part of a corporate-wide "balanced" performance management system.

The "bubbles" in figure 3-4 represent HR's objectives for each level of the Scorecard. These in turn are linked to measures at both the enterprise and SBU level (see table 3-4). Table 3-4 links the HR Scorecard at the SBU level with the HR Scorecard at the enterprise level. The directional arrows correspond to a strategy map for the HR function and tell the story of how GTE HR will implement its functional strategy. This HR linkage model does not have the kind of direct linkage to strategic performance drivers that would be possible if a larger Balanced Scorecard existed for the entire enterprise. Nevertheless, there are at least three points where the HR function Scorecard would tend to connect with the larger organization's strategy implementation efforts.

First, recall from chapter 2 that GTE HR developed five strategic thrusts for its HR strategy after close consultation with the organization's business leaders. The foundational role of these five strategic thrusts is reflected by their location at the bottom of the HR linkage model (see figure 3-4). Second, the HR function Scorecard focuses on more than efficiency goals. The two objectives (maximize human capital and minimize HR costs) in the financial category are an effort to capture both value creation *and* efficiency as drivers of firm performance. Finally, at the customer level the HR Scorecard identifies strategic support for business partners as a key objective. This too should have the effect of improving the alignment between the efforts of HR managers and the business problems faced by line managers.

We began this chapter with the observation that a well-developed HR Scorecard should allow HR managers to do a better job of managing HR as a strategic asset, as well as provide a better demonstration of HR's contribution to firm performance. In organizations that have not gone through the systematic development of a strategy map describing strategic performance drivers and opportunities for HR, it becomes more difficult to aggregate the relationships that easily describe HR's impact on firm performance. However, as GTE's HR Scorecard demonstrates, even a functionally oriented Scorecard can serve to refocus the management decisions of HR professionals. GTE HR credits its Scorecard, and the associated change in perspective, with dramatically improved relations between HR and business unit managers.

Likewise, while our emphasis has been on measuring HR's "strategic

Figure 3-4 GTE HR Linkage Model

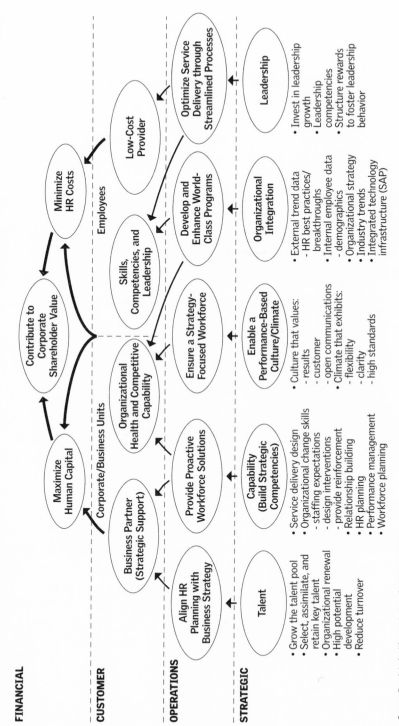

Source: Reprinted with permission of GTE Corporation.

Table 3-4 Measures for GTE HR Scorecard, by Objective

	Objectives	Enterprise Measures (Lagging Measures)	SBU Measures (Leading Measures)
Financial	F1 — Maximize shareholder value	• Total shareholder return • Revenue per employee	• Human capital value added
	F2 — Maximize human capital performance	• HR ROI (Index) • Total HR cost/employee	• Total labor cost percentage • Competitive capability index
	F3 — Minimize human resources costs	• Budget variance	
Customer	C1 — Business partner (strategic support)	• Rating on corporate service agreements	• Employee engagement index
	C2 — World-class standards	• Ranking of HR practice development/audit (vs. benchmark)	• Comparative analysis results—Hi-Tech, RBOC's, IT peergroups
	C3 — Responsive quality service	• Employee satisfaction survey results • Benefit center satisfaction percentage	• Hewitt—average time to resolve • Fidelity percentage resolved first call
	C4 — Low-cost provider	• HR cost factor indices	• Cost of service vs. benchmark
Operations	O1 — Align HR planning with business priorities	• % of HR strategic plans implemented	• Time spent with executives
	O2 — Provide quality consultative advice	• % of HR customized recommendations implemented	• % Service coverage/client
	O3 — Ensure a strategy-focused workforce	• Productivity improvement goals established • Compensation schemes aligned to strategy	• % Participation in goal setting process linked to strategy
	O4 — Develop and enhance world-class programs	• Benchmarking ranking • Programs executed	• Program development cycle time • Key initiative tracking vs. milestones
	O5 — Optimize HR services through alternative delivery channels	• Cost per delivery channel—HR interaction, automation, outsourcing • Cycle time to fill • Cost per transaction	• HR technology ROI and payback period • % Training delivered—CBT
Strategic	S1 — Capability (build strategic competencies)	• LD participation	• Critical skill attainment
	S2 — Talent (select, assimilate, and train)	• Voluntary separation rate/separation cost	• % New hires retention, 6 months/1 year ratio • Targeted workforce churn rate
	S3 — Performance-based culture/climate	• Rating on viewpoints survey • Organizational health index	• Internal promotion rate
	S5 — Organizational integration (information for decision making)	• Reporting % accurate first request • Turnaround time for ad hoc request	• Data availability
	S5 — Leadership	• LDP benchstrength • Diversity • Executive coaching	• High potential retention • Offer acceptance rate • Executive retention

impact," HR professionals have multiple roles, as Dave Ulrich has pointed out: strategic partner, administrative expert, change agent, and employee champion.[5] If HR professionals want a Scorecard that broadly touches on each of these roles, the functional emphasis illustrated by the GTE Scorecard is a good starting point.

BENEFITS OF THE HR SCORECARD

In constructing an HR Scorecard, avoid the temptation to merely "fill in the boxes." The key question to ask is, What would you like this tool to do for you? Or, put another way, How would you like managers outside of HR to think about your measures? We believe that the Scorecard offers the following benefits:

It reinforces the distinction between HR doables and HR deliverables. The HR measurement system must clearly distinguish between deliverables, which influence strategy implementation, and doables, which do not. For example, policy implementation is not a deliverable until it creates employee behaviors that drive strategy implementation. An appropriate HR measurement system continually prompts HR professionals to think strategically as well as operationally.

It enables you to control costs and create value. HR will always be expected to control costs for the firm. At the same time, serving in a strategic role means that HR must also create value. The HR Scorecard helps human resource managers to effectively balance those two objectives. It not only encourages these practitioners to drive out costs where appropriate, but also helps them defend an "investment" by outlining the potential benefits in concrete terms.

It measures leading indicators. Our model of HR's strategic contribution links HR decisions and systems to HR deliverables, which in turn influence key performance drivers in the firm's strategy implementation. Just as there are leading and lagging indicators in the firm's overall balanced performance measurement system, there are both drivers and outcomes within the HR value chain. It is essential to monitor the alignment of those HR decisions and system elements that drive HR deliverables. Assessing this alignment provides feedback on HR's progress toward those deliverables and lays the foundation for HR's strategic influence.

It assesses HR's contribution to strategy implementation and, ultimately, to the "bottom line." Any strategic performance measurement system should provide the chief HR officer (CHRO) with an answer to the question, "What is HR's contribution to firm performance?" The cumulative effect of the Scorecard's HR deliverable measures should provide that answer. Human resource managers should have a brief, credible, and clear *strategic* rationale for all deliverable measures. If that rationale doesn't exist, neither should the measure. Line managers should find these deliverable measures as credible as HR managers do, since these metrics represent solutions to business problems, not HR problems.

It lets HR professionals effectively manage their strategic responsibilities. The HR Scorecard encourages human resource managers to focus on exactly *how* their decisions affect the successful implementation of the firm's strategy. Just as we highlighted the importance of "employee strategic focus" for the entire firm, the HR Scorecard should reinforce the strategic focus of human resource managers. And because HR professionals can achieve that strategic influence largely by adopting a systemic perspective rather than fiddling with individual policies, the Scorecard further encourages them to think systemically about HR's strategy.

It encourages flexibility and change. A common criticism of performance measurement systems is that they become institutionalized and actually inhibit change. Strategies evolve, the organization needs to move in a different direction, but outdated performance goals cause managers and employees to want to maintain the status quo. Indeed, one criticism of management by measurement is that people become skilled at achieving the required numbers in the old system and are reluctant to change their management approach when shifting conditions demand it. The HR Scorecard engenders flexibility and change because it focuses on the firm's strategy implementation, which constantly demands change. With this approach, measures take on a new meaning. They become simply indicators of an underlying logic that managers accept as legitimate. In other words, it's not just that people get used to hitting particular sets of numbers; they also get used to thinking about their own contribution to the firm's implementation of strategy. They see the big picture. We believe that

that larger focus makes it easier for managers to change direction. Unlike in a traditional organization, in a strategy-focused organization, people view the measures as means to an end, rather than ends in themselves.

SUMMARY: TIPS FOR MANAGING WITH THE HR SCORECARD

Building an HR Scorecard should not be considered a one-time or even an annual event. To manage by measurement, human resource leaders must stay attuned to changes in the downstream performance drivers that HR is supporting. If these drivers change, or if the key HR deliverables that support them change, the Scorecard must shift accordingly. In building an HR Scorecard for your own company, you therefore may want to include a component indicating how up to date the HR deliverables are.

The same strategic perspective that guides the construction of the HR Scorecard should also guide the management of HR. In particular, human resource staff should keep line managers continually informed of the status of HR deliverables. Feel free to also invite line managers to identify potential deliverables on their own. This is all part of forging a powerful new partnership.

4

COST-BENEFIT ANALYSES
FOR HR INTERVENTIONS

ERHAPS ONE OF THE MOST important functions of the HR Scorecard measurement system is that it provides a means to identify, in
quantitative terms, the discrepancies between your firm's current
and ideal HR architecture. Such gaps may have arisen within the elements of the HR system itself, between the HR system and firm strategy,
or between desired and actual employee behaviors.

For example, in one firm we visited, the company's HR Scorecard
and planning processes indicated that they would face a shortage of
midlevel managerial talent as their business expanded and as a number
of midlevel managers reached retirement eligibility. (Business slow-
downs and a multiyear hiring freeze had shrunk the number of retiree
replacements in the pipeline.)

Senior HR managers in this firm quickly asked, How can we best
develop the employee competencies necessary to meet the firm's current
and future needs? Should we learn how to train employees in these competencies in-house, or should we use an external vendor? Should we
explore some other strategy entirely? In any case, what return on investment (ROI) can we expect from the various scenarios we're considering?

These kinds of questions form the focus of this chapter. In particular, we explore data-collection and analytical methods that can help you assess whether certain HR programs will pay off in the short and long run. Taken together, these methods make up what we call cost-benefit analysis. In many ways, cost-benefit analysis is a microcosm of the HR Scorecard framework. Determining which elements of your work should be "costed" is essentially a strategic task; thus you should tie it to the firm's competitive strategy and operational goals. For the sake of efficiency, you should also focus this decision process on only the vital few HR activities that really make a difference. In other words, the HR Scorecard will help to identify the most appropriate "doables" and "deliverables" that will become the focus of a cost-benefit analysis process.

Like most other human resource professionals, you probably already understand the importance of assessing the costs and benefits associated with investments in specific HR policies and practices. Indeed, for many years, HR practitioners have pursued this kind of information as if it were the Holy Grail. Many HR managers have even told us that the senior management team in their organization would be happy to fund more extensive HR initiatives and innovations—if only human resource leaders could provide economic justification for such policies.

Determining the ROI of specific HR interventions, whether as an end in itself or as a means of deciding on policies and practices, is not as difficult as it might first appear. Nevertheless, it does require some knowledge of finance, accounting, and the process of capital budgeting. It also requires a consistent, step-by-step process. In this chapter we will explore the thinking behind this process and then outline a recommended series of steps.

OPERATIONAL VERSUS STRATEGIC COST-BENEFIT ANALYSIS

We can think of most cost-benefit analyses as operational (designed to lower costs) or strategic (designed to help implement the firm's strategy). *Operational* cost-benefit analyses tell you how to improve activities that the firm already performs. By costing such activities, the organization can explore ways to lower recruiting-related expenses, compare the advantages of outsourcing the benefits function versus keeping it in-house, etc. In contrast, *strategic* cost-benefit analyses derive from the firm's strategy and operational goals and thus focus on questions such as, How can we best enhance employee strategic focus? You can easily identify the answers to such key questions from your firm's HR Scorecard—these are the deliverables that you have identified in the last chapter.

In most cases, cost-benefit analyses of either kind require the assembly of a special project team. Moreover, because you won't find the data you need in your firm's financial or managerial accounting system (as we've seen), you'll have to custom-design a data-collection method. The good news is that, while the "start-up" costs of designing such a system may prove relatively high, you can institutionalize your method and use it to ensure continuous improvement.

WHICH HR ACTIVITIES SHOULD YOU COST, AND WHY?

Many HR managers ask us, How can I determine the ROI on my investments in HR? This question often stems from well-intentioned efforts to demonstrate how investments in the HR *function* (as opposed to the HR *architecture*) create value throughout the organization. Invariably, we answer that cost-benefit analysis can prove both time-consuming and expensive and that human resource leaders should clarify their goals before embarking on a costing project.

Thus, before doing anything else, ask yourself what *types* (or categories) of HR activities should be "costed" and *why*. For example, is it important to know precisely what the ROI is for your training activities, or is it enough to know that the benefits of your firm's training activities exceed their costs? What is a more worthwhile activity: calculating your firm's cost-per-hire or determining the most effective way to increase employee competencies in a certain area, for example, financial literacy? Should you do one, both, or neither? Your HR Scorecard can be a powerful tool in this stage of the process. Specifically, the HR Scorecard should help you to identify the most salient HR doables and deliverables. These elements should be the primary focus of any cost-benefit analyses that you undertake.

The key objective at this stage is that you have a crystal-clear rationale for undertaking a costing project and that the effort is guided by the firm's strategy and the resulting HR Scorecard. To be meaningful, the project should have the following attributes:

- *Strategic importance.* The project has direct links to the implementation of the firm's strategy. Whether the project addresses an operational or strategic concern, the outcomes of the project should have a direct line of sight to the firm's overall strategy. You can determine whether this line exists by using the value-driver analysis method described in chapter 3.

- *Financial significance.* An effective costing project addresses an area of HR that involves significant and ongoing investments—for example, overall training and development, as opposed to a one-time training session.

- *Widespread impact.* The most valuable costing projects have the potential to affect a significant proportion of the firm's workforce. Alternatively, they target categories of employees (e.g., R&D scientists in a biotechnology firm) who have close links with the overall success of the business. For instance, a project to determine the ROI for a training program costing millions of dollars, affecting thousands of employees, and unfolding over many years can offer insights of significant financial magnitude.

- *Links to a business element of considerable variability.* Successful costing projects measure attributes of the firm's workforce or HR architecture that exhibit considerable variability in outcomes or performance levels. For example, if your firm's management development system is seen as highly successful in one part of the business but is a disaster elsewhere, then a cost-benefit analysis may help you understand why.

- *Focus on a key issue, problem, or decision facing line managers.* Finally, effective costing projects should provide an answer to a key question or problem facing the firm. For example, do we outsource our recruiting activities or continue to recruit in-house? Is our level of employee turnover optimal? Before beginning such a project, determine whether there is widespread interest in the results of the proposed study. If there isn't, then ask yourself why you want to conduct the study.

THE NEED FOR FINANCIAL SAVVY

HR managers requesting funds from senior line management teams encounter much tougher roadblocks than their peers in manufacturing, operations, and even marketing. Those other disciplines have a long tradition of quantifying the potential costs and benefits of their proposed programs and presenting these estimates in a language that all can understand—money. In contrast, most human resource professionals have little experience in quantifying what they do. In a world where numbers push aside intuition, such managers are at a distinct competitive disadvantage.

How can we remedy this situation? First, HR managers need to familiarize themselves with the concepts of finance and accounting, especially the process of capital budgeting. Organizations use capital budgeting to decide how to allocate capital among competing investments. For instance, do we buy a new building or lease space? Do we expand our production line or move to three shifts? Do we purchase another company or not? Not only does the capital-budgeting process help the rest of the firm determine its budgets, it also offers a strict discipline for rational decision making. Moreover, because this process requires managers to think in terms of the costs and benefits of each project over its entire useful life (as opposed to just this year), it encourages a longer-term focus on costs and benefits across multiple time periods. There are a wide variety of resources available for HR managers wishing to improve their financial literacy—from college courses to in-house program offerings. In chapter 7 we explore some of these delivery options in more detail.

DETERMINING THE ROI IN HR: A THREE-STEP PROCESS

In theory, determining the ROI in a particular HR policy or practice isn't complicated. Essentially, you need to assess the *total costs* and *total benefits* associated with the investment, and then calculate benefits less costs. You can do this by following this generic process:

1. Identify potential *costs*.

2. Identify potential *benefits*.

3. Calculate the ROI of the program using an appropriate index.

As with most seemingly simple processes, the "devil is in the details" for this one. In this case, the challenge lies in collecting or estimating data. Most firms don't regularly track cost and benefit data on HR activities, so they end up having to estimate. Here are some ways to get around this difficulty.

Identifying Costs and Benefits

By its very nature, identifying cost and benefit categories and attaching dollar value estimates to them is part art and part science. Potential benefits are particularly difficult to estimate because (a) they are likely to come some time in the future (while the costs are usually borne today) and (b) both the *level* of the benefits and the *probability* of receiving them are likely to be uncertain. That's okay. The trick is to come up with *plausible* estimates, as well as confidence intervals (a range of expected values for each estimate). Attaching a range to each estimate is important, as we will see. If your estimate of the ROI on a training initiative is 22 percent, plus or minus 3 percent, this would indicate a project with a very high probability of success. If your estimate is 22 percent, plus or minus 25 percent, this would imply that the project is much more risky.

Success at this stage hinges on the expert judgments—and careful analysis—of HR as well as line managers. There are a number of ways to generate these numbers. One effective method is first to develop a "straw man" of potential cost and benefit *categories*.[1] Then, using colleagues, subject matter experts, focus groups, and archival data, gather feedback on the categories and ask for help in generating dollar-value estimates for each of the categories that you have developed. It is important to recognize that some of these data may be available in full or part from your firm's HR information system. The trick is to have carefully developed the cost categories *before* you begin to develop the cost estimates.

A simple example can illustrate why this is important. If you were to ask most senior HR professionals how much they invest in training per year on a per-employee basis, they could probably generate a number based on the corporate training budget. However, if the firm is very large, there is often a considerable amount of training that is done at the division- or business-unit levels, and these investments are generally not tracked by corporate HR. In addition, there is often quite a bit of "on-the-job" training that is not tracked by the corporate *or* divisional financial statements. So, in most firms, the corporate budget for training and development can understate the true spending on training, and often by a considerable margin. This is why it is important to have defined your question carefully (e.g., Do we want to know the return on *corporate's* investment in training or the firmwide investment in training?) before you begin to collect actual data on costs.

UNDERSTANDING FIXED AND VARIABLE COSTS

If you ask an accountant to describe your firm's costs, you will quickly discover that there are a myriad of cost categories. Conventional managerial accounting systems often divide these categories into *fixed* costs (i.e., those that do not vary with the level of production or output) and *variable* costs (those that change directly with the level of production or output). Fixed costs include buildings, utilities, and insurance, as well as allocated staff "overhead" such as accounting, finance, legal, and human resources. Variable costs depend on the particular industry. For example, in the automotive industry, the costs associated with tires would be *variable* (because they change with the number of cars produced).

Why is it important for HR professionals to understand basic accounting conventions if they wish to perform cost-benefit analyses effectively? The answer is that we are really interested in whether a particular practice or intervention makes sense from an *economic* perspective (i.e., increasing shareholder wealth) as opposed to an *accounting* perspective. For a variety of reasons, accounting systems don't yield measures of true profitability the way that an economist might define it. For example, a charge for "depreciation" of physical assets (e.g., plant and equipment) effectively reduces a firm's reported net income (which is reported as the "bottom line" on a firm's income statement)—even though no one actually "paid" for depreciation. Depreciation is simply an adjusting entry that is designed to match current revenues with current expenses—whether real or estimated. The central concept is that since we have invested in buildings or machinery intended to provide us with economic benefits over many years, we should "match" (or depreciate) the cost of the building over its useful life. In contrast, many HR professionals are not aware that investments in people in any form are not considered long-lived assets, but are rather "expensed" in their entirety in the year in which they are incurred. As we noted in chapter 1, this is why managers are often reluctant to invest in people as opposed to buildings, especially if their pay is linked to the firm's net income.

Accounting systems are designed to allocate a firm's costs across a limited number of categories, primarily for the purposes of external reporting. The goal is to distribute these costs in a reliable and predictable manner, consistent with generally accepted accounting procedures (GAAP). Although firms have complete freedom to develop their own internal accounting systems, most companies use the same cost allocations for internal decision making as they use for external reporting.

This situation can distort the decision-making process. Since we are interested in estimating true economic profitability rather than following GAAP, we need to think carefully about the role of fixed costs in any cost-benefit analysis. Fixed costs are *economically* relevant only if we have to spend money directly on them *or* if they incur an opportunity cost elsewhere in the organization. For example, suppose your firm wants to determine the ROI of a new training program for midlevel executives. The firm currently owns an executive education center, which is generally booked at 60 percent of capacity. The program you propose will increase capacity another 20 percent, to a total of 80 percent of total capacity. In calculating the ROI of the training program, should the firm include a charge for the fixed assets associated with its training center? The answer is, it depends. If you want to allocate all of the firm's costs across a set of categories (as is done in conventional accounting systems), then the answer is yes. If, on the other hand, you want to know whether shareholder wealth will increase if the activity is performed, then the answer is no. Note that this situation changes if the training center is running at capacity and additional capital investments would be required to run the new program. In this case, it would always be appropriate to include an allocation for fixed costs. This distinction is important, as many firms (often inappropriately) require that new programs cover something called a "fully allocated fixed cost," effectively increasing the costs of the program and lowering the probability that it will have a positive ROI. As we have seen from our discussion of economic versus accounting costs, such an allocation of fixed costs is not always appropriate.

UNDERSTANDING SUNK COSTS

In addition to understanding fixed and variable costs, HR managers also need to gain perspective on *sunk costs*, or the total effort and resources that have been invested in a project to date. The easiest way to explain sunk costs is by example. For many years, one of us has nurtured a passion for the restoration of classic cars (a prime example of sunk costs if there ever was one!). As you restore an old car, the initial cost of the car and the subsequent restoration costs can in some cases exceed the market value of the completed car. To illustrate, suppose you've invested $25,000 in the purchase and partial restoration of a car. If you sold the unfinished car today, it would bring $15,000. Finishing the car would eat up an additional $20,000, but the car would then be worth only $30,000.

By selling the car unfinished, you would incur a loss of $10,000. Yet by investing additional time and resources to complete the car, you would lose $15,000 (plus the opportunity costs associated with the additional $20,000 investment). While an impartial observer would have no trouble arriving at the appropriate decision here, in the business world many managers pay entirely too much attention to sunk costs. Much like an impassioned car owner, HR professionals often fall in love with their projects and want to see them completed. In deciding whether to invest further in a project, they look at the sunk costs and figure that, since they've already invested so much, they simply can't abandon the effort.

How can you avoid this "fallacy of sunk costs"? The only solution is to periodically reevaluate your projects. Are the assumptions that you made still reasonable? Is the project costing what you had expected? Are you seeing the benefits that you had hoped for? Remember: At any given point in the life of a project, the only two things that matter are the amount of effort and resources required to *complete* the project, and the *present value* of the cash flows that the project will generate. As harsh as this may seem, the energy and effort already invested in the project are irrelevant. Goals and strategies change, and sometimes the most prudent course of action is to cut your losses and to move on to more value-creating projects.

UNDERSTANDING THE FINANCIAL IMPACT OF EMPLOYEE PERFORMANCE

In addition to grasping the importance of fixed, variable, and sunken costs, you also need to understand the financial impact of employee performance in identifying cost/benefit categories and estimates. At its core, determining the ROI in people entails comprehending the relative impact of high- and low-performing employees on the firm. Sometimes the impact is minimal. However, many managers underestimate it. For example, we recently worked with managers in the oil and gas pipeline industry who did not consider workforce management a potential source of competitive advantage in their firm. Because they were in a commodity business, they argued, their key sources of competitive advantage were access to pipelines and price of crude oil. Only when they saw that the level of pipeline throughput (a key strategic driver of firm profitability) differed substantially by shift—and that they could influence pipeline throughput via employee training, competencies, and supervision—did they perceive the potential impact of people on their firm's profits.

Most managers are already convinced that individual employee performance levels differ significantly. However, often they can't say with confidence *how much* difference better employees can make. For example, ask yourself this deceptively simple question: What is the relative economic value of an employee who performs at the fiftieth percentile compared to that of an employee who performs at the eighty-fourth percentile? (Such a shift—34 percent—reflects a *standard deviation* improvement. A standard deviation is a conventional measure of variability. Said differently, what is the relative economic contribution of *average* employees as compared to employees who are *well above average*?[2]

There are two important ideas here. First, you need to understand the *economic* contribution (valued added less salaries and other relevant costs) of *average* (fiftieth-percentile) employees. This provides a "reality check" on how your firm is deploying resources. For example, if the net benefits less costs of your direct sales force average $50,000 per employee, you should explore the possibility of adding to your sales staff because each salesperson is generating $50,000 more resources than she is consuming. If the benefits less costs are very close to zero per employee, you would explore other actions, such as restructuring or reassigning employees, or in the most extreme cases, downsizing.

The key question is whether, on average, employees in a particular job contribute a little or a lot to the firm's success. Economists generally use the average wage level for a given position as a proxy for its economic contribution to firm performance. For the firm to earn a profit, the argument goes, an employee must contribute at least her wages and benefits to the firm's success, as well as compensate shareholders for their risk. For example, stockbrokers usually make more than janitors because the former presumably contribute more profit to the firm's success.

Second, you must gauge the *variability* of the impact of employee performance on firm financial performance. Imagine a situation where the very best employees in a given job (eighty-fourth percentile or higher) have only a little more impact on firm performance than do average employees (an unusual scenario, we believe). In such a situation, the firm would not be likely to invest considerable resources in the attraction, selection, and development of those employees, because, quite simply, employee competencies and performance don't make a sufficient difference to the firm overall.

Let's take a closer look at how this works. Imagine that there are two kinds of employees in your firm. The first group has high average wages, relative to the rest of the firm's employees, and there is a high degree of variability in output from employee to employee. For example, in a large sales organization, it is not unusual for the highest output salesperson to sell ten times that of the lowest output salesperson. However, this group of high performers may be relatively small, perhaps only 500 of the firm's 50,000 employees.

Low wages and low levels of variability in the output among employees characterize the second group. Specifically, the best employees in this group have an economic impact on firm performance that is no greater than twice that of the worst employees in this group. However, there are considerably more of these employees throughout the firm.

You believe that, by specific changes in training programs, performance management processes, and the introduction of an incentive compensation plan, you might be able to raise the performance of the average employee in each group from the fiftieth to the seventy-fifth percentile. If each of your proposed programs has a positive ROI, you are going to want to implement both of them. And obviously, you will wish to focus on the one with the largest ROI first. But how would you decide among these proposed programs?

Clearly, estimating the impact of high and low employee performance on the firm is no simple task. Indeed, these estimates have been described as the "Achilles' heel" of the HR field.[3] Fortunately, you have a variety of methods at your disposal. An understanding of basic social-science research methods can help.[4] By putting on your social scientist "hat," you can observe "naturally occurring field experiments" in your organization and glean insights into the relative impact of employee performance. For example, an intervention might be happening in one part of the organization, but not in another. What outcomes do you observe in each situation? Or, as it was in the pipeline company we mentioned earlier, you might notice that productivity is high in one shift but low in another. Taking a closer look at why this is happening might yield important insights.

THE BECKER-HUSELID APPROACH FOR CALCULATING THE ECONOMIC VALUE OF HIGH AND LOW JOB PERFORMANCE

Academics have worked for many years to develop methodologies to help determine the economic benefits of high and low employee performance in a particular job. For example, scholars working in the field of utility analysis have devoted considerable effort to determining the economic benefit of the use of more effective (valid) selection tests on employee performance.

The general conclusion of this line of research is that employees considered to be high performers (i.e., those at the eighty-fourth percentile, or one standard deviation above average) have from 40 percent to 80 percent greater impact on firm performance than do average employees (i.e., those at the fiftieth percentile). The implications of this line of research are that high levels of employee performance have a greater economic impact than was previously believed.

While these results are based on studies that include many firms, it is also possible to develop estimates of the economic impact of employee performance within one's own firm. In 1992 Becker and Huselid developed a procedure to provide just such estimates. In a sample of 117 retail home products firms, Becker and Huselid used regularly collected data to determine that high-performing sales associates exhibited 74 percent to 100 percent greater economic performance than did average-performing employees.

This procedure can be used when there are financial data that can be isolated to particular divisions, units, or work teams. For example, departments within a retail environment, manufacturing cells or teams, or sales functions can often link sales or profits to specific units. Data that describe individual levels of employee performance, as well as any relevant control variables, such as employee education and experience, are also needed. It is especially helpful if these data can be collected over time. Once these data have been collected, multiple regression analyses can be used to determine the impact of the independent variable (employee performance) on the dependent variable (sales or profits).

Such analyses can be very helpful in determining which categories of employees create the most value in the organization, which can then be used to help provide focus for the firm's organizational intervention efforts.

Source: Brian E. Becker and Mark A. Huselid. "Direct Estimates of SDy and the Implications for Utility Analysis," *Journal of Applied Psychology* 77, no. 3 (1992): 227–233.

Calculating Benefits Less Costs

Let's say you've chosen cost and benefit categories for your HR project analysis and have come up with plausible estimates for each. The next step is to compare the costs with the benefits to determine the net benefit (or loss!) associated with the project or program.

If all the benefits and costs from a particular HR investment occurred in a single period (e.g., one year), then calculating a program's ROI would be very simple. You could either divide the dollar value benefits of the program by its costs (yielding a percentage) or subtract the program costs from its benefits (yielding a dollar value savings). For example, outsourcing your firm's benefits administration might save $1.2 million dollars of "in-house" costs while incurring $800,000 dollars in consulting fees, in addition to $100,000 in "transition" costs. The ROI of this endeavor expressed in a percentage is the following:

(($1.2MM - [$800,000+$100,000])/[$800,000+$100,000]) = 33 percent

Expressed in dollars of savings, the figure would be as shown:

$1.2MM - [$800,000+$100,000] = $300,000

You can conduct similar calculations to determine the *payback period* (the number of months or years before a program fully covers its costs). Following up on the same outsourcing example, assume that your benefits costs are currently the following:

($1.2MM / 12 months) = $100,000/month

The costs of transitioning to the outsourcing vendor are $100,000. Thereafter, the vendor will save the firm the following per month in benefits administration costs:

([$1.2MM - $800,000]/12) = $33,333

Thus, the payback period for this investment would be as shown:

($100,000/$33,333) = 3 months

Finally, HR professionals frequently calculate the *breakeven volume* (e.g., the number of participants who must attend a particular training program for the program to break even). For example, a consulting firm specializing in executive seminars calculated that a typical one-day course it offers requires an investment of $20,000 in advertising, staff support, salary for the presenter, and room and equipment rental. Each of these costs is essentially fixed, in that it remains constant if there is 1 paying participant or 100. Each participant pays $395 per day as a registration fee, and from this fee is deducted all variable costs (food, incentive compensation for the presenter and staff) of $100 per participant. Thus, the breakeven cost of this program would be the following:

$$(\$20,000)/(\$395-\$100) = 68 \text{ participants}$$

The managers in this firm use this number (and their considerable experience) to make a judgment about the viability of each new program. In essence, they ask, Are we sure that we can attract at least sixty-eight participants? If the answer is no, the program is cancelled.

But investments in HR are rarely this simple, in part because the costs— and especially the benefits—of such programs often unfold over more than a single year. For example, a management development program for an entire cadre of senior executives might well cost millions of dollars to develop and administer during its first year. Yet the firm may not begin to feel the impact of the program for as many as eighteen months down the road. A conventional, single-period ROI calculation for such a program would actually show a *negative* ROI (significant costs but no benefits in the first year).

Thus, a more appropriate cost-benefit calculation would incorporate multiple time periods (to reflect that investments today yield payoffs in future periods), as well as the time value of money (the notion that a dollar today is more valuable than a dollar sometime in the future). Money is more valuable today than in the future because of both *opportunity cost* (if I have the dollar today, I can invest it elsewhere) and *uncertainty* (the farther out into the future a project's estimated benefits are, the less likely they are to be realized).

Most organizations are willing to spend now for potential future benefits as long as they are adequately compensated for their opportunity costs and risk associated with the investment. Firms also require that a specific program compensate them for their *marginal cost of capital*—the amount of interest they would have to pay lenders if they borrowed money to pay for the program.

Net present value (NPV) analysis draws together all these factors—costs and benefits over multiple time periods, and compensation for uncertainty, opportunity costs, and the firm's costs of capital—to assess the overall potential value of a proposed HR program. In performing an NPV analysis on a program, you restate the program's costs *and* benefits in today's dollars.[5] Then, you subtract the present value of the program costs from the present value of its benefits, yielding a "net" present value for the program. In this way, you compare "apples with apples," while accounting for the likelihood that the program will yield benefits in the long run.

For example, imagine that you are considering the development and implementation of a new integrated performance management and incentive compensation program. The total development costs for this program will be $250,000. You estimate that this program will increase annual cash flow from operations (i.e., profits) a total of $270,000 each year for the next five years. However, because the program involves incentive pay, wages will increase a total of $130,000 per year for the five-year period. Assuming the firm's marginal cost of capital is 14 percent, should your firm roll out the new program? An NPV analysis of this situation would look as follows (Note: The present value "factors" shown in the example here can be found in any introductory financial analysis textbook. Alternatively, these values can be calculated via a spreadsheet or financial calculator.):

Year	Explanation	Amount	x	Factor	=	Present value
1	Program development cost	-$250,000		1		-$250,000
1-5	Increased wages	-$130,000		3.433		-$446,290
1-5	Increase in annual cash flow from operations	+$270,000		3.433		+$926,910
	Net present value:					$280,620

Based on these analyses, the program should be developed and implemented.

Cost-Benefit Analysis Procedures: A Hierarchy of Approaches

At this point, you may have gathered that there are a broad array of tools and methods for conducting cost-benefit analyses. Having to choose from among these various approaches does make this difficult task more challenging. However, by looking at the patterns in the ways other firms' HR departments grapple with this, we can glean some meaningful lessons.

We have explored this topic as part of our research. Specifically, we asked 968 senior HR managers what kinds of costs and benefits they measured and how they measured them. We also asked them to respond in one of three ways: (1) "we don't measure any element," (2) "we use a subjective estimate or intuition," and (3) "we use a formal procedure." Table 4-1 summarizes their responses.

As you can see from the table, most firms do not rigorously evaluate either the costs *or* the benefits associated with HR policies and programs. Indeed, the figures in the table may even *overstate* the extent to which firms use these procedures. (If a firm used a method once, their response may have implied that they use it regularly.)

Based on these data as well as our observations in a wide variety of firms, we believe that a range of cost-benefit analysis "quality" exists. This range starts at its low end with simple cost estimates and progresses

Table 4-1   What Firms Say They Are Measuring and How

	968 FIRMS		
	Don't Determine	Subjective Estimate or Intuition	Formal Estimation Procedure
Turnover costs	43.7%	43.1%	13.1%
Employee replacement costs	38.2%	48.8%	13.0%
Economic value of employees to the organization	67.4%	26.6%	6.0%
Cost of various employee behaviors (absenteeism, smoking, etc.)	48.3%	38.2%	13.5%
Economic benefits of developing a superior selection test	79.4%	17.1%	3.5%
Economic benefits of various training levels	47.2%	46.5%	6.3%
Economic benefits of additional recruiting	57.3%	35.4%	7.3%
Economic benefits of increasing job satisfaction, organizational commitment, or similar job attitudes	54.9%	42.3%	2.8%
Economic benefits of high, medium, and low performance on a particular job	54.2%	39.7%	6.1%

to benefits estimates and cost-benefit-index calculations. Firms showing the highest quality of cost-benefit analysis engage in these calculations on a regular, disciplined basis.

While theoretically some firms may combine these elements in various ways, our experience has revealed a number of typical combinations (see figure 4-1).

Level 1 organizations are by far the most prevalent. These firms do not routinely calculate the costs *or* the benefits associated with their HR programs. The recent downsizing of HR departments and the movement of HR resources closer to the line organizations have exacerbated this trend. Because these firms do little, if any, formal cost or benefit calculations, they do not calculate the ROI associated with their activities.

Level 2 organizations, in contrast, have begun to think systematically about the costs associated with their HR investments. However, they generally use intuitive or subjective estimates of these programs' potential benefits. In addition, they use relatively unsophisticated procedures, such as payback periods, breakeven volumes, or single-period ROI calculations. Finally, they conduct these analyses infrequently.

Level 3 organizations are the rarest of the three groups. These firms demonstrate a high degree of sophistication on all three elements: They identify the cost and benefits of their HR programs and use an appropriate

Figure 4-1 Hierarchy of Cost-Benefit Analysis Decisions

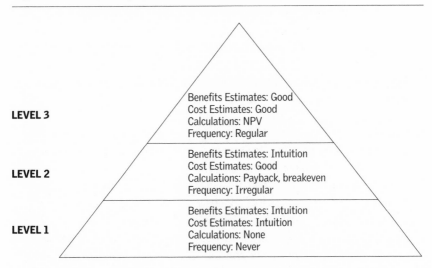

estimation procedure (e.g., NPV analysis) to calculate them. Because they see the value in such analyses, they conduct them regularly.

Should your organization perform Level Three analyses on *all* of its HR policies and programs? Our perhaps surprising answer is, *no*. Developing measurement competence means being able to match the depth and breadth of the data-collection and analysis procedures with the *importance* of the decision you're trying to make. For example, suppose you're mulling over whether to develop an on-site child-care center. You know that you will go ahead as long as the estimated benefits are at least equal to the costs (NPV = 0). In this case, you don't need to arrive at a precise estimate of the child-care center's ROI, if all indications suggest that the center's ROI is substantial and positive.

In contrast, imagine that you're trying to determine the viability of two competing options: outsourcing your benefits function or continuing to perform these activities in-house. In this case, more precision, and a move toward Level Three analyses, may serve you well. If a particular decision involves large dollars or has substantial strategic import, you may want to shoot for more precision there as well. Our point is that you shouldn't collect any more, but certainly no less, information than you need.

THE ROLE OF BENCHMARKING

Any discussion of the cost-benefit analysis of HRM investment inevitably raises the issue of *benchmarking*, or the process of collecting data on various aspects of a firm's HRM system from a variety of firms and then using these data to evaluate one's own firm.

Benchmarking studies can be grouped into those that focus on specific *levels* of a particular variable or attribute (e.g., What is our cost per hire relative to other firms in our industry?) and those that focus on specific *processes* (e.g., How does Wal-Mart operate its world-class logistics and distribution system?). Studies that benchmark *levels* of an attribute are often conducted via survey and include large numbers of firms; studies that benchmark *processes* generally include only a few firms and tend to be conducted via site visits or telephone interviews.

Our experience has been that studies that benchmark *processes* can provide a rich source of information, understanding, and often inspiration. While some have ridiculed such studies as "industrial tourism," we believe that observing exemplary processes *in situ* can be a very important learning experience for teams that have the responsibility for designing and implementing new processes within their own organizations. In contrast, we are less enthusiastic about studies that benchmark *levels* of a particular variable.

Why the reticence? A number of recent trends have made it more difficult to perform high-quality benchmarking studies that focus on "levels" of HRM practices or outcomes. The first is that many HR functions run much leaner than they have in the past, meaning that there are fewer HR professionals available to complete surveys. In addition, the movement of both HR resources and HR responsibilities to the line organization makes it harder than ever to ensure the comparability of the data across firms.

Can Benchmarking Ever Be Strategic?

For benchmarking to help an organization create a long-term source of competitive advantage, the information derived from this process would have to be rare, difficult to imitate, and valued by the firm's internal or external customers.* Yet almost by definition, if firms are readily willing to share such data, then it probably won't have much strategic value. Consider the case of Hewlett-Packard. HP is one of the most widely benchmarked companies in the world, and its business processes (especially its HR management philosophy and practices) have been widely reported in the business press and many academic books and articles. Why is HP willing to share such information, which will surely become available to their competitors? We believe that there are at least two important reasons. The first is that even if the firm is completely forthcoming about *what* they do, it doesn't help unless you know *how* they generated the solution, and the nuances of the context in which it has been implemented. Said differently, even if you had the recipe, you still might not be able to make the soup. Second, HP's management infrastructure relies heavily on leveraging employee competencies and talents in new and different solutions. In this context, the firm is continuously improving its intellectual capital, and by the time your firm has replicated what it learned in the benchmarking process, HP will have created new competencies to allow it to adapt to a new situation. In many industries, the firms that can learn the fastest are the winners. HP is a good example of just such a firm.

Our "bottom line" is that benchmarking of key processes can be very helpful, especially if it can help you learn about new processes and ways of doing things. And if the processes to be benchmarked come from industries other than one's own, they have the potential to grant even more useful insights. But benchmarking of "levels" of a particular attribute should be done with great care, if at all.

*See Jay B. Barney, "Firm Resources and Sustained Competitive Advantage," *Journal of Management* 17, no. 1 (1991): 99–120.

PUTTING IT ALL TOGETHER: AN EXAMPLE

We've covered a lot of different concepts and costing tools so far. How might they all come together in "real" life? An example may help. Because we have long believed that firms dramatically underestimate the costs of employee turnover (especially among high-performing employees), let's use this issue to construct a sample costing model.

To grasp the impact of your firm's turnover level, you must first have a sense for the performance levels of the leavers and whether you could have had any influence over an employee's decision to depart. Obviously, turnover among low-performing employees is desirable. However, in these times of high employee (and family) mobility and two-career couples, some employees may leave a firm for reasons unrelated to their job. In such cases, turnover is outside your control and may therefore be unavoidable. In fact, most scholars working in this area believe that there are four distinct categories of employee turnover.[6]

- *Undesirable, controllable.* Average- to high-performing employees leave, and the firm missed an opportunity to keep them. This is "bad" turnover.

- *Undesirable, uncontrollable.* Average- to high-performing employees leave, but the firm had no control over the situation (e.g., an employee's spouse was transferred to a much better job). This type of turnover is unfortunate, but it is also unavoidable.

- *Desirable, controllable.* Low-performing employees leave, with your assistance. This is "good" turnover.

- *Desirable, uncontrollable.* Low-performing employees leave by their own choice. This is also "good" turnover; however, in this category the firm was not aware of the employees' intentions or their performance levels and thus had no control over the departures.

To estimate turnover costs, you thus take stock of (1) the kinds of employees who typically leave the firm, (2) their performance levels, and (3) their reasons for leaving. We believe that turnover of average- to high-performing employees is very expensive, while turnover among low-performing employees can actually be beneficial—especially if the firm can then replace low performers with high performers. However, most firms find it more costly to retain unusually talented employees than average or untalented ones. Therefore, the type of turnover that you're "costing" will influence the costs of your intervention as well. In our experience, personnel records, along with exit interviews, can help you sort the "leavers" into the four categories just described. Most firms will then focus on estimating costs and benefits of the "undesirable, controllable" category.

Consider the example of an organization that successfully expanded its business but then became troubled by what it saw as an exodus of high-potential midlevel managers. The firm employs 1,000 managers, 400 of whom it considers "high performers." Thirty percent of these high performers leave the firm in any given year, so the company must hire 120 managers as replacements. (Note that this example focuses only on high-potential managers—total turnover costs would be much higher.) Assume that each manager earns $100,000 per year. Further assume that all turnover in this group is voluntary. Therefore, there are no costs associated with severance pay or increased unemployment premiums. Because the "leavers," by definition, are high performers, we can also assume that their replacements will, on average, exhibit lower performance—at least at first. Table 4-2 shows the cost categories and related estimates.

Turnover among high-performing midlevel managers costs this firm an estimated $6.7 million per year, or approximately $55,500 per employee. This is consistent with recent estimates suggesting that replacing a midlevel manager can cost about 50 percent of his or her salary, not including opportunity costs. It is certainly a lot of money. But is it too much money? Or is it simply a cost of doing business? To make this determination, we need to figure out whether efforts to reduce turnover might prove cheaper. To do this, we would compare the *marginal costs* associated with a reduction in turnover with the *marginal benefits*. And because "retained"

Table 4-2   Cost Estimate of Replacing 120 High-Potential Managers

Year 1 (hire 120 new managers)	
Separation costs	$60,000
Recruiting costs	$900,000
Selection costs	$900,000
Training and acculturation costs	$600,000
Lower productivity—acculturation	$1,200,000
Lower productivity—long run	$3,000,000
Total	**$6,660,000**

Note: All figures in present value.

employees will stay with the firm more than a year, our estimates must take into account multiple time periods as well.

Table 4-2 estimates only the *costs* of employee turnover. These data have meaning only when we compare them with the *benefits* associated with efforts to reduce this undesirable turnover. Even in the best of situations, turnover rarely reaches zero. However, a number of interventions could easily cut turnover by half. Let's say that, based on exit interviews and analysis of company records, our example firm has determined that it could reduce turnover among high-potential managers from 30 percent (120 managers per year) to 15 percent (60 managers per year). How? By offering higher wages, competency development, and enhanced promotional opportunities to the highest-performing employees. Clearly, some of these costs will occur just once; others will require continuing investments.

Should the firm invest in the turnover-reduction program for the high-potential managers? Suppose that, at this point, line managers express skepticism about the proposed program. They value the performance of talented managers, but they're not convinced that the investment required to *retain* these managers would pay off sufficiently. Tables 4-3 and 4-4 show the cost and benefit estimates, respectively, of reducing turnover in this group from 30 percent to 15 percent. (The cost estimates shown in table 4-3 need to be applied to all employees in this category, since you won't know in advance which employees you will get to keep. However, the benefit estimates in table 4-4 apply only to the 60 additional employees in the first year whom you expect to retain.)

These tables illustrate that investments in human capital often require expenditures in the current year that are not recovered until some years in the future. This is especially salient in HR, because, as we have discovered, most accounting systems focus managers' attentions on the current period. This makes sense if we think about it from a number of perspectives. First, as Yogi Berra once eloquently observed, "It's tough to make predictions, especially about the future." This is as true for HR as it is for baseball. People leave, strategies change, new competitors enter the marketplace. Each of these elements makes investments in HR more risky. At the same time, smart managers know that new business opportunities arise all the time. Further, the only way that their firms can take advantage of these opportunities is to cultivate a competent, capable, and flexible workforce. Thus, managers generally compare the present value (PV) of an intervention's benefits with the present value of its costs, so as to be compensated for their efforts and risk. Table 4-5 shows how this would work for our example firm.

Table 4-3 Cost Estimate of Reducing Turnover from 30 Percent to 15 Percent

Year 1	
Increased variable pay for high performers	$1,200,000
Enhanced promotional opportunities	$360,000
Additional training (competency development)	$600,000
Year 2	
Increased variable pay for high performers	$1,200,000
Enhanced promotional opportunities	$360,000
Additional training (competency development)	$600,000
Year 3	
Increased variable pay for high performers	$1,200,000
Enhanced promotional opportunities	$360,000
Additional training (competency development)	$600,000
Present Value of Costs (3 years @ 10% cost of capital)	**$5,858,381**

Table 4-4 Benefit Estimate of Reducing Turnover from 30 Percent to 15 Percent

Year 1 (60 Employees)	
Enhanced productivity and lower replacement acculturation costs	$3,000,000
Year 2 (120 Employees)	
Enhanced productivity and lower replacement acculturation costs (current and prior year's retained employees)	$6,000,000
Year 3 (180 Employees)	
Enhanced productivity and lower replacement acculturation costs (current and prior years' retained employees)	$9,000,000
Present Value of Benefits (3 years @ 10% cost of capital)	**$13,320,929**

Table 4-5 Net Present Value of Reducing Turnover from 30 Percent to 15 Percent

Present Value of Benefits	$13,320,929
Present Value of Costs	−$5,858,381
Present Value of Benefits Less Present Value of Costs	**$7,462,548**

In this particular scenario, the NPV of the proposed turnover-reduction program is substantially greater than zero ($7.5 million). Thus the data indicate that this investment would make sense even under the most restrictive of assumptions. In the case of "mixed" results, where the investment appears warranted given optimistic assumptions but questionable under conservative ones, we suggest gathering more data carefully and conducting more rigorous analysis. A specific methodology for developing very detailed and precise cost estimates, *activity-based costing*, has become a popular tool for management accountants.[7]

SUMMARY: COMPARING COST-BENEFIT ANALYSIS AND HR SCORECARD DEVELOPMENT

In this chapter we made the distinction between developing an HR Scorecard and calculating the return on investment of a specific HR program or intervention. These two activities help the HR function create value. However, they involve different processes and require different competencies from practitioners.

Cost-benefit analyses are different from HR Scorecards in their breadth (they are much narrower and more project focused) and in their longevity (they provide one specific answer only). Moreover, generally only the decision makers involved see the results of costing analyses. In contrast, the HR Scorecard is broad in scope and lays out a theory about how people create value throughout the business. It is also used by a much wider audience, viewed and updated regularly, and employed as a tool for following the progress of strategy implementation.

Both cost-benefit analysis and HR Scorecard development are important; indeed, they are complementary. Most firms use them sequentially, however. They develop a Scorecard to identify where they want to be in the future and where they are now, then they conduct ROI analyses to choose the most efficient way of getting to their desired future. HR managers need to hone their ability to use both of these powerful tools.

In the next chapter, we show you how to combine the knowledge you gain from developing measures to track your firm's strategy implementation with the insights you gain from cost-benefit analyses.

HRSP/RUTGERS UNIVERSITY HR COSTING PROJECT

Can most firms accurately determine how much money they invest in people? And if they could, would they then make better decisions about those investments? In a recent project sponsored by the Human Resource Systems Professionals (HRSP) and Rutgers University, Charles Fay, Steve Director, Paul Hempel, and Mark Huselid developed an integrated, spreadsheet-based costing model to evaluate the true economic costs and benefits associated with investments in people—whether these investments originated in the HR function or elsewhere in the organization. The goals of the model were twofold:

1. To develop estimates of the cost of human-resource-related activities to the firm; and

2. To allow the user to estimate the costs associated with changes in various human-resource-related practices.

Fay and colleagues showed that developing such a model is not as straightforward as might be imagined, however. In a firm's financial statements, investments in people are usually reflected in cost of goods sold (COGS) or selling, general, and administrative expenses (SG&A). For most firms, what this means is that the true costs associated with the firm's investments in people—whether you consider total costs or the costs associated with a particular HRM practice—are very difficult to isolate because these costs are "embedded" in larger cost categories. Indeed, many firms would find it difficult to determine the true cost of investment in training, because these costs are distributed throughout the firm and conventional accounting systems are not designed to capture these costs.

Compounding this problem is the fact that investments in people—even those investments that are designed to create value over the long term—are expensed in their entirety on the income statement during the current period. Because firms don't track investments in people over the long run, they have little incentive to pay careful attention to these investments.

Thus, in developing the HRSP/Rutgers costing model, the authors were obliged to develop mutually exclusive and exhaustive categories for HR costs. They then developed a methodology for collecting the relevant data and then validated their model in a sample of six large firms. In contrast to previous research (which has most often attempted to estimate the costs of a single human resource activity), their approach focused on the costs and benefits of the entire HRM system.

(continued on the next page)

(continued from the previous page)

In the HRSP project the authors conceptualized costs of and benefits from any type of HRM intervention as a number of interrelated components (see figure):

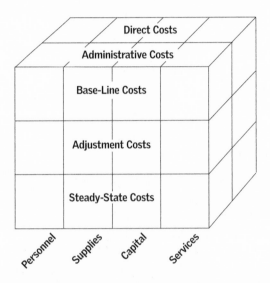

Base Line Operating Costs: These are annual costs associated with human resource management processes and activities. They represent the "starting point" and serve as the benchmark against which proposed changes in human resource management processes and activities will be compared.

Adjustment Costs: These costs occur only once as the result of the implementation of a human resource management initiative.

Steady-State Costs: These are recurring costs associated with implementation of a human resource management initiative plus those unrelated to the new initiative.

Administrative Costs: These are the costs associated with designing, piloting, implementing, administering, and evaluating a human resource initiative or ongoing HR activity.

Direct Costs: These are additional costs incurred as a result of a human resource initiative or ongoing HR activity. For example, a pay increase requires some administrative cost to design and implement; the extra payroll resulting from implementation is a direct cost.

Both administrative and direct costs are divided into the following four components:

- personnel

- supplies

- capital

- outside services

Key Lessons from the HRSP Project

In developing and validating this model, the authors concluded the following:

1. The true costs associated with a firm's investment in people were not apparent in the budgeting and accounting systems of most HRM departments. Indeed, the HR department budget dramatically underestimated the firm's true levels of investment in people, because (1) they are not well captured by accounting systems in general, and (2) much investment in people is distributed throughout the firm in the operating budgets of line managers. Because most accounting systems are very imprecise in how they allocate costs for investments in people and because many of those costs are distributed throughout the organization, the budget for a firm's HR department dramatically underestimates a firm's total level of investment in people, perhaps by as much as 50 percent. As a result, most firms cannot easily determine their true levels of investment in some fairly common categories, such as training.

2. The discipline imposed by a movement from considering only investments in the HR function as tracked by the accounting function to thinking about the economic investments in people (wherever they may occur in the firm) can be very helpful in the process of cost-benefit analysis.

3. It is possible to determine the firm's true level of people-related investments, but it requires considerable resources. Before embarking on such a project, firms should have a very good reason for doing so, as the process is very labor-intensive.

Sources: C. H. Fay, P. S. Hempel, S. M. Director, and M. A. Huselid, "Costing Human Resource Initiatives" (School of Management and Labor Relations, Rutgers University, 1997); and C. H. Fay, P. S. Hempel, S. M. Director, and M. A. Huselid, "Rutgers Human Resource Costing Model Software (Version 1.3) User's Manual" (School of Management and Labor Relations, Rutgers University, 1997).

5

THE PRINCIPLES OF
GOOD MEASUREMENT

T HE HUMAN-RESOURCE performance-measurement system you
use plays a key role in determining HR's place in your firm—
including securing HR's credibility. It also influences the organization's ability to capitalize on HR as a strategic asset. For these reasons,
you must ground that measurement system in some essential principles.
Let's take another look at HiTech, the company we first met in chapter 3,
to see what can happen when a firm ignores these principles.

HiTech is a large manufacturer headquartered in the western United
States. Its innovative products have earned it recognition as an industry
leader. Like many companies, HiTech for several years had emphasized
the importance of people as a source of competitive advantage. However, although the company had prominently emphasized some "people
policies," it had not articulated the cause-and-effect relationships that
might link its HR architecture to customer and shareholder value. As a
first step toward measuring these relationships, HiTech's HR leadership
conducted a feasibility study to explore what it would take to develop a
strategic measurement system. The following are the problems they
encountered in this project. As we'll see, this list provides insight into
the necessary ingredients for an effective measurement effort.

Available data—not relevant data—drove HiTech's key decisions.
Because HiTech had not articulated the processes through which
people create value throughout the business, it did not manage (and
therefore measure) the relevant drivers within that value chain. Not
surprisingly, the measures it *did* have available were designed for
other purposes. The company used people measures from the traditional annual employee survey, for example, and financial measures
that included budget variance. The feasibility project was focused on
one of the few business units that currently collected data on all three
components in the value chain. To that end, HR chose a service/call-
center operation because of the close relationship between front-line
employees (HiTech's service contracts) and customers. Though the
call center was a *convenient* source of data, it was clearly not
HiTech's "core business." Nevertheless, HR had no other data to
work with.

*By incompletely articulating its causal story, HiTech undermined its
measurement results.* By relying on measures that were available
rather than appropriate, HiTech found it very difficult to draw even
tentative inferences about important relationships. For example, the
call center generates revenue through a fee-for-service arrangement
with the regional sales office. It may also generate additional revenue
through new sales of additional products to existing customers. Call-
center "profitability" is thus the net of the combined revenue from
these two sources minus budgeted costs. The company assessed customers' perception of value by using two available efficiency measures (call volume and speed per answer) and by gauging service
accuracy and customer satisfaction.

   This is a typical set of metrics that you would find in a company
that uses measurement to monitor activities against some standard,
particularly cost control. These metrics are not so helpful to an organization that wants to understand the value-creation process. For example, the HiTech call center really has three ways to drive "profitability."
First, it can increase revenues by providing outstanding service, which
over time will add to the overall product value perceived by HiTech's
customers. But there is likely to be a significant delay between call-
center performance and changes in product purchases. Indeed,
HiTech might more accurately link its call-center performance to

product sales rather than service billing, since service billing is ultimately an internal cost that HiTech would like to reduce. In other words, the call center's gain becomes a charge against the product sales business unit.

Second, the call center generates revenue through service sales that lead to top-line growth, that is, new service sales that are not tied to a preexisting customer purchase. Here, HiTech could expect the time lag between the customer's service experience and buying decisions to be relatively short.

Third, HiTech included budget variance as a measure of cost control (and thus a measure of profits, indirectly). While cost control is one traditional measure of financial performance, it may well conflict with "new sales" revenue. For example, measures of efficiency and speed may drive down costs, but they do not necessarily represent the most *effective* way to generate new revenues. HiTech's simple causal model combines these conflicting effects into one relationship.

In its measurement system, HiTech included what we might term the operational or internal process measures of a Balanced Scorecard (speed and volume) in the "customer" segment, along with customer satisfaction. A more appropriate model would have had those process measures *driving* customer satisfaction, which in turn would drive financial performance. This more realistic causal connection would have given managers actionable results that they could then use to adjust the implementation of the call center's strategy at the appropriate point in the system.

Finally, the people metrics HiTech used highlighted a common problem many HR managers face when trying to make business sense of their HR measurement system. HiTech relied on employee attitude surveys that contained a substantial number of questions. However, these questions represented just one large and ill-defined measure of employees' attitudes toward the company and their supervisors. Because the survey responses could not be divided meaningfully into separate determinants of employee strategic behavior (competencies, motivation, strategic focus), HiTech had no idea how to align the HR system to drive change. Even if the senior HR management team believed that people could generate value at HiTech, the measures they used provided little insight into how the HR system should be aligned to influence people results.

HiTech didn't communicate HR's strategic value up front. HiTech's HR VP required the cooperation of other business units to collect the necessary data for the feasibility study. However, because the organization had not gone through Steps 2 through 5 in our model (described in chapter 2), the VP had no way to convince these other units that the results of his project would make a difference in the performance of line operations. Therefore, these units saw the project as a diversion and not a priority. As a result, the feasibility-project team collected useful data on just a few units out of a much larger population. This limitation made it nearly impossible for the senior HR management team to draw meaningful inferences about the potential relationships in the model.

Multiple problems compounded to limit the value of HiTech's feasibility study. The feasibility study's small sample size was compounded by the CHRO's over-reliance on available data. Moreover, those data were not necessarily available in the appropriate time periods. The unit of observation was the supervisory group within the call center. But the measures that the CHRO chose to focus on required data that became available on different cycles. For example, the operational process measures of speed, efficiency, and volume were available monthly. Revenue and customer satisfaction measures were gathered quarterly. And the employee survey data came up annually. These disparities in timing forced the feasibility-project team to annualize all the measures so as to conform to the employee data cycle. Thus, instead of having thousands of unit observations over several years, the project team had access to less than thirty.

Taken together, these flaws in HiTech's measurement-system feasibility study hamstrung the project. Not surprisingly, the results of the pilot project provided little to reinforce HR's status as a strategic asset or to guide HR's strategic effectiveness. The pilot project was not extended to a more comprehensive analysis, and HiTech missed an opportunity to sharpen the strategic focus of HR.

WHY BETTER MEASUREMENT?

A sound performance-measurement system does two things. First, it improves HR decision-making by helping you focus on those aspects of the organization that create value. In the process, it provides you with feedback that you can then use to evaluate current HR strategy and predict the impact of future decisions. A well-thought-out measurement system thus acts as both a guide and a benchmark for evaluating HR's contribution to strategy implementation.

Second, it provides a valid and systematic justification for resource-allocation decisions. HR can't legitimately claim its share of the firm's resources unless it can show how it contributes to the firm's financial success. An appropriately designed performance-based measurement system lets you explicate those links and thus lay the groundwork for investment in HR as a strategic resource, rather than HR serving as a cost-center to be retrenched.

For example, suppose you measure your firm's standing on the High-Performance Work System index (described in chapter 2). The HPWS index is a summary indicator of the "performance" orientation of key HR practices. You find that your firm's HR system falls in the forty-fifth percentile among all firms and the fifty-sixth percentile in your industry group. A good measurement system will let you predict *how much* improvement in firm performance you can expect if you boost your HR system to a higher target-percentile level. Or, let's say you find that your firm is already in the ninetieth percentile on the HPWS index. You can then calculate how much of the company's shareholder value is attributable to your outstanding HR system, compared to the value created by a HR system at the fiftieth percentile.

This approach is a sophisticated form of benchmarking, because it goes beyond measuring just the "level" of the HR system. It lets you attach dollar values to the gap between your firm's current HR system and some target level. Still, it suffers from the same weakness as any benchmarking approach for measuring HR's strategic influence. It doesn't tell you much about how narrowing that gap actually *creates* the predicted gains in shareholder value. In effect, there's a "black box" between HR and firm performance—and preventing HR from gaining the credibility it needs to become a true strategic partner.

Ultimately, you must have a persuasive story about what's in the black box. You must be able to throw back the cover of that box and reveal a plausible process of value creation from HR to firm performance. The strategic HR architecture we have described, aligned with the strategy implementation process, forms such a story. Telling this story—through the measurement system you design—will help you identify actionable goals and performance drivers.

THE MEASUREMENT CHALLENGE:
ATTRIBUTES *AND* RELATIONSHIPS

When we speak of measurement as a strategic resource for HR managers, what do we really mean? For example, many firms identify one or two "people-related" measures, such as employee satisfaction, in a balanced measure of corporate performance. Line managers, even HR managers, might be held accountable for these measures, which could also be incorporated into the managerial bonus plan. Such measures capture the quantity, or level, of a particular attribute—in this case, employee satisfaction. How much is there? Does it change over time? How does it compare with that of other firms, or across SBUs? Most of us would assume that more of this attribute is a good thing. We say "assume," because in many firms there is probably little *evidence* supporting the link between employee satisfaction and firm performance. Such organizations emphasize the *level* of the attribute, rather than the *relationship* between the attribute and some strategic outcome (performance drivers or firm performance).

Good measurement requires an understanding of and expertise in measuring both levels *and* relationships. Too many HR managers under pressure to demonstrate the HR-firm performance relationship rely on *levels* of HR outcomes as proxies for measures of that *relationship*. In other words, they can't show the direct causal links between any HR outcome and firm performance, so they select several plausible HR measures as candidates for strategic drivers—and then simply assert their connection to firm performance.

This inability to demonstrate these relationships is sometime obscured by diagrams that vaguely suggest cause and effect. Figure 5-1 shows a common example of what might be called a superficial strategy map. A firm might include one or two measures under each of these three categories and do a good job of measuring the levels of those attributes. But what does doing well on those measures really mean? The arrows imply that better performance on the "People" dimension improves performance on the "Customer" dimension, which in turn will improve "Profits." But the real story of value creation in any firm is much more complicated,

Figure 5-1   A Superficial Strategy Map

PEOPLE   ➡   CUSTOMERS   ➡   PROFITS

so this "story" is incomplete. It provides only the most superficial guide to decision making or performance evaluation. It's only marginally better than traditional measures that make no effort to incorporate a larger strategic role for HR. Boxes and arrows give the illusion of measurement and understanding, but because the *relationship* measures are so limited, such diagrams—and the thinking behind them—can actually help to undermine HR's confidence and credibility.

Even though relationship measurement is the most compelling assessment challenge facing HR managers today, attribute measures should form the foundation of your measurement system. Why? Because evidence of a strong relationship between A and B is worthless if the measures of A and B themselves are worthless. But words such as "worthless" or "useful" or "appropriate" aren't precise enough for our discussion about the elements of good measurement. In fact, there are well-defined principles delineating effective measurement practice. Understanding those principles lets you take that essential first step in developing a strategically focused HR measurement system.

NUMBERS WITH MEANING

Let's begin with a simple definition of what we mean by measurement. Typically, measurement is defined as *the assignment of numbers to properties (or characteristics) of objects based on a set of rules.* Numerical representation is important, because often we are interested in quantities. But, we are interested in quantities that have meaning. For example, knowing that average employee satisfaction is 3.5 on a 5-point scale is numerical, but it doesn't have much inherent meaning. Is 3.5 good or bad? Or consider an employee turnover rate of 15 percent. Percentage points have more inherent meaning than 5-point scales, but simply observing the number doesn't reveal much about whether 15 percent is a problem.

To add meaning to these levels, we need context. This is the appeal of a benchmark. If we find that our 3.5 on a 5-point scale is considerably better than our industry peers' ratings, we can begin to attach some significance to that measure. However, we might also observe that our 3.5 is considerably below our own historical level on this measure. We're doing better than our peers but not maintaining our historical performance. Of course, in both cases we have made interpretations about *relative* value only. That is, we are better or worse than some standard. In neither case do we have any measure of *managerial* value. In other words, what difference does it make whether we have a 3.0 or 4.0 value on a 5-point employee satisfaction scale? To have managerial value, the measure must be expressed in numerical units that have inherent performance significance (such as dollars). Barring that, we have to be able to translate the measure into performance-relevant units.

Consider this simple example: Suppose you want to demonstrate the dollar cost (new hiring and training costs, lower productivity) associated with each additional percentage point in your firm's turnover. To get managerial value out of this exercise, you would have to link HR measures to performance drivers elsewhere in the firm, and ultimately to firm performance. Recall the Sears story. The key "people" measures in Sears' measurement model reflected employees' attitudes toward their jobs and the company overall. Sears could have benchmarked those attitudes against similar *levels* at other companies, or perhaps against Sears' own historical norms. From this, the company might have identified a gap. However, then it would have had to ask, so what? Unlike most companies, Sears had an answer to this question, because it could translate *changes* in those attitude measures into *changes* in firm performance. The "people" numbers thus had business meaning.

Measuring relationships gives meaning to the levels, and to potential changes in those levels. However, those relationships are very likely to be firm-specific. Therefore, the more the magnitude (the impact of one measure on another) of those relationships is unique to your firm, the less useful it is for you to benchmark on levels. Benchmarking on measurement levels assumes that the relationships among these levels are the same in all firms, and hence that they have the same meaning in all firms. That's the same as saying that the strategy implementation process is a commodity, or at least that HR's contribution to that process is a commodity. For this reason, we find benchmarking on HR strategic measures to be misguided at best and counterproductive at worst.

MEASURES VERSUS CONCEPTS OR VISIONS

For our purposes, the "objects" in our definition of measurement are a firm's HR architecture and strategy implementation systems. The "properties" of those objects that most interest us are the value-creating elements in those two systems—in other words, the HR deliverables and the firm's performance drivers that the deliverables influence. We can think of these properties as abstract concepts, but also as observable measures. First, an organization or top management team can identify key links in the value-creation chain by taking what we call a "conceptual" or "vision" perspective. For example, the simple relationship between employee attitudes and firm performance serves as the foundation of the Sears measurement model described earlier. Sears refined its model further with brief vision statements about the important attributes of each element in its model. If you recall, the company's top management decided that Sears must be a *compelling* place to work, a *compelling* place to shop, and a *compelling* place to invest (the "three C's"). As another, more specific example, a retail bank that we've worked with identified "superior cross-selling performance" as a key performance driver.

Such concepts and visions—let's refer to them collectively as "constructs"—are properties of the strategy implementation process. However, they are so abstract that they provide little guidance for decision making or performance evaluation. To illustrate, identifying "superior cross-selling performance" as a key performance driver may take things one step beyond the vision stage, but it's still too conceptual to be operational. What does it mean? How will we know it when we see it? Will two different managers both know it when they see it? In short, how do we measure it?

Compelling and easy-to-grasp constructs are important because they help you capture and communicate the essence of powerful ideas. They're like simple but evocative melodies that everyone can hum. Nevertheless, they are not measures. Rather, they constitute the foundation on which you *build* your measures. Clarifying a construct is the first step in understanding your firm's value-creation story. But you must then know how to move beyond the construct to the level of the measure.

One way to detect a good measure is to see how accurately it reflects its underlying construct. Earlier, we said that a measure of the *relationship* between A and B is worthless if the underlying measures of A and B themselves are worthless. A or B would be worthless if they did not reflect the constructs behind them. For example, if Sears measured the construct "compelling place to work" simply by assessing the level of employee satisfaction with pay, the measure would not have very much relevance. Why? Because it omits key dimensions, such as the understanding of business strategy or relationships with supervisors, of the underlying idea that it is designed to tap.

One way to avoid this kind of mistake is to use multiple measures that reflect different dimensions of the same construct. In Sears' case, managers used a seventy-item survey, which they then distilled down to ten items as their measure of "compelling place to work." Next they consolidated those ten items along two dimensions—employee attitudes about the job and employee attitudes about the company. Figure 5-2 illustrates this technique. This approach gave the organization an explicit way to assess how well it was realizing its vision of being a "compelling place to work."

Figure 5-3 illustrates another problem that can arise in choosing metrics. In the figure notice that the measure does *not* correspond to its underlying construct for two reasons. First, the measure doesn't fully capture all of the properties of the construct of interest. This "deficiency" is the dark area on the left. Second, the measure is capturing something beyond the construct of interest. In other words, the measure is contaminated (lighter area on the right). This kind of measurement error is all too common. For example, recall the retail bank that identified "cross-selling performance" as a key performance driver. How should the firm measure

Figure 5-2   An Example of Multiple Measures Reflecting Different Dimensions of the Same Construct: A Compelling Place to work

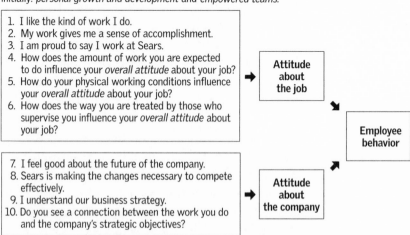

Responses to these 10 questions on a 70-question employee survey had a higher impact ont. employee behavior (and, therefore, on customer satisfaction) than the measures that were devised initially: *personal growth and development* and *empowered teams*.

1. I like the kind of work I do.
2. My work gives me a sense of accomplishment.
3. I am proud to say I work at Sears.
4. How does the amount of work you are expected to do influence your *overall attitude* about your job?
5. How do your physical working conditions influence your *overall attitude* about your job?
6. How does the way you are treated by those who supervise you influence your *overall attitude* about your job?

Attitude about the job

Employee behavior

7. I feel good about the future of the company.
8. Sears is making the changes necessary to compete effectively.
9. I understand our business strategy.
10. Do you see a connection between the work you do and the company's strategic objectives?

Attitude about the company

Source: Adapted from Anthony J. Rucci, Steven P. Kirn, and Richard T. Quinn, "The Employee-Customer-Profit Chain at Sears," *Harvard Business Review* 76, no. 1 (January–February 1998): 90.

this construct? It might use total sales, under the assumption that employees or branches with more cross-selling skill would have higher total sales. But total sales would also include sales *other than* those derived from cross-selling performance by tellers; those other data would thus contaminate the metric. What about assessing "total number of different products sold per customer," or "new sales to existing customers"? In either of these cases, the bank would still have to develop a measure that tapped the important attributes of the performance driver in question *without* blurring the picture with unrelated influences.

These sorts of measurement errors severely reduce the value you can derive from your measurement system. If you use a deficient measure, it's very likely that employees will ignore or misinterpret a particular performance driver. For example, if a key driver is "positive customer buying experience," you might use "time with customer" as a measure. Indeed, market research shows that customers appreciate it when sales staff do not pressure them to make a quick purchase. On the other hand, if this is your *only* measure of the customer's buying experience, sales-people might be tempted to needlessly drag out their encounters with customers. It's still true that what gets measured, gets managed. Simply put, we can't measure A and hope for B.[1]

METRICS THAT MATTER

Suppose you've developed a clear strategy map describing your firm's strategy implementation process, identified the key performance drivers involved, and even have a good idea of what measures you might use to capture the HR enablers of those drivers. You still have several important

Figure 5-3 Misalignment of Construct and Measure, Causing Contamination/Deficiency

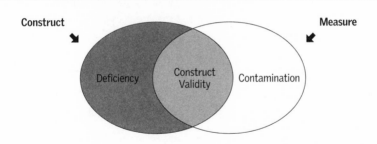

decisions to make regarding the structure of those measures—decisions that will dramatically affect their eventual usefulness. The measurement process is not an end in itself. It has value only if its results provide meaningful input into subsequent decisions and/or contribute to more effective performance evaluation. Therefore, as you think about the choice and form of a particular measure, stop for a moment and think carefully about what you would do with the results. Imagine receiving your first report summarizing this measure. What key decisions will these results inform? Will another manager, particularly outside HR, consider recommendations based on this measure to be persuasive? Would these results provide a compelling foundation for a resource-allocation decision within your firm?

We have defined "measurement" as the process of assigning numbers to properties of objects by following certain rules. Numerical measures are appealing because they describe quantities, which play a central role in most decisions. But not all measures provide information about quantities. Here are some pointers to keep in mind as you choose metrics for your own system:

Nominal Measures. Nominal measures are the lowest level of measurement and tell us nothing about quantity of a particular attribute. They simply indicate differences or categorizations across certain properties. For instance, classifying employees by gender indicates a difference between males and females. It doesn't say anything about whether one category is "more" or "less" than the other on the property of gender. Nominal measures are useful only for counting. Any numbers attached to these categories are used as labels, as in "category 1" or "category 2." In HR, gender counts would most likely be used to assess compliance activities, such as adherence to EEO policies, but they would have little value in measuring HR as a strategic asset.

Ordinal Measures. Ordinal measures represent the next level up of measurement. They provide the first, but least-sensitive, measure of quantity. Think of ordinal measures most easily as rank-order assessments. If we know that A exceeds B on the underlying property in question, we can "rank" A above B. We just don't know by how much. In addition, we know that if B is greater than C, then A is also greater than C. We can say nothing, however, about how the difference between A and B compares to the difference between B and C.

Rank-order measures are probably most useful in performance evaluations, such as "good," "better," and "best." Promotion recommendations provide another apt example: The top candidate is better than the rest, but this top ranking says nothing about how *much* better. (Note that for the purposes of succession planning, this may not matter.)

Interval Measures. Interval measures are an improvement beyond ordinal measures because they let us assume that the interval between "scores" of 1 and 2 is equal to the interval between 2 and 3. Many common business performance measures expressed in time, dollars, units, market share, or any combination of their ratios are interval measures. For instance, a 1-point percentage change in market share means the same *number* of customers going from 34 to 35 percent as it does going from 67 to 68 percent. (Note that these examples are also ratio measures, which we describe next.) The more common—and purest—form of interval measure is one of those scales on which "1" means "strongly agree" and "5" means "strongly disagree."

Ratio Measures. In the cases of distance, dollars, and time just described, you can see that ratio scales have an important advantage over interval scales, because they have a true zero point. This point of reference lets you make meaningful comparisons between two values. For example, you could describe one result as two-thirds the quantity of another result. Ratio measures are also appealing because the units of measure tend to have inherent meaning (dollars, number of employees, percentages, time, etc.). Finally, these measures are relatively easy to collect. (Note, though, that just because they're readily available doesn't necessarily mean that they'll accurately reflect the underlying concept or vision that you're trying to assess—as we saw earlier.)

Ideally, you will develop a measurement system that lets you answer questions such as, how much will we have to change x in order to achieve our target change in y? To illustrate, if you increase training time by 20 percent, how much will that change employee performance and, ultimately, unit performance? Or, if you reduce turnover among key technical staff in R&D by 10 percent, how long before that action begins to improve the new-product-development cycle time? A measurement system that can provide this kind of specificity is not easy to develop and, indeed, may be beyond the reach of some firms. But measurement quality is a continuum, not an absolute. As with most decisions, developing a strategic HR measurement system involves trade-offs. To make the correct trade-off, you need to choose the point along the measurement-quality continuum that you think your firm can reasonably achieve.

MEASURING CAUSATION

Why are accounting numbers and financial measures so compelling? It's not so much that they guide decision making, but that they are expressed in units that directly reflect the bottom line—dollars. We can object to the supposed shortsightedness of the "bean counters," but there is still something to the adage that "a dollar saved is a dollar earned." As we've seen, this characteristic makes it particularly challenging to manage intangible assets (such as human capital), for which you can quantify costs much more easily than benefits. For example, how would you measure the value of developing and implementing a new competency model? As with many large investments, you may not realize the benefits for several years, and even then they might manifest themselves only indirectly, through improved levels of performance drivers elsewhere in the firm. Since HR will always tend to be further upstream in the value-creation process, measuring the value of human resource decisions means assessing their impact on strategic drivers that are linked more closely—if not directly—to the bottom line.

Quantifying these relationships is by no means an easy task. However, even if you can't empirically verify a five-link chain of causation from HR to firm performance in your organization, establishing HR's influence on key interim performance drivers (such as customer retention or R&D cycle time) has clear financial implications. As HR managers validate an increasing number of such links, they begin to establish the central connections between HR and firm performance. Having systematic and quantifiable evidence of HR's contribution to seven out of twenty strategic performance drivers, for example, is not the complete story of HR's strategic influence, but it is a significant improvement over zero out of twenty!

But what does "measuring a relationship" actually mean? Terms such as *association, correlation,* or *causation* might come to mind—though they are sometimes used too loosely and aren't always helpful. Two variables are *related* when they vary together, but you may not know for sure that one actually *causes* the other. You don't have the luxury of arguing over such nuances, though. You have to make decisions, and your colleagues expect those decisions to produce results. At some point, your job requires you to draw a causal inference about the relationship between a decision and its result. After all, you're not interested in whether a mere "association" exists between a particular incentive system and employee performance. You need to know whether the system in question will produce a change in employee performance and, if so, by how much.

In short, you need relationship measures that are "actionable." One of the most common measures of a statistical relationship is the *correlation coefficient*. Ranging from −1.00 to +1.00, correlation coefficients describe the extent to which two variables change together. Unfortunately, correlation coefficients have little actionable value. First, they are not expressed in units that have any inherent meaning. To illustrate, how would you interpret a correlation coefficient of .35? Has your CEO ever asked you to describe HR's contribution in terms of correlation, or its equivalent statistical term "explained variance"? Second, correlation coefficients typically describe the relationships between just two variables. Since most business outcomes have more than one cause, these measures simply can't capture the complexity of real-world questions. For example, suppose you're the head of HR at a major retailer, and you're interested in the relationship between hours of sales training and the customer buying experience. In addition, store outlets offering more training have implemented a new computer system that reduced customer transaction time by 30 percent. The variables "training time" and "customer satisfaction" might well show a strong positive correlation. However, much of it may be due to the influence of the new technology!

So what are the alternatives? There are many to choose from—but all of them have a couple of important features. For one thing, unlike the simple correlations just described, they all measure relationships from a multivariate, rather than bivariate, perspective. This means that if you were interested in understanding the individual effect of a particular HR deliverable on a performance driver, the measure of that relationship would accurately reflect the *independent* effect of that individual HR deliverable. Moreover, these causal models measure relationships in actionable terms.

For example, you need to know that a 20-percent change in competency A will increase employee cross-selling performance by $300 per employee per week, not that the two are "positively and significantly correlated."

So, you *can* operationalize your causal inferences—you just need to carefully consider the plausible alternatives to the HR effect you are interested in. For *x* to be a cause of *y*, for example, you have to be confident that the effect on *y* is not due to some influence other than *x*. If you can keep those other influences from varying, your confidence in your causal inference will increase. You will also be able to express your inference in actionable terms.

Measuring Causal Linkages in Practice

Let's take a look at how some firms devised ways to measure causal linkages.

THE EXPERIENCE AT GTE

GTE provides a very interesting illustration of how an organization can estimate linkages across several performance drivers in a strategy map. GTE's Network Services unit (approximately 60,000 employees) "hypothesized" that market share was driven by customer valuation of its service, which in turn was driven by customer service quality, brand advertising, and inflation. The driver (the leading indicator) for customer service was a set of strategic employee behaviors focusing broadly on employee engagement. GTE HR created what it called the "employee engagement index" (EEI) based on a subset of seven questions from the GTE employee survey as a measure of these strategic behaviors.

The analysis supported the hypothesis and demonstrated the wisdom of HR's "balanced" approach to performance measurement and management. For example, GTE found that a 1 percent increase in the EEI resulted in nearly a ½ percent increase in customer satisfaction with service. In other words, GTE examined a key section of its "strategy map" and explicitly tested its hypothesis that employee behaviors are indirect leading indicators of key strategic measures (market share).

GTE was able to do this for three reasons. First, unlike at HiTech, the HR department had a clear story in mind of how employee behaviors actual drive strategy in its organization. Second, HR recognized the need to collect and merge information from multiple sources and multiple time periods. Third, it had access to the technical expertise necessary to make these statistical estimates.[2]

THE EXPERIENCE AT SEARS

Sears was one of the first companies to actually quantify the hypotheses in a strategy map. It has further refined its firmwide work-shop-invest model to include a focus on specific relationships within stores (see figure 2-6 in chapter 2 for an example of their full-line store strategy map). For example, at Sears the Brand Central department specializes in consumer durables (TVs, refrigerators, etc.). These items tend to be expensive and complex, are purchased infrequently, and require high levels of prepurchase advice from salespeople, who are paid on commission. In contrast, in the Women's Ready to Wear(RTW)/Intimate Apparel department, products tend to be inexpensive and uncomplicated, customers generally make their own selections with limited input from salespeople, and customers tend to purchase items more frequently. Here the sales associates are paid on an hourly basis.

Steve Kirn, VP for innovation and organizational development, and his staff wanted to know: Do the relationships differ among the Work, Shop, and Invest categories between these two departments? Because Sears collects data on each of these elements by department, they were able to generate some surprising answers. The willingness of customers to recommend Sears as a place to shop to others (which they call customer advocacy) is a key driver of profitability. For example, in Women's RTW/Intimate Apparel, a 1 percent increase in customer advocacy was linked to a 7.4 percent increase in revenue, and in Brand Central to a 4 percent increase. However, the drivers of customer advocacy differed across departments. In the RTW/Intimate category, working conditions and a belief that the company's pricing is a competitive strength significantly affected overall attitude toward Sears and had a favorable impact on customer advocacy. In Brand Central (a commission-based category), pay and a willingness to recommend Brand Central emerged as significant drivers. The presence of attentive and responsive managers was a core driver of sales associate attitudes and, ultimately, economic value across all of the departments studied. Such analyses are critical for helping Sears to gain an increasingly sophisticated understanding of its strategy map and to help implement that strategy faster.

DRILLING DEEPER AT SEARS

A fuller understanding of the relationships between people, strategy, and performance may also require some innovative thinking in the analysis of data. At Sears, customer satisfaction is a key driver of store performance, not only because satisfied customers are more likely to become repeat customers, but also because they are more likely to recommend Sears to others as a good place to shop. Thus, as we described in this chapter, customer advocacy is a key driver of profitability at Sears. But as Sears found, the relationship between customer satisfaction and advocacy is nonlinear. For example, when customers rated their overall satisfaction with the shopping experience as a "10" on a scale of 1 through 10, 82 percent of them were likely to recommend Sears to friends or family—a key driver of business success in retailing. However, when customers rated Sears a "9," only 33 percent were likely to recommend Sears as a place to shop. While Sears managers initially believed that a "9" on a 10-point scale was a high rating on customer satisfaction, analyses showed otherwise. Thus, satisfied customers were not enough—what they needed were *enthusiastic* customers to drive referrals. Understanding these relationships helped Sears managers understand how much customer satisfaction was "enough."

Increasing Your Confidence in Causal Relationships

Despite the wide range of influences on any management phenomenon, the question remains: Is it really possible to isolate the effect of a particular HR management policy or practice on firm performance? When you're dealing with complex, living systems in the real world, it's not possible to completely isolate variables. In even the most rigorous social-science laboratory experiments, certain factors still lie outside the researchers' control. The best you can do is to improve your confidence in such judgments. Here are some points of encouragement to keep in mind:

> *Just because it can, doesn't mean it does.* Just because an organizational outcome can be influenced by a wide range of other influences doesn't necessarily mean that it is. In most cases, there are only a few key influences on your outcome of interest. If you understand your business, you can easily identify these vital few. In our example of the relationship between cross-selling skills (an HR deliverable) and cross-selling sales performance (a driver for the firm's strategic goal

of increased revenue growth), cross-selling sales performance may also be strongly influenced by the availability of timely product information to employees. Does this mean that the relationship between skills and performance might be contaminated by the influence of product information availability? No, if all employees have the same product information available to them. Yes, if product information availability varies with *both* employee skills and cross-selling performance. In this case, it doesn't vary with either. On the other hand, if it turned out that, for some reason, employees with better skills also had better product information, then it would be more difficult to isolate the independent influence of skills on performance.

If it can be measured, it's much less of a problem. So what can we do if there is another influence, such as product information availability, that we think might be confounding our estimate of the relationship between skills and employee performance? Fortunately, if you can measure this other influence—for example, if you can assess the *level* of product information availability—you can then use a variety of techniques to estimate the *separate* (or independent) *effects* of both skills and product information availability on employee performance.[3] As a manager, you don't need to be an expert in those techniques, but you should understand the circumstances under which they may have value.

All other causes are not created equal. A potential other cause becomes more of a concern when it affects *both* variables of interest. Think of this other cause as a *joint influence*. For example, product information availability might confound the relationship between skills and performance only when it can be shown to influence both. If it affects just cross-selling performance but does not vary with skills, then it won't affect the estimated relationship. Likewise, if it varies with employee skills only but has no apparent effect on sales performance, it will not affect the relationship between the two variables.

You can account for joint influences. Clearly, the real challenge in measuring causal relationships lies in handling *joint influences* that you can't measure. If you *could* measure them, you could control their confounding effects using statistical techniques. However, simply by understanding the logic behind your causal model and the basic principles of measurement, you will have a much better grasp of the magnitude of the problem and, in fact, whether there really is a problem.

IMPLEMENTING YOUR MEASUREMENT SYSTEM: COMMON CHALLENGES

Now that you have an overview of the foundations of good measurement, let's highlight some common problems managers encounter when they attempt to implement these ideas. These problems focus on the more technical challenges surrounding the implementation of these systems, rather than the organizational hurdles associated with change efforts in general. We leave a discussion of these latter challenges for chapter 8.

Out with the Old, In with the New

Much of the challenge surrounding the introduction of a more strategically focused measurement system involves the complexity of introducing any new IT system. Your current system and measures are comfortable, and changing them can prove expensive. This is particularly true for measurement systems that let you assess relationships as well as levels. In addition, managers tend to become very attached to the metrics they create, and we have frequently seen firms continue to use these *legacy metrics* long after they have become inappropriate. Unfortunately, as we've seen, there is probably an inverse relationship between the *accessibility* of your current measures and their *value* in a strategic measurement system. Recall our earlier argument: *If your measures don't fully capture the underlying organizational process or outcome that really drives strategy, they will have little value.* This means you really have to understand the story of value creation in your organization and accurately measure the HR drivers in that process. This process takes time and resources, but if the organization isn't willing to make that investment, it will have nothing more than "garbage in, garbage out."

HR managers may often find themselves at the head of this change effort, and we discuss these challenges in some detail in chapter 8. But one of the first hurdles such managers might face is simply building consensus that such change is necessary. While fortunate to have the strong support of CEO Arthur Martinez at Sears, Tony Rucci, the former vice president for administration, has observed that CHROs must learn to build their support wherever possible. In his experience, about two-thirds of the employees in any organization are going to be indifferent or actively opposed to such initiatives.[4] He argues, however, that effective change comes through time and energy devoted to the one-third who support change rather than attempting to convert the two-thirds who are not supportive.

The Temptation to Measure It All

Don't let the fact that it may be impossible to measure *every* relationship prevent you from making *wise* use of available data. For example, Sears was able to precisely express the relationships among employees, customers, and profitability in part because it is in the retail service industry. The causal link between front-line employees and profitability was not only relatively direct for this firm, it was also relatively short. In other words, there was not an overwhelming number of links between employee behaviors and financial performance.

In manufacturing or other industries where the links in the value chain are more complex and probably more numerous, HR managers may want to begin with easily measured relationships. For example, even if the larger company information system is unable to link new-product cycle time to customer satisfaction and ultimately profitability, establishing the first several links between the HR system and R&D cycle time would say a lot about HR's strategic influence (see figure 5-4). By establishing even just the few links shown in the figure, HR managers could begin to talk about deliverables that make a difference in the business.

Figure 5-4   An Example of Establishing Links between the HR System and Performance Drivers in a Strategy Map

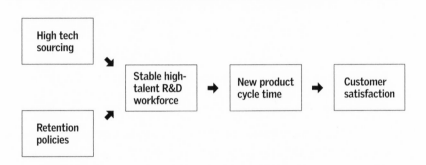

Matching Data to the Appropriate Level of Analysis

To measure relationships, you have to assess cause and effect at the same *level of analysis*. Examples of levels of analysis include the employee, team or group, project, unit, branch, division, and SBU. The problem is that HR measures might be available at just one level of analysis (the employee), while higher-order performance drivers, such as customer satisfaction, might be available only at the level of the unit or larger organizational division. Or, certain process or development measures might be available at the team or project level, but profitability is measured at a higher level.

This is where understanding the value-creation story comes in. If you can grasp how strategy is really implemented in your firm, you should be able to create parallel measures at the appropriate level of analysis. For example, an international package delivery service uses a complex "time in transit" index to measure operational performance at the level of the firm. This calculation means nothing at the level of the truck driver. However, at that individual level, "number of off-route miles" is one of many measures that cumulate to the "time in transit" index. HR decisions that influence "number of off-route miles," such as training or reward strategies, have strategic value because this variable drives the ultimate "time in transit" index.

Alternatively, you may need to aggregate lower-level measures to higher levels of analysis. So, for example, if financial or customer satisfaction data are available only at the level of the unit or division, individual-level HR measures can be aggregated to that level. That is, you could cumulate the individual-level measures into a summary measure at the unit or division level—in this example, the mean of all individual employee measures could represent the "team" measure. Ultimately, you have to think about what you are going to do with the results and ask yourself whether the outcomes of a particular level of analysis will really give you the answers you need. Otherwise, you may be diverted by measurement convenience, at the expense of measurement effectiveness.

Separating Leading from Lagging Indicators

You can logically distinguish leading from lagging indicators as you develop a causal model of your firm's strategy implementation process.

However, to identify and quantify relationships within the model, you need to know more than just that "HR" is a leading variable and "customer satisfaction" is a lagging variable. Accurately gauging the relationship between the two requires some sense of the magnitude of the time lag between changes in the leading indicator and subsequent changes in the lagging indicator. Don't worry about calculating an exact figure for the delay, but do understand the implications of leads and lags when developing your measurement system. The key is to collect measures over multiple time periods, so that you can evaluate the relationship between HR at time T-2 with performance driver x at time $T+1$. You will probably have to collect some data more often than you have in the past. Employee surveys, for example, have little value when collected only annually.

SUMMARY: THINKING STRATEGICALLY ABOUT MEASUREMENT

Thinking strategically about measurement means understanding whether the measurement system you are considering will provide you with the kinds of information that will help you manage the HR function strategically. This lesson is the same theme we've been reinforcing throughout the entire book. In addition, "think top down, not bottom up" should guide the technical decisions underlying your measurement system. Understanding the value-creation process and developing construct-valid measures of that process form a "top-down" approach. Starting with available measures and making the best of a bad situation is a "bottom-up" approach that in most cases will be a waste of time and, in the long run, will only undermine HR's strategic credibility. This chapter should provide you with the essential principles of measurement that will enable you to move beyond the limits of the "best available" approach. In the next chapter, we'll apply these principles to the problem of measuring HR alignment with the firm's strategy implementation system.

6

MEASURING
HR ALIGNMENT

THROUGHOUT THIS BOOK we have emphasized that for human resources legitimately to be considered a strategic asset, the HR architecture must be aligned with the requirements of the firm's strategy implementation process. We've also developed an HR performance measurement system that helps organizations to manage this strategic asset and evaluate its contribution to overall firm success. This performance measurement system also requires an attention to alignment—first, to shift focus away from traditional operational measures to more strategic measures and, second, to develop alignment measures that might serve as leading indicators in your HR Scorecard.

TWO DIMENSIONS OF ALIGNMENT

Figure 6-1 depicts the two dimensions of alignment that your HR architecture must achieve in order to become a strategic asset. These dimensions provide the foundation and focus for developing actual alignment metrics.

The first, and perhaps most critical, of these two dimensions is alignment between strategy implementation and the HR system. You can see this dimension on the vertical axis of the diagram. To achieve this alignment, your organization must emphasize strategy implementation and recognize it as a source of competitive advantage. To use Kaplan and Norton's term, you need to be a "strategy focused organization." This further requires that the company understand strategy implementation as a balanced process of value creation rather than simply as an exercise in financial control. As we saw earlier, this means being able to tell the story of "how the firm makes money." It also means incorporating both financial and nonfinancial variables, as well as leading and lagging indicators.

The "strategic" HR system is designed not from the bottom up (i.e., "best practices") but from the top down. In figure 6.1, HR deliverables represent those products of the HR architecture that are integrally linked to the successful implementation of the firm's strategy. The unique requirements of an organization's strategy implementation determine the particular HR deliverables, which in turn shape the HR system.

The horizontal axis depicts a dimension of alignment within the HR architecture that influences the overall development of human resources as a strategic asset. This is the alignment between the strategic role the HR function can

Figure 6-1 HR Alignment

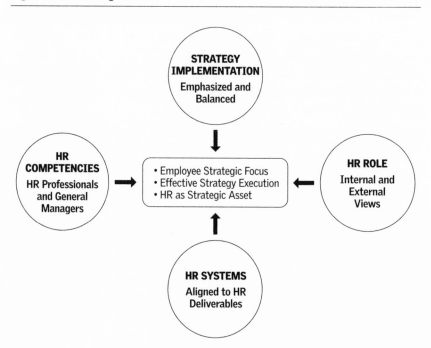

play and the level and mix of human resource competencies available among HR professionals and line managers. In figure 6-1, "HR Role" designates the degree to which HR professionals in an organization perceive themselves as strategic partners and the extent to which managers outside HR share the same view. Alignment requires that human resource *and* line managers develop a shared view of HR's role. HR can then crystallize that shared view by developing a business case for its part in value creation throughout the company (Step 2 in the model described in chapter 2).

Implementing HR's strategic role often requires the involvement of both human resource professionals and line managers. Indeed, many firms rely on the participation of line managers to implement the HR system in a way that reflects the business demands of the enterprise. At the same time, an organization is not likely to view HR as a strategic asset if the firm lacks a core group of human resource professionals who have the competencies to deliver on that role. Therefore, alignment along the horizontal axis focuses on the competencies needed to implement a *shared* view of HR's strategic potential.

In sum, figure 6-1 tells us that if an organization expects to develop HR as a strategic asset, it needs to think about alignment in two ways. The first is the alignment between the HR system that produces key HR deliverables and the requirements of the firm's strategy implementation system. This chapter shows you how your organization can measure this kind of alignment. The second is the alignment between the role expectations for the HR function and the individual competencies required to put that role into action. Chapter 7 describes those competencies in considerable detail. Together, both types of alignment produce a strategically focused workforce, which drives superior strategy execution and, ultimately, shareholder value.

ASSESSING INTERNAL ALIGNMENT

Measurement systems can serve a number of purposes. As we've seen, they can guide management of HR's contribution to strategy implementation. They also provide a "scorecard" that validates HR's contribution to firm performance. Measurement can serve another purpose as well. For managers who want to quickly assess the potential of their firm's HR system as a strategic asset, a simple measure of the *internal* alignment of that system can help.

The Case of Stilwell Manufacturing

The example of Stilwell Manufacturing is a composite of our experience at a number of firms. This case describes a relatively simple diagnostic process for evaluating the internal alignment of the HR system—that is, whether elements of the HR system reinforce each other rather than work at cross-purposes. The Stilwell story also sheds light on the destructive impact of misalignment on an organization's labor force.

Stilwell is a diversified manufacturer with an international production and distribution system. While the company has been very successful in recent years (it generated $2 billion in revenues in 2000), the senior management team has developed a new strategic plan for the business that forecasts double-digit increases in both revenues and cash flow over the next three years. Most members of the organization consider this plan extremely aggressive, especially in light of the fragmented and highly competitive nature of Stilwell's industry. Moreover, these projections have come at a time when Stilwell has faced considerable difficulty in hiring and retaining the best workers (especially in R&D capacities).

To achieve their two optimistic financial goals, Stilwell's top management team has identified four strategic drivers they believe should guide the business during the next five years:

- Shorten new-product development times.

- Enhance customer focus and responsiveness.

- Enhance productivity.

- Develop and successfully manage several joint ventures.

We can characterize Stilwell's current organizational structure and HRM system as follows:

- The organizational structure consists of many functional "silos," with little cross-functional communication or coordination.

- The HR function has a silo structure as well. Recruiting, selection, performance management, compensation, and HR planning and strategy generally operate autonomously and efficiently.

- HR managers reliably and properly administer compensation and benefit programs and hire people as requested, but line managers frequently describe them as overfocused on compliance and cost reduction at the expense of business-problem resolution.

- Jobs reflect traditional (i.e., narrow) definitions; for example, machinists tend to work on only one machine or type of part. The company has few team-based work structures and decision processes.

- Recruiting and selection efforts center on filling current openings. The company gives little consideration to hiring for potential or "promotability." Managers make hiring decisions on the basis of resume screening and interviews; they use no formally validated selection tests.

- The organization devotes considerable resources to skills development for new and continuing employees. Training systems emphasize general skills and are provided to all employees.

- Performance-appraisal and management-development systems have existed for many years at Stilwell. However, many employees describe the performance-management process as "routinized" and not particularly influential on individual, team, or business-unit behavior. In addition, line managers frequently complain about the time required to complete these evaluations.

- Compensation is generally not contingent on individual, work group, or firm performance. Any pay increases go proportionally to all workers. As a rule, the company does not differentiate pay between the lowest- and highest-performing workers in any given job.

Diagnosing Stilwell's Internal HR Fit

What conclusions can we draw about the internal alignment of Stilwell's HR system? Measures of internal alignment are best focused on those who "live with" the HR system and those whose behaviors that system is designed to influence—line managers and front-line employees. To assess internal alignment within Stilwell's HR system, we generally ask individuals from these two groups to estimate the degree to which the various HR management subsystems work together. Here's a simple way to begin this process: Think of the degree of "fit" and internal consistency as a continuum from –100 to +100, and assign a value in that range to each relationship using the measurement tool shown in table 6-1.

(We've added some responses to the boxes to show how Stilwell might assess its internal HR alignment.) The data in the chart can be collected in a variety of ways. However, in most companies a short survey of 100 or so individuals, followed by one or two focus groups of mid- and senior-level employees, gives a comprehensive picture of the current internal alignment of the company's HR system.

If we take a close look at Stilwell's entries in the chart, we can see that several elements in the HR system are internally inconsistent. For example, both the selection and performance-appraisal processes are outdated and do not generate the kind of competencies Stilwell needs now or will require in the future. Similarly, Stilwell does not have the level and mix of compensation to attract the requisite talent, nor is its compensation structure designed to reflect the current team structure. While the HR system provides the VP of HR with the kind of efficiency numbers she has traditionally been asked to provide the CEO, the human resource system is undermining HR's ability to contribute to value creation. The process of filling out this chart would send a very clear message that the Stilwell HR system is not currently configured to implement the company's proposed strategy, or perhaps any strategy.

The Sources of Internal Misalignment

Even a simple diagnostic process such as the one just described can be a surprising wake-up call for many human resource managers. It can reveal that the HR system is sending conflicting signals about what the organization values and that it has failed to support a strategic focus among employees.

How does such misalignment develop, even in companies where HR professionals are knowledgeable, perhaps even expert, in current human resource practices? The most common explanation we hear is that HR managers simply have not thought much in these terms. Their focus traditionally has been operational, not strategic and systemic. A functional specialization in compensation or development that places little attention on linkages and that conflicts with other policies only worsens the situation. What's more, an operational emphasis on consistency and uniformity often overrides any concerns about the potential impact of internal misalignment. At the extreme, managers dismiss such concerns with a

Table 6-1 Diagnosing Internal Fit

In the chart below, please estimate the degree to which the various HR management subsystems work together harmoniously or "fit" together. Think of the degree of fit and internal consistency as a continuum from –100 to +100, and assign a value in that range to each relationship. Examples of the extremes and midpoints on that continuum are as follows:

–100: The two subsystems work at **cross-purposes.**

0: The two subsystems have **little or no effect on one another.**

+100: Each subsystem is **mutually reinforcing and internally consistent.**

DNK: Don't know or have no opinoin.

	HR Planning	Recruiting and Selection	Training and Development	Performance Management and Appraisal	Compensation and Benefits	Work Organization (e.g., teams)	Communication Systems	HR Performance Measurement Cost	HR Performance Measurement Value Creation
HR Planning	—	-30	0	-20	0	0	0	0	0
Recruiting and Selection		—	0	-10	-20	-30	0	+30	-40
Training and Development			—	0	0	0	0	+30	-10
Performance Management and Appraisal				—	0	-30	-20	0	-20
Compensation and Benefits					—	-50	0	+40	0
Work Organization (e.g., teams)						—	0	0	0
Communication Systems							—	0	0
HR Performance Measurement								—	

casual "Come on—how bad could it be?" HR has a tradition of telling line managers what they can't do, and there is a long-held belief that HR's problems don't affect anything important in the firm. Today, even though many of these professionals have embraced the idea of playing a strategic role, they find themselves burdened with a misaligned HR system—a remnant of an earlier period.

Interestingly, misalignment within the HR system can also stem from too much emphasis on benchmarking. Again, the strategic elements of the HR system must be developed from a top-down perspective—meaning from an analysis of the *unique requirements* of a firm's strategy implementation process. When you benchmark, you look to other firms. This approach effectively treats practices (and measures) as commodities, because it assumes that what works in one company will work in another. But as you may recall in our earlier discussion about systems thinking, removing a component from its larger system can have unexpected consequences for both the component and the system. Specifically, you diminish the value of the component if you evaluate it in the context of another system that was not designed for the same purpose as your original system. Benchmarking may help you understand processes, once you design your HR system from a top-down strategic perspective. Nevertheless, too often it becomes the primary input to a bottom-up development process.

ASSESSING EXTERNAL ALIGNMENT

Diagnosing internal alignment can help you quickly spot potential problems within the HR system and can highlight the need for action. However, it provides little remedial guidance. This is because internal alignment follows from the external alignment of the HR system—that is, the extent to which the HR system is designed to implement the firm's strategy. In other words, you should design your company's HR system only after you carefully analyze the *firm's* strategic drivers and the relevant HR deliverables that contribute to those drivers. By doing this, you create a kind of strategic fabric that weaves the HR system together. This process can even give you a rationale for allowing occasional misalignments. For example, the rewards and development practices for one deliverable may require a different approach from those of another deliverable.

The HR Scorecard includes a set of measures designed to assess the degree of *external* alignment between the HR system and the requirements of the firm's strategy implementation process (see Steps 5 and 6 in chapter

2). In building your firm's HR Scorecard, you arrive at a *design* for a strategic HR system, as well as a measurement system that will let you *manage* HR effectively. But to gain both of these Scorecard benefits, you have to understand how HR deliverables drive strategy implementation in your organization and which HR system elements produce those deliverables.

Scale and Perspective

In choosing measures to evaluate external HR alignment in your Scorecard, you need to consider two things: scale and perspective. *Scale* refers to the specific measurement tool you choose. For example, in chapter 3, we discussed using toggles to indicate whether elements of the HR system are aligned in a general sense with the HR deliverables required by the strategy implementation process. Toggles (rank-order scales) simply indicate the presence or absence of alignment, rather than the *degree* of alignment. If you consider degree of alignment important in your own organization (for example, during a large change initiative), you would want to choose a different measurement scale (perhaps a 0 to 100 range to reflect the firm's progress toward alignment).

Perspective refers to individual viewpoints. Alignment, like beauty, is in the eye of the beholder. It represents a nexus between HR and the rest of the organization. It is crucial that judgments about alignment reflect both sides of this divide. For example, you may well see your firm's HR system as aligned with the required deliverables, but if the rest of the organization doesn't see things that way, you don't have alignment. Therefore, as you construct your external alignment measures, test your assumptions about alignment against the experiences and impressions of managers and employees outside of HR.

The External Alignment Matrix

To measure the external alignment of your HR system, we recommend a two-step process: (1) test alignment of HR deliverables within the strategy map, and (2) test alignment of your HR system with HR deliverables. In both steps, you collect information from focus groups or other cross-sections of employees, though the second step might rely more heavily on HR's perspective. As you'll see, this process helps you find out whether certain HR deliverables are in fact the key performance drivers for each respective element in your firm's strategy implementation process. It also shows you whether the HR system is providing the correct skills, motivation, and work structures to produce those deliverables. (Again, review chapter 2 to see how these steps relate to the measurement-system design process.)

Table 6-2 shows the kind of information you might solicit to test alignment between HR deliverables and the firm's strategy implementation process.[1] This chart asks respondents to indicate the degree to which each HR deliverable enables the appropriate strategic driver, on a scale of –100 to +100. Note that respondents evaluate only those HR deliverables and strategic performance drivers that you have linked by *identifying and locating HR deliverables within your firm's strategy map* (see Step 4 in chapter 2). The actual values in the matrix reflect what Stilwell Manufacturing might have discovered had they analyzed HR's role using our model in chapter 2.

Stilwell Manufacturing has a lot of work to do. Even this simple analysis highlights the misalignment between what the HR system is producing and what Stilwell needs to implement its high-growth strategy. For example, the firm is experiencing considerable turnover among its most senior research technicians, which is making it difficult to shorten product development cycles. As it turns out, Stilwell pay levels have

Table 6-2   Testing Alignment of HR Deliverables within the Strategy Map as Illustrated by Stilwell Manufacturing

Please indicate the degree to which each HR deliverable in the chart below would *currently* enable each strategic driver, on a scale of –100 to +100. Empty cells indicate this is not a "key" deliverable for a particular driver. Examples of the extremes and midpoints on that continuum are as follows:

–100:	This deliverable is **counterproductive** for enabling this driver.
0:	This deliverable has **little or no effect** on this driver.
+100:	This deliverable **significantly enables** this driver.
DNK:	Don't know or have no opinoin.

HR DELIVERABLE

Strategic Performance Drivers	Employment Stability among Senior R&D Staff	Team-based Behaviors	Strategy-focused Performance	High-talent Staffing Level
1. *Shorten product development times*	–80	–30	+30	
2. *Enhance customer focus and responsiveness*	–20		–20	
3. *Enhance productivity*		–10	–50	–40
4. *Develop and successfully manage joint ventures*	–10	–50		

fallen behind the market, and the company is losing its most senior people to the competition. In addition, the R&D unit has moved to a cross-disciplinary team-based system in an attempt to leverage new ideas across the entire Stilwell product line. However, the R&D staff lacks the team skills to make this work, causing further delays. The one bright spot is that while reward *levels* are below market, the rewards are structured to motivate strategic behavior (unlike in the rest of the firm)—in this case to encourage shorter product development times. While this analysis has been limited to the R&D function, it could easily be extended to the broader organizational focus of the remaining performance drivers.

Once you've assessed the fit between your HR deliverables and strategic performance drivers, you then measure the extent to which the HR system is producing the appropriate elements of human performance required for these deliverables. There are several ways to approach this analysis, depending on how fine-grained you wish it to be. One approach is to link deliverables with their respective elements of human performance and then examine how the HR system is influencing those elements of human performance. For example, strategic human performance in organizations is a function of three interrelated elements:

- *Employee Skills:* Do employees have the skills required to perform their roles?

- *Employee Motivation:* Are employees motivated to apply those skills?

- *Employee Strategic Focus:* Do employees understand how their job contributes to the successful implementation of the firm's strategy and have the opportunity to apply that knowledge?

In other words:

$$\text{Strategic Human Performance} = \text{Employee Skills} \times \text{Motivation} \times \text{Employee Strategic Focus}$$

Yet this approach requires a second step to make these results "actionable," namely, that these dimensions of human performance must be linked to the elements of the HR system that produce them.

A more direct approach is described in table 6-3, where the measure of alignment would go directly from the human resource deliverable to the HR system. This approach assumes that HR has framed the analysis of its deliverables (as in table 6-2) to emphasize the dimensions of strategic

Table 6-3   Testing Alignment of the HR System with HR Deliverables as Illustrated by Stilwell Manufacturing

Please indicate the degree to which the following elements of the HR system facilitate the HR deliverables shown, on a scale of –100 to +100. Examples of the extremes and midpoints on that continuum are as follows:

–100: This dimension is **counterproductive** for enabling this deliverable.

0: This dimension has **little or no effect** on this deliverable.

+100: This dimension **significantly enables** this deliverable.

DNK: Don't know or have no opinion.

HR Deliverable	HR Planning	Recruiting and Selection	Training and Development	Performance Management and Appraisal	Compensation and Benefits	Work Organization (e.g., teams)	Communication Systems
Employment stability	0	0	0	0	-50	-20	0
Team-based behaviors	0	0	-30	-20	-40	0	0
Strategy-focused behaviors	0	0	0	0	+40	0	0
High-talent staffing level	0	-50	0	-50	0	0	0

human performance. Again, responses are on a scale of –100 to +100. You can then use these data to determine whether the elements of the HR system designed to produce those deliverables are appropriately aligned.

The sample data in table 6-3 are designed to highlight the "vital few" points of alignment between the HR system and a set of HR deliverables. The matrix describes an HR system that is not externally aligned with the requirements of the firm's strategy implementation process. To cite just a few examples: The hiring process is not producing the types and quantity of talent required by the firm's high-growth strategy. The recent reorganization into a team-based structure has not been adequately supported by focused development efforts or changes in the traditional performance management and reward systems. Compensation levels are not sufficient to maintain necessary levels of employment stability.

To summarize, we have described one measure of internal alignment and two measures of external alignment. Each captures a different, but important, dimension of the alignment process. Figure 6-2 locates each of these alignment measures on the continuum between the HR system and the firm's larger strategy map.

A STEP UP IN SOPHISTICATION:
THE SYSTEMS ALIGNMENT MAP

The alignment measures we've explored so far are based on very simple principles of measurement. Their advantage lies not so much in their degree of sophistication, but in their ability to help you focus on the

Figure 6-2 Internal and External Alignment Measures on Continuum between HR System and Strategy Map

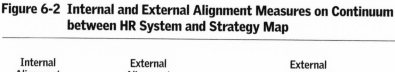
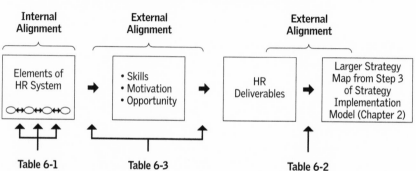

activity of measurement in general. All of these tools prompt you to think about how your company's HR system is aligned with the unique demands of the firm's strategy implementation process. Most important, these simple measures "align" your attention with strategic rather than operational matters.

There are more sophisticated measures of alignment available that capture the subtle interrelationships between the HR system and employee behavior. The earlier measures focus on individual elements of the system. They don't give you a complete picture of the overall alignment of the HR system, other than as a sum of the individual elements. A systemic perspective is essential for figuring out how to change the system in order to improve alignment. There is a myriad of interrelationships both *within* the HR system and *between* the HR system and the firm's strategy. Whenever you start fine-tuning any system, you have to think through the possible unintended consequences of your changes and the ways in which adjustments may ripple through the system and beyond.

To address these concerns, we have developed a measure that we call the Systems Alignment Map (SAM). This metric offers several important benefits:

- *It lets you visualize alignment.* How do you recognize alignment when you see it? SAM features a measurement process that lets you create a "picture" of your firm's HR system and its alignment with the company's strategic goals. Visualizing strategic alignment lets you see exactly where changes are required and what the nature of those changes might be. Visual depictions of multidimensional phenomena have long been understood to have two key advantages. First, they make it easier for the observer to see patterns in the data. This is particularly important for managers who are not familiar with more traditional data-analysis techniques. Second, when data are portrayed in this fashion, they are simply more accessible to the human eye and therefore more interpretable.[2]

- *It incorporates perspectives from the entire organization.* As we've indicated, alignment is very much a matter of perspective. It is very difficult for HR professionals to fully understand the influence of the entire HR system on employees at different levels in the organization. SAM incorporates all of those perspectives and lets you design alignment measures for specific employee groups, divisions, or processes.

- *It measures alignment systemically and yields realistic action steps.* The SAM methodology incorporates all of the links that make up the external and internal alignment of the HR system. As a result, it lets you simulate how changes in one element in the system will affect the alignment of the *whole* system. More important, SAM helps you identify ways to bring a single element into alignment—without generating unintended consequences.

- *It's relatively easy to administer.* The SAM methodology does not require employees to think outside of their own organizational experience. As a result, the tool gives you an aggregation of individual perceptions about alignment, from every facet of the organization. The data-collection process is no more intrusive than traditional employee surveys. Indeed, it is probably less threatening than typical surveys because it does not require sensitive evaluations.

- *It's based on best scientific principles of measurement.* The SAM technique relies on a well-developed, multidimensional scaling technique called Galileo.[3] Galileo allows us to manage some very difficult measurement challenges, yet produce actionable results.

The Galileo method of measurement was developed to provide greater precision and reliability than traditional Likert-type (5-point) metrics. Because it generates ratio rather than just interval measures (i.e., includes an absolute zero and can be positive or negative), it is particularly suited to our focus on alignment, where we want to understand that X is twice as far from A as Y. The results of a Galileo analysis can be represented both numerically and visually. Both are important for a complete analysis of strategic alignment, but the visual representation tends to provide the best intuitive insight into what are often very complex phenomena. The most common use of Galileo in a business context is in marketing, where customers provide a perceptual map of the proximity of various product attributes to the product in question.[4]

Galileo relies on an aggregation of individual perceptions. Individually, these perceptions may be imperfect reflections of the larger organizational experience, but taken together, they provide a remarkably accurate picture. You can get a sense of the power of the Galileo technique by considering a famous example from the field of cognitive psychology called the Johnson-Laird room demonstration.[5] In this demonstration, individuals are given a description of a room. The text is necessarily imprecise (what Johnson-Laird calls "indeterminate"). Based on the description, the individuals are asked to estimate the distances between pairs of objects throughout the room (e.g., bed, gas ring, radio, wardrobe, bookcase, window, door, etc.) using the Galileo technique. While each person's cognitive map of the room will be distorted and unbalanced, when aggregated across the entire sample of subjects, the many individual maps result in a room that is reasonable, balanced, and in proper proportions (that is, there are no locations inconsistent with the original description). Thus, each individual's mental model reflects inconsistencies and distortions, but the aggregate mapping reflects the actual physical positioning of objects in the room with surprising accuracy.

This strategy—obtaining the Galileo representation and then returning to the original representation (as judged by the individuals and their perceptions)—resembles the practice of mapping the validity of cross-cultural research materials through one translation and then a second translation back to the original. Just as Galileo can be used to aggregate individual maps of physical imagery, so it can be used to aggregate individuals' cognitive maps of attitudes or beliefs in order to obtain a fuller representation of actual relationships among concepts. The final cumulative effort is remarkably accurate. We use the same approach to build an organizational alignment map, based on individual employees' perceptions of alignment from their own locations within the organization.

Using SAM

Why is alignment so important to strategy? Without it, an organization cannot expect its employees to have the strategic focus required to implement the firm's strategy. But employees sharpen their strategic focus only by experiencing the various organizational systems that guide their behavior. The SAM approach lets you understand employees' perceptions of these systems. To develop a Systems Alignment Map, we recommend the following steps:

1. *Identify the key strategic drivers in the firm.* Drivers could be the strategic goals of the firm or specific performance drivers in your strategy map. The choice will depend on how these concepts have been communicated and understood throughout the organization.

In any case, these are the strategic "targets" of the HR system and the basis for any judgments about alignment.

2. *Identify the key elements of the HR system expected to drive strategy implementation.* These are the same elements of the HR system we used in tables 6-1 and 6-3. Generic categories would include compensation, rewards, performance management, career development, competencies, hiring and selection, and training and development, but the specific choices are likely to vary by organization.

   In the previous section, we highlighted the two stages of external alignment: from HR system to HR deliverable, and from HR deliverable to strategic performance driver (see figure 6-2). Steps 1 and 2 here have consolidated those two stages. However, there is no reason why you can't include HR deliverables as a third set of comparisons. Doing so would provide a richer picture of alignment, but at the price of making the analysis more difficult for the respondents.

3. *Ask a representative sample of employees to provide a list of paired "alignment" evaluations for all elements you identified in Steps 1 and 2.* To do this, provide respondents with a matrix resembling that shown in table 6-4. We've filled in some examples of HR system elements and strategic goals, along with sample evaluations in some of the boxes. Unlike with the other alignment measures, respondents are asked to describe the "distance" between a series of paired comparisons, such as pay versus customer service, using a 0 to 100 scale. The value 0 is used to signify "close" or "similar," while 100 means "dissimilar" or "far away."

Respondents are also provided with a "benchmark" to calibrate their ratings. For example, they might be given the example of "CEO" and "customer service" and told that they should consider those two concepts to have a distance of 30. There are several rules of thumb in selecting a benchmark. First, it ought to be drawn from the concepts being rated. Second, you should select two concepts that all employees will be familiar with and preferably a benchmark that most will agree with. Finally, it is better to choose a pair for which the distance benchmark will be toward the middle of the 0 to 100 scale.

The ratings in table 6-4 illustrate the perceptions of just one employee.

Table 6-4 The SAM Matrix

Think about your work experience at this company during the last three months. You experience and observe a wide range of policies, communications, and interactions with other members of this organization. We are interested in your judgments about how these different experiences fit together. In other words, are we "all on the same page"? Your responses, along with those of hundreds of others in the company, will help us answer that question.

On a scale from 0 to 100, please describe how different or "far apart" each of the following organizational concepts is from the others. The more different, or farther apart, they seem to be, the larger the number you should write. To help you calibrate your ratings, assume that the CEO and customer service are 30 units apart. If two words or phrases are not different at all, please write zero (0). If you have no idea, please leave the space blank.

	Strategic Goal 1: Enhance Product Development	Strategic Goal 2: Enhance Customer Focus	Last Strategic Goal	First Element of HR System: Recruiting and Selection	Second Element of HR System: Compensation and Benefits	Last Element of HR System	Me	My Supervisor
Strategic Goal 1: Enhance Product Development	—	50		20	80			
Strategic Goal 2: Enhance Customer Focus		—			20			
Last Strategic Goal			—					
First Element of HR System (Recruiting and Selection)				—	10			
Second Element of HR System (Compensation and Benefits)					—			
Last Element of HR System						—		
Me							—	
My Supervisor								—

Note: This is a truncated version of the original matrix. Shaded cells indicate where portions of the matrix have been omitted.

Note that we have also included columns for the individual employee and his or her supervisor. This step will give you an insight into how employees perceive the alignment of the organization's systems and how they view themselves ("Me" in table 6-4) in relation to those systems. This latter perspective is the key to employee strategic focus. The supervisor/employee alignment measures provide insight into the kinds of messages—intentional or not—that managers may be sending to employees. Supervisors at any level have a powerful influence on employee behavior, in large part because of the signals they give about what the organization considers appropriate and valuable. An all-too-common impediment to organizational change is managerial reluctance to get on board with a change effort because it isn't understood or it threatens managers personally. Without necessarily intending to, supervisors communicate their reluctance to direct reports, and the change effort stalls out as a result. Including supervisor information in the Systems Alignment Map helps you account for this influence.

Marketing and Refining at Mobil Oil: An Example of SAM

To illustrate the possibilities of the SAM approach, let's consider the marketing and refining (M&R) group within Mobil Oil.[6] Although this group did not explicitly employ the SAM method, its use of the Balanced Scorecard has been well documented. Therefore, the organization's experience lends itself to illustrating the SAM methodology.

At Mobil, the M&R group developed a number of strategic themes for the organization. To keep our SAM illustration simple, we'll focus on just these four, as expressed in these slogans:

- Financially Strong

- Delight the Customer

- Safe and Reliable

- On Spec, on Time

To use SAM, M&R would translate these themes into the strategic drivers that make up the causal flow of a balanced performance measurement system. Then they would identify the HR deliverables and the necessary alignment of the HR system required to produce those deliverables.

Let's now imagine that M&R identified *competencies* as the single most important HR deliverable required to implement the firm's strategy. Again, for simplicity's sake, we'll limit the analysis to the following elements of the HR system: *compensation*, *rewards*, and *training and development*. Assuming that M&R might identify these three functions as major enablers of competencies, let's focus on this subset of the HR system in our sample analysis.

EXAMPLE I: A SYSTEM IN MISALIGNMENT

Figure 6-3 shows a Galileo representation of a somewhat misaligned HR system.[7] (The data that went into this graphic would be obtained through an employee-survey matrix like that shown in table 6-4.) This figure depicts the possible *aggregate* perception of all employees surveyed regarding the alignment among the company's strategic goals, the HR deliverable "competencies," and the HR system elements designed to produce that deliverable.

How might we interpret this picture? First, we can see that employees generally consider competencies as closely aligned with the "Financially Strong" and "Delight the Customer" strategic goals. Perceived alignment between this deliverable and the "Safe and Reliable" and "On Spec, On Time" goals is not as strong. In this case, if the company expects competencies to equally influence *each* of the four stated strategic goals, it will

Figure 6-3   Galileo Map of Misaligned HR System

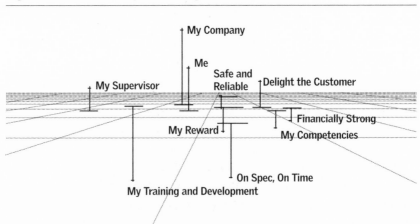

need to strengthen those competencies that specifically support "On Spec, On Time" and "Safe and Reliable."

Second, consider the location of "Me" (the aggregate of all individual respondents) relative to the firm's strategic goals. This positioning indicates the extent of *employee strategic focus* we described earlier. If you can imagine the average employee in this example, he or she stands some distance away from the firm's strategic goals. This finding probably reflects the combined impact of the compensation system, the firm's development policies, and the employee's supervisor—none of which are aligned with those strategic goals. For example, perhaps training and development policies reflect an earlier strategy or generic training that is not considered relevant to the new strategic goals. Similarly, the immediate supervisors for most employees are simply reinforcing the importance of those goals. This is one of the most valuable insights a Systems Alignment Map can offer. It not only provides an image of employee strategic focus but also highlights the conflicting signals that lie at the core of any misalignment. It doesn't explain the reason for a particular misalignment, but it highlights the presence of a problem that can prompt further investigation.

How might SAM provide actionable results? For one thing, it gives a visual and intuitive summary of how the human dimension of the organization is aligned with the firm's larger strategic goals and the HR system. It thus alerts you to any alignment problems and provides some guidance for how you might address these problems. Note, though, that because this is a perceptual map, it doesn't tell you whether the HR system elements are *in fact* out of alignment; it just shows employees' understanding of those elements. You, the HR professional, have to determine whether the misalignment is structural or just misunderstood by the employees. In our experience, once HR professionals identify a misalignment, they have no trouble supplying the motivation and skill required to resolve it. The big hurdle, which the Systems Alignment Mapping helps to surmount, is capturing the *nature* of the alignment problem by pinpointing those parts of the organization that are in alignment and those that are not.

The SAM approach leads to actionable results in another way as well. Specifically, the methodology is based on precise measures of the "distances" and interrelationships among the perceptions depicted in the Galileo graphic. In effect, these perceptions of alignment somewhat resemble the planets in a solar system. Like the planets, the concepts in the Galileo depiction exert a gravitational pull on one another. Shifting one concept toward a second will not only influence the relationship between them but also change their relationship to other elements in the system. For instance, in the example of misalignment just described, it may be that training priorities are largely based on feedback from line managers. If line managers become more "strategically focused," this will draw the training and development policies closer to the strategic goals, which will further reinforce the movement of the average employee toward those same goals. By understanding the potential impact of this "gravitational pull" among the many different elements within the HR system and the rest of the firm, you can craft wiser interventions to resolve alignment problems.

EXAMPLE 2: A SYSTEM IN ALIGNMENT

Figure 6-4 illustrates relatively good alignment between employees and the elements of the strategy implementation process. Any Galileo picture necessarily describes the relative position of various elements within the larger system. In this case, both *rewards* and *training and development* are somewhat out of alignment. However, in contrast to figure 6-3, you can see that the strategy implementation system of this organization is fairly well aligned internally.

One advantage of the Galileo methodology is that you don't have to rely on just the graphics in comparing two alignment maps. The method provides numerical estimates that let you precisely compare the degree

Figure 6-4   Galileo Map of Aligned HR System

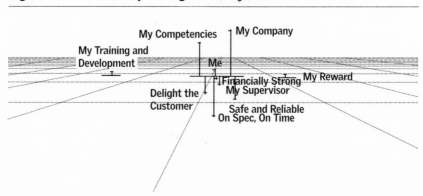

of alignment between two maps. (This aspect of Galileo is beyond the scope of this chapter, but you can learn more about it in the works cited.) Galileo is thus particularly useful for measuring changes in strategic alignment over time within your firm as you implement HR interventions. It is very easy to then incorporate these measures into the alignment dimension of the HR Scorecard. One of the most effective ways to reinforce HR's strategic role is by conducting a monthly or quarterly alignment-review session—with a Systems Alignment Map as the focus of discussion.

EMPLOYEE STRATEGIC FOCUS AS A PERFORMANCE DRIVER: USING SAM METRICS TO MANAGE PERFORMANCE

The SAM results provide several metrics that you can track. One is overall HR alignment. You can calculate *aggregate* distance between the HR system and strategic goals. More important, you can measure changes in this kind of alignment over time. You can also use the aggregate "me" relative to each strategic goal as another measure of "employee strategic focus." Again, measuring changes in these relationships over time is particularly valuable. Finally, you can calculate ESF (employee strategic focus) measures at lower organizational levels, including at the individual level, to help analyze performance problems. We don't recommend using responses to SAM metrics to judge employees' performance, however. SAM metrics are self-reported data and hinge on employees' providing honest opinions about strategic alignment within the firm. If these measures became part of individual performance evaluations, it would be too easy for employees to report these data in a self-serving way. Nevertheless, much as some managers are held accountable for the employee survey results of their subordinates, ESF metrics could be used as a measure of performance for managers responsible for improving the ESF of others.

SUMMARY: A PORTFOLIO OF METRICS

The word *alignment* seems to be on everyone's lips in the business world these days. As a theme, it runs throughout this book as well. We have tried to demonstrate why alignment is so important to HR's role as a strategic asset. We have also emphasized the importance of measurement as a foundational capability for realizing that role.

The need for better measures becomes particularly acute in evaluating alignment. In this chapter, we introduced several different approaches to the measure of alignment. First, we discussed alignment measures as diagnostic tools. The emphasis here was on *internal alignment* as an indicator of the more fundamental alignment between HR and the firm's strategy. Next, we explored a two-step process for assessing *external alignment*. This process involved gauging both the HR deliverable–strategic driver fit and the HR deliverable–HR system fit. Finally, we described a unique approach to capturing the entire HR-strategy fit through a visual depiction of alignment. Each of these metrics contributes an important piece of the puzzle and enriches your overall view. We encourage you to build on all of these ideas and to adapt them to the unique challenges of your own organization.

7

COMPETENCIES FOR
HR PROFESSIONALS

N OW THAT YOU'VE WORKED with a template for designing a
strategic HR architecture in your firm and explored a measurement system for managing that architecture, how do you make
sure you have the skills to actually implement this strategic perspective?
Doing so requires competencies that may be new to you. In this chapter,
we discuss the skills you'll need to forge a strategic partnership with line
management. We'll also review examples from companies that have successfully honed those competencies.

TRANSFORMING THE PROFESSION

All professions establish standards that determine entrée and certify proficiency. In the last decade, those interested in the discipline of human
resources have moved aggressively and boldly to define it as a profession.
These moves have included the remarkable growth of the national Society
for Human Resource Management (SHRM), which now boasts more than
150,000 worldwide members; a certification assessment sanctioned by
SHRM, which enables entrants to demonstrate knowledge of fundamental
principles; and specialized graduate degrees in human resources (e.g., at

Cornell, University of Illinois, Michigan State, University of Minnesota, Ohio State, Rutgers, University of Wisconsin, and a number of other universities). Underlying this movement toward professionalism are a body of knowledge, a set of expected behaviors, and specific outcomes for those doing HR work. We can think of these expected knowledge and behaviors as *competencies*. To serve as valuable business partners, HR professionals need to define and measure these competencies systematically.

WHAT IS HR COMPETENCE?

Competence refers to an individual's *knowledge, skills, abilities,* or *personality* characteristics that directly influence his or her job performance. The concept of individual competence has a long tradition in the managerial field. Most of this work has focused on leaders and general managers.[1] Other research has sought to specify HR competencies through interviews with executives within a single firm or from a limited set of firms.[2] Many companies have tried to identify critical HR competencies by asking line managers within the company what they expect from HR and the kinds of competencies HR professionals should exemplify (e.g., what line managers need from HR). This approach assumes that each company may have unique expectations of its human resource professionals and that, as clients, line managers play a central role in defining those expectations.

Defining HR competencies company by company through executive interviews has some advantages. For one thing, it anchors the findings in behaviors, because the questions asked in the interviews can target actual cases in which HR professionals within the company demonstrated competence. It also tailors the process to the specific needs of the companies in question. However, the danger is that executives may not know what they don't know. That is, they may identify only those competencies they have seen, when in fact other HR competencies may have more importance for their firm if they only knew about them. This approach may also lead to biased results, depending on the sample of executives chosen for interviews. Executives' managerial orientation, rather than the actual needs of the business, may influence their expectations of HR. For example, line managers that have never seen HR professionals in a strategic role may not be able to think of HR as anything other than administrative overhead. Firms generally have idiosyncratic requirements for implementing strategy. Therefore, while firm-specific studies may yield some interesting examples, these case studies alone will not provide an overall competency model for the HR profession.

Three large-scale HR competency studies, conducted in the 1990s, have shed some interesting light on the status of this profession. In the first study, Towers Perrin collaborated with IBM to survey 3,000 HR professionals, consultants, line executives, and academicians about a broad range of HR issues.[3] The work revealed a rather diverse perspective on HR competencies. Among the four groups surveyed, the most commonly identified competencies included the following:

- Computer literacy (line executives)

- Broad knowledge of and vision for HR (academics)

- Ability to anticipate the effects of change (consultants)

- HR's education of and influence on line managers (HR executives)

The second study was recently sponsored by the Society of Human Resource Management Foundation.[4] This work focused on the *future* competency requirements of HR professionals. Based on data from 300 HR professionals from different industries and companies of different sizes, this study concluded that core human resource competencies center on leadership, management, functional, and personal attributes that must be augmented by level- and role-specific competencies.

The third and most extensive of the HR competency surveys was conducted at the University of Michigan School of Business in three rounds over a ten-year period (1988 to 1998). This work involved more than 20,000 HR and line professionals and identified human resource competencies across HR functional specialties, industries, firms, and time. The study aimed to create a competency template for the entire HR profession, not just for a single firm. Let's take a closer look at this research.

Michigan's HR Competency Research

The Michigan research team, led by Wayne Brockbank, Dale Lake, Dave Ulrich, and Arthur Yeung, initially developed and pilot-tested an HR competency model based on a careful review of the literature. Next, they field-tested this model in a wide variety of industries, HR functions, and regions. Their first round of data collection, in 1988, included more than 10,000 individuals in 91 firms.[5] The team concluded that HR competencies could be divided into three distinct domains: knowledge of the business, delivery of HR practices, and ability to manage change. Interestingly, the results at this point indicated that, of these three areas, the ability to manage change ranked highest in importance in predicting the overall effectiveness of HR professionals.

As this project progressed, the researchers continued to explore competencies for HR professionals on a company-specific basis. As the findings from these case studies accumulated over several years, a clear pattern of an evolving change in competency requirements emerged: HR professionals were effective if they also demonstrated personal credibility, if they allocated their time to key strategic issues more than administrative processes, and if they mastered rapid change. These findings prompted a second round of surveys in 1992 and 1993 that focused on global firms and included more than 5,000 participants. The results underscored HR's new strategic role at the close of the twentieth century. Specifically, the researchers observed a dramatic increase in the amount of time that HR professionals devoted to strategic issues, and a relative decline in the time they allocated to more traditional issues.[6] For example, HR professionals needed to be more knowledgeable than ever about financial management and external competitive and customer demands. They also had to be able to work with line executives to send clear and consistent messages about their firm's goals and directions.[7] Finally, this research found that the highest-performing firms reduced time and effort spent on HR transactional issues by outsourcing, automating, and reengineering their HR activities.

The third phase of the project continued to focus on the evolution of HR competencies and culminated in the most recent survey of 5,000 HR professionals in 1997 and 1998. These results described a continually changing profession that is increasingly taking on a strategic role in organizational life. The data continued to support the importance of the competency domains as originally defined—knowledge of the business, professional mastery of HR, and change management. However, they also pointed to two additional domains: culture management and personal credibility.[8] We will briefly describe each of these five domains:

KNOWLEDGE OF THE BUSINESS

HR professionals add value to an organization when they understand how the business operates. Why? Because that understanding allows them to adapt HR and organizational activities to changing business conditions. Only by knowing the financial, strategic, technological, and organizational capabilities of your organization can you play a valuable role in any strategic discussion. HR professionals who have mastered industrial, employee, or human relations may be fully competent in their discipline but still fail to grasp the essentials of the business in which their firms compete. For example, some HR professionals know how to *use* human resource technology such as multiple rater performance appraisal systems but not how to *adapt* that technology to specific, changing business conditions. Some firms are now doing performance appraisal over the Web and include customers and suppliers as well as supervisors, peers, and subordinates in the appraisal process. Business acumen requires knowledge, if not direct operational experience, in functional areas such as marketing, finance, strategy, technology, and sales, in addition to human resources. By "knowledge of the business" we don't mean the ability to *manage* all these business functions, but the ability to *understand* them. To implement the model we described in chapter 2, HR professionals need to comprehend both sides of the nexus between HR deliverables and business/strategic problems. In short, to be valuable business partners, HR professionals need to know much more about the business than line managers need to know about HR.

DELIVERY OF HR PRACTICES

Like any other staff members, HR professionals at the very least must be experts in their specialty. Knowing and being able to deliver state-of-the-art, innovative HR practices builds these professionals' credibility and earns them respect from the rest of the organization. It is the sine qua non for cultivating a professional "brand" for HR. However, as we've discussed in earlier chapters of this book, the dimensions of this professional expertise are shifting rapidly over time. Therefore, HR professionals must be dedicated enough to continually master the underlying theory of HR and agile enough to adapt that theory to their unique situation. For example, we spoke at a chief learning officer conference recently and spent some time talking about how some of the foundational concepts by Chris Argyris helped organizations build learning disciplines. At the end of our session, some chief learning officers from large firms approached us and asked how to spell "Argyris." Their questions indicated little understanding of Argyris's seminal work—a bit surprising given that these were the people tasked with helping to transform their firms into learning organizations. To the extent such questions demonstrate a lack of knowledge about the theories behind learning, and how to build on those theories, HR professionals may have some work to do.

MANAGEMENT OF CHANGE

This competency is another example of the increasing role of HR as business partner. Perhaps the most compelling challenge facing most CEOs is the need to refocus the organization in response to new strategic directions. Human resource professionals are well positioned to drive that change—if they are prepared. An HR professional who can orchestrate change processes demonstrates the following abilities: the ability to diagnose problems, build relationships with clients, articulate a vision, set a leadership agenda, solve problems, and implement goals. This competency involves knowledge (of change processes), skills (as change agents), and abilities (to deliver change) essential for moving the "people" side of the organization.

MANAGEMENT OF CULTURE

Management researchers John Kotter and James Heskett found that firms with "stronger" cultures (as measured by the extent to which employees share the values of the firm) tend to achieve higher performance.[9] We have described the strategic role of HR architecture and emphasized the role of systems. Ultimately, the employee behaviors produced by these systems become woven into the culture of the company. In that sense, a high-performance HR strategy is a leading indicator of a high-performance culture. HR professionals need to understand that they are the "keepers of the culture" and that their impact reaches well beyond their functional boundaries.[10]

PERSONAL CREDIBILITY

If the other four domains can be thought of as the pillars of HR competence, personal credibility might be described as the foundation on which those pillars rest. The Michigan research project found that successful HR professionals were seen as personally credible both inside and outside their function. But what does credibility mean? We believe that it comprises three dimensions. First, it requires that human resource professionals "live" the firm's values. This, of course, goes hand in hand with being the "keepers of the culture." We once visited a firm where the head of HR was being sued for sexual harassment based on compelling evidence against him. In this case, no matter how much this executive knew about business, HR, culture, and change, he utterly lacked personal credibility. Organizational values that often trip up HR executives are openness, candor, ability to be a team player, capacity to treat individuals with respect, concern for due process, and insistence on the highest performance for HR executives themselves and their staff. If the HR professionals do not live these values in their work, they can hardly expect others to give them much credibility.

Second, HR professionals build credibility when their relationships with colleagues are founded on trust. Trusting relationships emerge when HR professionals serve as valued partners on management teams, when they have "chemistry" with the management team and are able to work well as team members and exert influence without authority, and when they skillfully support business objectives.

Third, HR professionals earn the respect of their colleagues when they act "with an attitude."[11] What we mean by "with an attitude" is having a point of view about how the business can win, backing up that opinion with evidence (a primary purpose of this book), presenting innovative and unsolicited ideas and solutions, and encouraging debate about key issues. Human resource leaders especially need that attitude when engaging in Step 2 of our model in chapter 2—building a business case for why and how HR matters in strategy implementation.

Prioritizing Competencies

In the most recent round of research in the Michigan project, the researchers analyzed the relative impact of the five domains just discussed on the overall effectiveness of the HR professional. Table 7-1 describes the behavioral indicators of these competencies and shows how they rank in their perceived contribution to the effectiveness of HR professionals. All of these domains are considered important competencies for the HR professional. However, research indicates that they range from least to most important as follows: knowing the business (allows HR professionals to join the management team), mastering HR practices (lets them define and access best practices within HR), managing culture (helps them to shape the firm's identity), orchestrating change (allows them to "make things happen"), and demonstrating personal credibility (earns them respect and goodwill). This ranking holds true across industry, level of HR professional, and specialty area.

Table 7-1 Description and Relative Importance of HR Competency Domains

Competency Domain	Importance Rank (1 = highest)	Specific Competencies (in order of importance)
Personal Credibility	1	Has track record of success.
		Has earned trust.
		Instills confidence in others.
		Has "chemistry" with key constituents.
		Demonstrates high integrity.
		Asks important questions.
		Frames complex ideas in useful ways.
		Takes appropriate risks.
		Provides candid observations.
		Provides alternative insights on business issues.
Ability to Manage Change	2	Establishes trust and credibility in relating to others.
		Is visionary.
		Takes a proactive role in bringing about change.
		Builds supportive relationships with others.
		Encourages others to be creative.
		Puts specific problems in context of the larger system.
		Identifies problems central to business success.
Ability to Manage Culture	3	Shares knowledge across organizational boundaries.
		Champions culture-transformation process.
		Translates desired culture into specific behaviors.
		Challenges the status quo.
		Identifies the culture required to meet the firm's business strategy and frames culture in a way that excites employees.
		Encourages executives to behave consistently with the desired culture.
		Focuses the internal culture on meeting the needs of external customers.
Delivery of Human Resource Practices	4	Expresses effective verbal communication.
		Works with managers to send clear and consistent messages.
		Expresses effective written communication.
		Facilitates the process of restructuring the organization.
		Designs development programs that facilitate change.
		Facilitates design of internal communication processes.
		Attracts appropriate employees.
		Designs compensation systems.
		Facilitates dissemination of customer information.

Competency Domain	Importance Rank (1 = highest)	Specific Competencies (in order of importance)
Understanding of the Business	5	Understands the following: • human resource practices • organizational structure • competitor analysis • finance • marketing and sales • computer information systems

The Michigan research is supported by evidence from other companies that have developed their own competency models. As table 7-2 shows, the experience of General Electric, and other Fortune 500 companies is consistent with the Michigan model.

Table 7-2 HR Competencies by Company

	General Electric	Large Consumer Products Manufacturer	International Pharmaceutical Manufacturer
General categories of competencies identified by company	1. Knowledge of Business 2. Delivery of HR 3. Management of Change 4. Personal Credibility	1. Leadership 2. Knowledge of the Business 3. HR Strategic Thinking 4. Process Skills 5. HR Technologies	1. Knowedge of Business 2. Individual Leadership 3. Process Practices 4. HR Practices 5. Other Strategic Planning
Competencies related to knowledge of the business	• Business acumen: knows business objectives, cycle, global developments. • Customer orientation: knows who customers are and how they make buying decisions. • External relations: works with key constituents (media, schools, government) and public policy.	• Understands corporate business (structure, vision, values, strategies, financial and performance measures). • Understands internal and external customers. • Understands key business disciplines, value-based management, HR implications of global business, information technology.	• Understands corporate and division vision, mission, culture, goals, values, strategies, and financial and performance measures. • Knows company products. • Understands the health-care industry and current challenges it is facing. • Understands company's key policies

(continued on the next page)

(continued from the previous page)

Table 7-2 HR Competencies by Company

	General Electric	Large Consumer Products Manufacturer	International Pharmaceutical Manufacturer
		• Understands the strategy- and business-planning process.	• Understands the strategy and business-planning process.
		• Understands and is able to apply a systematic HR planning process.	• Applies systematic HR planning process.
Competencies related to managing culture	• Continually assesses organization issues and trends for improvement. • Champions Work-Out as way to support sustained change. • Consulting and coaching: leverages resources to meet business needs. • Introduces new ways of thinking.	• Understands the environment (external and internal) of corporation and individual businesses. • Selects, designs, and integrates HR systems or practices to build organizational mind-set, capability, and competitive advantage for respective business. • Develops and integrates business HR strategies within framework of corporate HR strategies. • Has knowledge of management processes in business.	• Demonstrates effective project management skills. • Understands and applies principles of organization design. • Displays systems and process thinking; works to build integrated procedures.
Competencies related to HR technical expertise	• Organization design: knows structure, work teams. • Selection and staffing: knows succession planning, encourages diversity, identifies and assesses talent, conducts orientation, encourages retention.	• Has a generalist perspective on HR systems and practices as they relate to achievement of business competitive advantage. • Designs, integrates, and implements HR systems to build organizational capability.	• Displays technical expertise in HR disciplines. • Is knowledgeable about "best in class" HR practices. • Designs and delivers leading-edge practices. • Measures effectiveness of HR systems and practices.

	General Electric	Large Consumer Products Manufacturer	International Pharmaceutical Manufacturer
	• Measurement and reward: manages performance, compensation, feedback. • Negotiation and conflict resolution: manages labor relations. • Learning and development: supports individual and team development, career development, training, experience-based learning. • Employee relations: handles employee issues, HR policies and practices. • Communication: builds communication plan, shares information.	• Designs and delivers leading-edge practices to meet competitive business needs. • Measures effectiveness of HR systems and practices.	
Competencies related to personal credibility	• Credibility: maintains confidentiality, meets commitments. • Judgment: sets priorities, acts on key issues, makes data-based decisions. • Courage: stands up for beliefs, delivers honest news. • GE values: advocates and models GE values.	• Understands the nature and styles of leadership and displays appropriate leadership characteristics. • Demonstrates leadership at multiple performance levels: individual, team, unit.	• Builds partnerships and collaborative relationships with clients by working toward mutual goals. • Initiates discussions and takes action on the HR implications of business strategy. • Sells ideas and HR approaches to line managers in a manner that builds commitment.
Competencies related to being able to make change happen	• Change advocacy: encourages support for new ideas, seeks new ideas. • Facilitation: manages personal conflicts, encourages creativity.	• Has competence in company's processes. • Understands key process skills such as consulting, problem-solving, evaluation/diagnosis, workshop design, and facilitation.	• Demonstrates effective consulting skills: works to understand needs, engages in constructive problem solving, clarifies roles and responsibilities, partners with client, follows through on commitments.

(continued on the next page)

(continued from the previous page)

Table 7-2 HR Competencies by Company

General Electric	Large Consumer Products Manufacturer	International Pharmaceutical Manufacturer
	• Understands the principles and processes of organizational change and development. • Balances, integrates, and manages under conditions of uncertainty and paradox.	• Demonstrates effective facilitation skills: facilitates teams, tasks forces, etc.; designs processes to accomplish goals at a meeting or other forum. • Designs and facilitates organization change: understands process of organization change, initiates and leads change, designs plans for change, is able to manage change under conditions of paradox. • Demonstrates analytical and problem solving skills. • Displays verbal and written communication skills.

We can draw several lessons from the competencies described in table 7-2. For one thing, even though the large-scale Michigan studies necessarily relied on relatively generic competency labels, they closely map to the experience of the companies in this table. This gives us confidence that the underlying model accurately reflects the challenges that HR professionals typically face. Moreover, the information in table 7-2 makes the competency model more actionable because it reveals behaviors required for each competency domain. Finally, these results highlight what has become an ongoing debate in the HR profession. The debate centers on how much one needs to master HR technical competencies (such as the intricacies of team-based incentive systems) to be a truly effective human resource professional. Most firms expect technical proficiency, though some give it relatively little weight overall. In our view, technical competencies must be represented in a company's HR-competency port-folio. However, such competencies are probably not essential to HR pro-fessionals' ability to serve as business partners and strategic architects. In these roles, it is more important to understand the implications for HR of the firm's strategy, in general, and the appropriate strategic drivers, in particular. This understanding may well require a sixth competency: strategic HR performance management.

STRATEGIC HR PERFORMANCE MANAGEMENT: A NEW COMPETENCY

This book is not primarily about a new *role* for HR; the notion of HR as a strategic partner was with us for much of the 1990s. However, it does imply a new *competency*—in strategic HR performance management—which we might add to those five already enumerated. What do we mean by strategic performance management? We mean the process of orches-trating the firm's strategy implementation through balanced performance measurement systems. Notice that we use the term *management* rather than *measurement* in defining this competency. That's because the pur-pose of the measurement systems we've discussed in this book is more effective *organizational* management. Nevertheless, the ability to imple-ment balanced performance *measurement* systems, such as the Balanced Scorecard, is also essential for this competency.

Increasingly, firms that understand the importance of strategy execution to their long-term success are adopting strategic performance management as a key competency and emphasizing measurement-led management. Yet this emerging trend also represents a challenge. On the one hand, it holds out hope that HR will indeed become a legitimate strategic asset. On the other, as we've seen from the recent history with the Balanced Score-card, HR traditionally has been the weak link in the performance meas-urement system. We believe that this weakness can be transformed into a strength, if HR professionals develop a competency in strategic perfor-mance management.

To build this competency, human resource managers must under-stand strategic measurement along two dimensions: *what* to measure and *how* to measure it. *What* refers to strategy implementation, emphasized throughout this book. A focus on strategy implementation provides the bedrock for the strategic management of HR. As we saw in chapter 5, the *how* of measurement can be somewhat more technical. You may not need to master each nuance, but you should at least appreciate the many aspects of measurement in order to make informed decisions regarding their results.

The Dimensions of Strategic Performance Management

The dimensions of a competency in strategic performance management are probably a little different from those of most competencies that HR professionals have considered in the past. They strongly support our argument that human resource managers must learn to think differently about HR. Moreover, they confirm the idea that these leaders have to be able to demonstrate HR's strategic influence to senior line managers. We divide the strategic performance management competency into four dimensions discussed in the following sections.

CRITICAL CAUSAL THINKING

In chapter 2, we noted that the strategic link between HR architecture and firm performance is the strategy map that describes the firm's strategy implementation process. Remember that this map is a collection of hypotheses about what creates value in the firm. HR professionals must begin to think in these causal terms in order to evaluate how HR is driving firm performance. This ability is especially important because HR deliverables are often positioned upstream in those causal linkages. The line of sight between HR and firm performance is long enough that if HR doesn't explicate the connections between them, others might not either.

UNDERSTANDING PRINCIPLES OF GOOD MEASUREMENT

A key foundation of any management competency is a reliance on better measures. As we saw in chapter 5, HR professionals need to be comfortable distinguishing between the conceptual *constructs* that lie behind the drivers shown in a strategy map, and the *measures* that reflect those constructs. In particular, the measures must appropriately describe those constructs. As we've seen, you can't measure A and hope for B.

ESTIMATING CAUSAL RELATIONSHIPS

Thinking causally and understanding measurement principles help you estimate causal relationships between HR and firm performance. In practice, such estimates can range from judgmental to quantitative inferences. While most HR professionals we work with would like to move beyond judgmental assertions about HR's strategic impact, don't underestimate the power of those arguments. Even if you're presenting your case on just a hypothetical basis, your argument will carry weight if you base it on the logic behind your firm's value-creation story. Ideally, you will also eventually have quantitative estimates of the link between HR and firm performance, or at least be able to point to specific links in the strategy map. However, your most important tasks are to realize that those estimates are possible and to calculate them as opportunities arise.

For example, imagine that you're the head of HR at a pipeline company in which maintenance tends to be reactive rather than predictive. As a result of this reactive stance, the company suffers frequent shutdowns, high maintenance costs, low customer satisfaction, and, ultimately, reduced profitability. You propose a possible change in the training and reward system for pipeline maintenance workers as a way to reverse these problems. To assess the potential of this intervention, you could simply calculate the expense of the proposed program and compare it with that of other training/reward programs in the company. Or perhaps you calculate the cost per trainee and find that your cost is 20 percent *below* the average training cost in the industry. However, if you had a competency in strategic performance management, you would tackle this challenge very differently. You would (1) recognize the strategic implications of a change in HR architecture around the maintenance workers, (2) identify the opportunity to link HR changes in maintenance to changes in pipeline reliability, maintenance costs, and, ultimately, customer satisfaction and profitability, and (3) understand the measures required to estimate those relationships.

HR professionals must also be able to see patterns in seemingly unrelated data. As it turns out, common themes often emerge when you examine trends using different analyses. For example, as part of our HR assessments, we often collect data from multiple sources (interviews, observations, surveys, reports). As a team, we identify what we observed in the data we collected, post that observation, and see whether others who collected data from a different source made similar observations. This technique, called triangulation of analyses, lets you draw richer and more confident inferences from the data.[12]

COMMUNICATING HR STRATEGIC PERFORMANCE RESULTS TO SENIOR LINE MANAGERS

To manage the strategic performance of HR in your firm, you have to be able to effectively communicate your understanding of HR's strategic impact to senior executives and line managers. This continues our theme of top-down thinking. Specifically, you need to understand what questions managers outside HR want answered and how the results of your strategic HR measurement system will supply the answers to those questions. Don't get distracted by the array of available measures and the mechanics of data collection. Instead ask yourself, "What am I going to do with these measures when they become available? How will I use them to manage HR's strategic performance? How will I use them to demonstrate HR's strategic impact?" Alternatively, as new strategic issues come to the attention of senior managers, think about how the measures you're currently using might be structured in fresh ways to shed new light on those issues.

Integrating Strategic Performance Management with the Five Core HR Competencies

How might you integrate this new competency in strategic performance measurement with the five core HR competencies described earlier? We offer some ideas in the next few sections.

KNOWLEDGE OF THE BUSINESS

As a competency, strategic performance management must leverage the other core competencies. Any effective HR professional needs to understand the financial indicators of business success (shareholder value, profits, balance-sheet management, earnings, return on assets), customer success measures (customer satisfaction and commitment surveys, segmentation criteria, buying criteria, market and customer share data), competitor analysis (industry trends, competitor strengths and weaknesses), and process improvement. All HR professionals should also be able to translate their work into the same financial and customer-focused language used to describe the rest of the business. This does not mean that every HR decision has direct links to shareholder return on equity, but you should know how HR decisions drive shareholder value *in principle*. In short, you need to be able to describe your work from the perspective of the CFO or CEO. For example, chapter 4 shows you how to use basic financial-analysis principles to evaluate HR decisions.

As we've seen, HR professionals too often want to measure their success by their activities rather than by business results. With a stronger competency in strategic performance management, you can hypothesize how an investment in the HR system might influence your firm's financial outcomes, customer value proposition, or competitive advantage. However, when we ask HR professionals to illustrate the relationship between an HR investment and a subsequent strategic impact, using a two-axis graph, many have trouble doing so. They are unclear about how to measure the HR investment (i.e., label the x-axis) and how to determine what the investment will influence (i.e., label the y-axis). Further, they don't know how to depict the potential relationship between the two variables on the graph (i.e., determine whether the line on the graph would be linear or curvilinear). In short, they can't describe HR's strategic impact crisply and succinctly in terms that line managers will find persuasive.

We saw this difficulty firsthand in a firm where the line managers resisted investments in HR. They didn't believe that HR had a direct influence on business performance, and the HR managers couldn't make a persuasive case otherwise. To get the line managers thinking differently about HR, we asked each of them to plot the expected impact of improved quality of management on business results. We posed the question, "If the quality of management in this organization went up 10 percent, what would the impact on business results be?" As the managers thought about this and then plotted their scores, they soon realized that the business case for HR was not hard to make. All of them agreed that improved management quality would ultimately drive better business results. The ranges they anticipated went from 10:3 to 10:10, with an average of 10:7. In other words, for every 10 units of management-quality increase, this group of otherwise cynical managers believed that 7 units of business results would follow. As we became more specific about which HR initiatives would improve management quality, and what kinds of business results the managers could expect, these leaders became far more supportive of HR investments.

DELIVERY OF HUMAN RESOURCE PRACTICES

A strategic performance management competency strongly emphasizes measurement. This emphasis in turn supports HR professionals who need to make informed choices about which HR systems should receive more

or less investment. As the examples in chapter 4 showed, a rigorous assessment system compares the potential outcomes of one pay program or
training opportunity over another. HR measurement lets you define the
quantifiable trade-offs associated with particular HR investments. In other
words, not everything worth doing is worth doing superbly. At some point,
diminishing returns will set in. Measuring the value created by different
HR practices helps you identify which practices offer the highest return
on investment, which have the greatest employee or financial impact,
and which should receive the most management attention. Within a functional area such as training, this kind of assessment is crucial. A firm
with a $4,000-per-employee training budget might have a number of
choices—external programs, technology programs, technical training,
managerial training, coaching, etc.—for how to allocate this money. Using
strategic performance measurement, human resource executives can evaluate the trade-offs for each of these choices and get the highest possible
returns on their ultimate investment decision.

MANAGEMENT OF CULTURE

We know that what gets measured, gets managed. But what gets measured also defines a company's culture. Why? Because it describes what
is valued. For example, a global insurance firm was embarking on a
strategic shift from selling products to designing customer solutions. The
top managers' goal was to create intimacy with target customers and
inspire those customers to buy a broader array of financial service products. In other words, their goal was larger customer "share of wallet." To
make this strategic shift, the organization's culture had to move from one
focused on products and cost to one focused on customer service. This
move required a significant change in the performance measures used
throughout the company. Also, someone had to tell the story of how this
new strategy might be implemented. That job fell to the firm's HR professionals, who because of their competency in strategic performance
management proved quite successful at this task. They were able to
articulate how a new culture and value set could burnish the company's
reputation with investors and customers. They also gave credible explanations for why employee commitment to this new culture was critical
for success. Perhaps most important, they understood how new measures
of employee performance would play a central part in implementation of
this new strategy. At the same time, they could explain these changes to

employees in a nonthreatening way. Finally, the HR professionals were able to communicate how and why an extensive team-based learning experience could kick-start this cultural change. They recommended that customers be involved in the learning experience—as designers, participants, and presenters. They also suggested customer-focused projects for the session and showed how the projects might best be allocated among the session participants. Last, they proposed using customer-solutions performance indicators as a basis for compensation.

MANAGEMENT OF CHANGE

HR professionals with a strategic performance management competency are well positioned to facilitate the pace and extent of change in their organizations. HR systems can be impediments or enablers of rapid organizational change, but HR professionals with this competency will at least understand the business case for HR's leading these change efforts. In one example, the HR leadership team in a global manufacturing firm created a visual model that let them measure various manifestations of "speed." The model resembled a hub surrounded by spokes, with "individual commitment" at the center. The HR professionals suggested that if employees could rid themselves of impediments to their work, their commitment and discretionary energy would go up. Their "speed," or ability to respond quickly to new situations, depended in part on HR-created forums in which employees could identify and rid themselves of bureaucratic controls, which impeded their work. The spokes of this model represented other key processes that the firm had to manage, for example, order delivery time, product innovation cycle time, and hiring of key talent. The HR team measured success by defining a world-class speed standard for each process (e.g., the order delivery time of 48 hours was world-class, but the firm was operating at 96 hours). In short, the firm considered organizational "speed" a strategic capability that drove other key processes. HR led the effort to bring that capability to world-class standards. Furthermore, its model turned the concept of "speed" into a set of measurable results (more committed employees and faster key processes) that the firm could then compare over time and link to other strategic outcomes.

PERSONAL CREDIBILITY

We've seen that the personal credibility of HR professionals holds the key to the acceptance of their role as business partners. HR professionals with a strategic performance management competency will increasingly be sought out for their advice and counsel on business issues that have a strong "people" component. Because these managers will be living the firm's values, their colleagues will view them as trustworthy, dependable, and aligned with the rest of the organization's management.

MANAGING HR COMPETENCIES

Developing competency models for HR professionals is an important first step in the evolution of the profession. Nevertheless, the way in which those competencies are managed and nurtured in practice will ultimately determine whether the profession advances further. Managing those competencies includes cultivating the performance of HR professionals, assessing HR performance and rewarding it appropriately, and designing HR development programs. Let's briefly review each of these.

Performance Management of HR Professionals

An old adage that we hope is quickly buried forever holds that someone who can't make it elsewhere in business ends up in HR. This perception of HR changes only when HR managers begin to "make a difference" in their organizations. This transformation of HR's role is closely tied to transformation of HR as a profession. As a profession, HR rests on a legitimate body of knowledge, a predictable set of outcomes, and a model of competencies. These three "pillars" shape who is hired into HR, how their performance is assessed, and how they are compensated.

When hiring HR staff, human resource executives can choose from among a number of candidate sources. New hires may come directly from college and then be promoted through an internal, HR-succession system. They might also transfer from other functions within the firm or be hired away from other firms. Decisions about where to source talent may vary depending on how much an HR function wants to maintain or change its identity. For example, an HR function that wants to build on its past may hire more internal candidates than an HR function that feels a need to create a new future. However, the competency framework required for HR professionals should remain constant.

To illustrate, using the five-dimension competency model described earlier, senior line executives of a global financial service institution decided to dramatically shift the direction of the firm's HR function. They chose an executive from outside HR to head the function. She in turn replaced 60 percent of her direct reports with individuals from outside HR. She took care to ensure that the entire new team had outstanding business acumen, an ability to shape the firm's culture and manage change, and personal credibility. But, she realized that the team lacked deep technical expertise. Accordingly, she encouraged her staff to surround themselves with talented HR professionals, then to aggressively hone the general business skills they needed to meet HR's requirements. This meant that new members of her staff from outside HR assured themselves that their direct reports were technically proficient and then worked diligently to master the theories underlying HR for themselves. By adopting this approach, she improved the credibility of the function, crafted a more business-oriented HR plan, and empowered the function to generate innovative HR practices. In this example, the strategic performance management competency developed over time through the informal synergy between managers with general business skills and the new HR staff.

Assessment of HR Performance

An HR competence framework also serves as a tool for assessing HR performance. Jack Welch, CEO at General Electric, took a unique approach to this by advocating measurement of results according to a manager's ability to "live" the firm's values. He argued that successful GE leaders had to score high in both achieving results and embodying the core values that the organization had identified. The greatest challenge, he conceded, lay in clarifying those values so that the company could measure the degree to which each of its leaders demonstrated the values in their daily behavior.

Like other organizational leaders, HR professionals should be assessed on both the results they achieve and the behaviors they exhibit. In this book, we've explored a model for measuring HR's strategic impact. Behaviors come from competencies, which we've explored in this chapter. But how do you actually measure HR competencies? A number of assessment tools exist. As part of the Michigan study discussed earlier, the researchers developed an instrument for gauging the performance of HR professionals. This instrument consists of about sixty behaviorally anchored questions that

explore the extent to which an HR professional demonstrates a competence. It has been used in more than thirty firms and has generated valuable
feedback for the HR professionals, their immediate supervisors, and HR
executives within those firms. Tracked annually, this information can help
firms design development plans at the individual and overall HR function
level. Other similar assessment tools exist (e.g., the Society for Human
Resource Management has an assessment tool), or firms can and have
developed their own tools. In each case, the tool becomes a visible guide to
the competencies HR professionals should demonstrate and a mechanism
to assess the extent to which they do.

In assessing its HR competencies, a company must also tie rewards to
demonstrated competence. As the adage states, "That which gets rewarded
gets done." But, it is hard to reward something if you can't measure it.
And, it is hard to measure something unless you can clearly operationalize
and define it. By defining HR competencies in behavioral terms, a company can use any number of assessment tools (such as the 360-degree
feedback technique) to judge the extent to which an individual demonstrates the competency in question. Then, the firm can allocate rewards
based on overall competence, improvement in competence scores, or competence compared to that of other HR professionals in a group.

Development of HR Professionals

To build the talents of its HR professionals, a firm can use any number of
internal and external training programs, as well as specific development
experiences. In-house programs generally are attended by a large percentage of the HR community. They may range from one-day workshops to
two-week seminars. Table 7-3 shows the prototypical design for a one-
week seminar. As the table indicates, programs typically include modules
on business strategy, HR's role, strategic HR, best HR practices (staffing,
development, measures and rewards, organization design, communication), consulting or change skills, and interactions with line managers.

Several companies have developed their own innovations to this
basic design. For example, Eastman Kodak's HR-development program
consisted of five one-day sessions spread over eight weeks. Each partic-
ipant was asked to bring a client (either a line manager served by a generalist or an HR generalist served by an HR specialist) to the afternoon
of the first day and to the closing session on the fifth day. On day one,

participants asked their clients to list their expectations of HR professionals at Kodak. This activity generated feedback about what clients wanted and what HR could provide. On the last afternoon, clients returned and met again with their HR professional. During this encounter, they formed a contract about expectations, standards, and deliverables for the future.

As another illustration, General Electric ran a two-week HR program. Prior to the program, the three senior HR executives who sponsored the course provided the program coordinator with a business/HR challenge they were currently facing (e.g., team rewards, global organization, product cycle time). During the program, participants formed teams, who then visited the relevant sponsoring HR executive, collected data, formed recommendations, and provided advice on how to resolve the problem. In this vivid example of action learning, participants applied their knowledge to real issues. Moreover, in this program, senior HR executives and their line-manager clients often made joint presentations. These team presentations provided participants with role models and practical examples of line/HR coordination.

Other company examples reveal the richness of these programs. At Digital and Amoco, for instance, HR professionals received a sequential development experience. In both companies, the first week of training

Table 7-3 Prototype of a One-Week HR Seminar

	Day 1	Day 2	Day 3	Day 4	Day 5
A.M.	Welcome by senior HR executive Business challenges HR vision	Strategic HR: turning business goals into HR priorities, with a focus on shared mind-set and organization diagnosis	HR best practice: measures and rewards	Being a change agent or consultant in HR: learning and applying a change model	Personal leadership: building credibility
P.M.	HR roles and deliverables Competencies for HR professionals	HR best practice: staffing and development	HR best practice: organization design and communication	Measuring HR effectiveness	Action planning for the business, the HR function, and the individual Making commitments to act

focused on state-of-the-art HR practices. The second week emphasized strategic and business thinking as it applied to HR. In both companies, the course sponsor was the senior HR executive who attended, presented his vision of HR, and answered questions. General Mills, for its part, asked participants to do a 360-feedback session on the roles of HR before attending the program. During the program, this data helped participants to identify HR's strengths and weaknesses and arrive at specific action items. At Saudi Aramco, an HR-role survey was administered to clients and participants and then used as a benchmark for HR quality. Six months after the program, the company measured progress by readministering the survey to clients and participants.

In addition to internal HR-development opportunities, numerous external learning opportunities exist. These programs may emphasize general HR knowledge or technical skills. For example, WorldatWork offers programs on compensation trends. They may be offered through associations, universities, consulting firms, consortia (e.g., Cornell University's School of Industrial and Labor Relations), or public offerings (e.g., the University of Michigan's Human Resource Executive programs).[13] These external programs parallel closely the internal programs, except they allow participants to experience how other companies deal with similar issues. For example, in a recent Michigan two-week HR executive program, the forty-two participants were from twelve countries, varied industries (consumer products, financial services, utilities, high tech), and different firm cultures. The participants were able to see how a core set of principles applied to each unique setting. They were also able to learn from each other. For example, a number of the participants had been through mergers and acquisitions and distributed to the entire class their "HR due diligence" checklist in pre- and post-merger activity. The five checklists that were shared allowed participants who had not been directly involved in a merger to learn from others and create their own checklist if required for their business.

Finally, HR professionals can also develop their skills through specific assignments and experiences. For example, at PPG Industries, top leaders believe that the company's HR professionals can build critical competencies through on-the-job responsibilities and experiences, through classroom experience, or both. Table 7-4 shows PPG's development guidelines according to the following time frames: first year, 2 to 4 years, and 5 to 9 years. This company believes that honing the indicated competencies within these time frames is the joint responsibility of the individual HR professional and his or her supervisor. (PPG's time frames are provided as a guide and might well vary in other firms based on individual and organizational circumstances.)

Table 7-4 PPG Industries' Development Guide for HR Professionals

Function	First Year	2–4 Years	5–9 Years
Recruiting and selection	• Selection techniques	• College recruiting • Nonexempt hiring • Reductions in force	• Internal consulting on staffing and structure • Hiring experienced professionals
Training and development	• Quality process training • Corporate training and education	• Program development and presentation • Meeting leadership • Team management, empowerment, self-directed work teams, etc. • Training of operators and maintenance personnel	• Leadership training • Individual development planning process
Compensation and benefits	• Benefit program content • Corporate benefits • HRIS/PC training	• Job description preparation	• Job evaluation and compensation administration
Labor and industrial relations	• "Floor" skills	• Contract administration and grievance investigation • Preventive labor-relations practices	• Arbitration • Negotiation preparation and participation • Labor relations (NLRB) process • Strike preparation
Personnel administration and systems	• Policy and administration • Regulatory areas (EEO/AAP, ADA, Wage and Hour)	• Recognition systems • Workforce diversity issues • Compliance reviews and discrimination charges	• Performance management and appraisal systems and practices

(continued on the next page)

(continued from the previous page)

Table 7-4 PPG Industries' Development Guide for HR Professionals

Function	First Year	2–4 Years	5–9 Years
Safety, health, and environment	• OSHA and workers' comp • Plant operations and operating hazards	• Americans with Disabilities Act	• Security issues
Communications	• Employee publications and meetings		
Government and community relations		• Community relations initiatives	• Government relations practices
Business management skills			• Budgeting and financial reporting • Business strategy and planning process

General Electric is another apt example. This company has identified twenty developmental experiences that it considers important for building HR competency (see sidebar "GE's HR-Development Opportunities"). As GE sees it, HR professionals can hone their talents through job assignments, job rotation, task-force assignments, and networking with other managers. In addition to these development experiences, GE has prepared a reading list to reinforce specific development activities with work from leading HR theorists such as Chris Argyris, Richard Beatty, Wayne Brockbank, Lee Dyer, Edward Lawler, George Milkovich, Jeffrey Pfeffer, and Craig Schneier.

SUMMARY: NEW PROFESSIONAL COMPETENCIES

This book brings some new perspectives and methodologies to the most pressing problems facing HR managers. We believe that the ideas explored herein are especially appropriate at this point in the development of the HR profession. Specifically, we feel confident that these perspectives and tools will help to move the profession along the exciting and rapidly changing course it has taken in recent years. In this chapter, we argue that if HR professionals are going to successfully navigate this new course and take full advantage of the ideas in this book, they will have to

---

GE'S HR-DEVELOPMENT OPPORTUNITIES

1. Employee-relations problem-solving assignment

2. HR-generalist assignment

3. Technical-specialization assignment

4. Organization-effectiveness intervention experience

5. Process-consulting experience

6. Community-relationship experience

7. Stretch job assignment

8. Exposure to global issues

9. Staff assignment

10. Cross-functional experience

11. Fix-it assignment

12. Start-up assignment

13. Large-scale change effort

14. Organization-structuring assignment

15. Corporate assignment

16. HR functional-leadership assignment

17. Business-team partnership experience

18. Business-leader support assignment

19. Exposure to role models

20. Extended professional network

---

broaden their professional competencies to include what we call strategic performance management. However, the other five dimensions of HR competency discussed earlier are also essential for HR to serve as a legitimate strategic partner. Paired with an understanding of how to manage these HR competencies, this six-dimension model can serve as a development template for HR professionals in the future.

8

GUIDELINES FOR
IMPLEMENTING AN
HR SCORECARD

D EVELOPING AN HR SCORECARD and actually implementing
one are two different things. As our colleague Steve Kerr points
out, any change effort has two generic elements defined by this
equation:

Effective Change = Quality x Acceptance (or EC = Q x A).

Quality means that the technical aspects of the change have been clearly
defined. In the previous chapters, we defined the technical elements of an
HR Scorecard. We showed you how the Scorecard must link to your
firm's strategy, be congruent with the company's HR architecture (HR
function, HR systems, and employee behaviors), and pass validity and
reliability tests. However a high-*quality* HR Scorecard is not enough to
ensure success. Without *acceptance*, this change effort might begin with
enthusiasm and excitement but will quickly fizzle out.

This chapter explains how to build the acceptance element of your
HR Scorecard, that is, how to be disciplined in applying lessons of change
management to the implementation of the Balanced Scorecard you develop.
It serves less as a road map to what is on the Scorecard and more as a guide
to implementing the Scorecard. This chapter gives those charged with
implementing an HR Scorecard a blueprint for action.

GENERAL LESSONS OF CHANGE

Most efforts at change fall short of their goals. As Peter Senge and his colleagues report, many of their efforts to create learning organizations did not accomplish the intended results.[1] Ron Ashkenas writes that only 25 to 30 percent of change efforts actually succeed.[2] James Champy shares similar findings about his work on reengineering, reporting success rates of about 25 to 33 percent.[3] Clearly, interventions—no matter how well intentioned and carefully thought out—are far more difficult to put into action than we may think.

Likewise, we have visited many companies that believe that HR measurement matters and that genuinely want to create and use an HR Scorecard. Often these companies express enormous initial interest in this approach, conduct a workshop or two about how to use Scorecards, begin to sort out which HR measures matter most, and track them once or twice. Soon, however, they discover that the commitment to the HR measurement work was more rhetoric and hope than reality and action. In most cases, the "Q," or technical aspect, of the Scorecard is manageable. (Executives can identify the right measures and create indices to assess them.) But high-quality *thinking* about the HR Scorecard as a change program never occurs. These companies fail to apply change-management lessons to their implementation of the Scorecard.

Much has been written about how to ensure that desired changes actually happen. In work at General Electric, Steve Kerr, Dave Ulrich, and their colleagues drew on an apt metaphor for effecting successful change. They suggested thinking about change as a pilot's checklist. Any pilot preparing for a flight rigorously follows a checklist to ensure that the aircraft is ready to fly. This checklist is not meant to be a teaching tool. Indeed, most of us would refuse even to climb into the airplane if we discovered that the checklist was teaching the pilot. In other words, the checklist should contain few surprises. In addition, the pilot should complete each and every action on the list, without fail, every time she or he prepares to go for a flight. Like seasoned pilots, most managers know from both experience and research how to make change happen. The challenge is to figure out how to turn what they *know* into what they *do*. At General Electric, Kerr and Ulrich created a "pilot's checklist" for making change happen and then helped managers develop the equivalent of a pilot's discipline to apply this checklist to change projects.

Jeffrey Pfeffer and Robert Sutton picked up on this theme in their work on avoiding the "smart trap" (this very problem of not knowing how to translate knowledge into effective action).[4] To avoid this trap a human resource executive who wants to implement an HR Scorecard should rigorously follow a change checklist. This will increase dramatically the probability that the company will not only design but also use the Scorecard.

Of course, extensive debate has arisen on how to define the critical features of successful change. Douglas Smith identifies ten characteristics of change leaders; John Kotter suggests eight keys to successful leadership of change; Michael Beer's change model features five core factors.[5] But we would argue that *using* a checklist—any checklist—is more important than choosing one particular checklist over another. Trouble in implementing change comes not from misunderstanding *what* to do, but from a lack of discipline about *how* to do what needs doing.

Because we have had experience with the change checklist used at General Electric, let's use this list to sketch out some guidelines for creating and sustaining an HR Scorecard.[6] A team of internal and external change agents designed the GE change checklist.[7] They reviewed more than 100 articles and books on individual, team, organizational, and society change and then synthesized the findings into seven key factors. These factors have convergent validity in that they are consistent with the research on other change models; in fact, they are drawn from them. Moreover, these factors have face validity—in other words, managers at GE have confirmed that these factors help make change happen. Finally, the factors also have deployment validity. They have been used in their present or adapted form for thousands of change projects at hundreds of companies. Table 8-1 shows these seven factors and their definitions.[8]

The seven factors in table 8-1 have been applied in multiple settings and thus offer some general lessons for successful implementation of an HR Scorecard. First, the organization must attend to all seven factors in order for the Scorecard to succeed. The process of initiating and sustaining the Scorecard may be iterative, that is, you may need to cycle back through some of the earlier steps several times. But, in general, the process unfolds in the sequence shown in the table.

Second, you can use these factors to create a profile of your firm's present capacity for change on any given project, not just the HR Scorecard. You can generate this profile by scoring the extent to which each of

Table 8-1 Keys and Processes for Making Change Happen

Key Success Factors for Change	Questions for Assessing and Accomplishing Change
1. *Leading change* (who *is responsible*)	Do we have a leader . . . • who owns and champions the change? • who demonstrates public commitment to making it happen? • who will garner resources to sustain it? • who will invest personal time and attention to following it through?
2. *Creating a shared need* (why *do it*)	Do employees . . . • see the reason for the change? • understand why the change is important? • see how it will help them and/or the business in the short and long term?
3. *Shaping a vision* (what *will it look like when we are done*)	Do employees . . . • see the outcomes of the change in behavioral terms (that is, what they will do differently as a result of the change)? • get excited about these outcomes? • understand how the change will benefit customers and other stakeholders?
4. *Mobilizing commitment* (who else *needs to be involved*)	Do the sponsors of the change . . . • recognize who else needs to be committed to the change for it to happen? • know how to build a coalition of support for the change? • have the ability to enlist the support of key individuals in the organization? • have the ability to build a responsibility matrix to make the change happen?
5. *Building enabling systems* (how *will it be institutionalized*)	Do the sponsors of the change . . . • understand how to sustain the change through modifying HR systems (e.g., staffing, training, appraisal, rewards, structure, communication)? • recognize the technology investment required to implement the change? • have access to financial resources to sustain the change?
6. *Monitoring and demonstrating progress* (how *will it be measured*)	Do the sponsors of the change . . . • have a means of measuring the success of the change? • plan to benchmark progress on both the results of the change and the implementation process?
7. *Making it last* (how *will it be initiated and sustained*)	Do the sponsors of the change . . . • recognize the first steps needed to get started?

Key Success Factors for Change	Questions for Assessing and Accomplishing Change
	• have a short- and long-term plan to keep attention focused on the change?
	• have a plan for adapting the change over time to shifting circumstances?

the seven factors exists, using a range of 0 through 100, and plotting those scores as shown in figure 8-1. We recommend that change leaders routinely assess the progress they are making on each of the dimensions of the change process using a simple profiling system such as the one illustrated in figure 8-1. During the planning phase, the profile could be used to inventory the strengths and weaknesses of your company's *current* change process. When you consider past change efforts, where has the company been particularly effective and where have those efforts fallen short? This will give you a chance to concentrate on those areas where remediation is required.

For example, the experience reflected in figure 8-1 is probably typical of many companies. There is a reasonably enthusiastic cadre of change

Figure 8-1 Profiling the Change Process

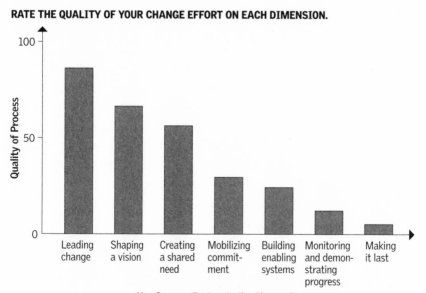

RATE THE QUALITY OF YOUR CHANGE EFFORT ON EACH DIMENSION.

Key Success Factors in the Change Process

leaders, but they are only modestly successful at creating a shared sense of urgency around the need for change and communicating a coherent vision of the future if the change is successful. The change leaders understand the need for change and what the future might look like, but they haven't been effective at articulating that vision to the rest of the organization. Because the foundational elements are not as effective as they should be, the rest of the change process is undermined. It is very difficult to mobilize commitment to change outside the core group because the message for change is not persuasive. As a result, there is little support for changing other institutional levers, such as reward systems, that will reinforce and provide momentum for change. Not surprisingly, there are no early successes to demonstrate progress, and ultimately the change effort never really takes hold and becomes just another "flavor of the month." Recommendations for successfully accomplishing each of the steps in the profile are summarized in table 8-2.

Third, the change checklist provides a disciplined approach to monitoring the key factors that need more attention. For example, in many HR measurement initiatives, the reason for using the measurement is clear to a broad range of people (that is, the need is already high), but the vision of what the measurement will entail is vague. In these cases, instead of rolling out speeches, conferences, and workshops about the need for the measurement, the organization would be wiser to focus on clarifying and communicating the vision behind the HR Scorecard.

Finally, the change checklist can serve as a powerful new language for talking about how the company might actually implement its HR Scorecard. To illustrate, at General Mills, human resource professionals who work as change agents help their clients through the profiling exercise shown in figure 8-1 on an array of initiatives. In doing so, they familiarize these managers with a new way to think about and discuss change. They can then talk with these clients about how to ensure that good ideas translate into effective, enduring change.

APPLYING CHANGE MANAGEMENT LESSONS TO THE HR SCORECARD

When a company conceives of its HR Scorecard as an initiative or project, it can apply each of the seven factors to improve the project's chances. Let's look at some hints for how to manage each factor.

Table 8-2 Guidelines for Implementing an HR Scorecard

Change Checklist Item	Guiding Questions for Change Sponsors	Suggested Guidelines for Implementation
1. *Leading change*	Who is in charge of the effort? Who sponsors? Who champions?	1. Need two sponsors (line manager, head of HR). 2. Require measurement champion: someone specializing in HR measurement. 3. Need advisory team to supervise work.
2. *Creating a shared need*	Why do the HR Scorecard? How does it fit with our business?	1. Create business case for HR and for HR measurement. 2. Share this case with line management and HR. 3. Allocate 3 to 5% of HR budget to measurement.
3. *Shaping a vision*	What is the desired outcome of the Scorecard?	1. Define desired outcomes of the HR Scorecard. 2. Prepare the key measures that will be tracked and monitored, and clarify how they will be tracked. 3. Define decisions that will be made using these measures. 4. Create a mechanism to collect the data behind the measures.
4. *Mobilizing commitment*	Who needs to support the project?	1. Identify key players whose support the project requires. 2. Figure out how to engage these key players so they will support it.
5. *Building enabling systems*	How do we build systems to sustain the change?	1. Put the right people on the project. 2. Ensure that we have the right incentives to do it. 3. Make sure that the HR measurement group reports to the right people. 4. Create a communication plan for HR measurement. 5. Invest in technology requirements to execute the HR Scorecard. 6. Make the financial investments required.
6. *Monitoring and demonstrating progress*	What will we use to track the implementation process?	Develop a project plan for HR measurement.
7. *Making it last*	How will we sustain the effort?	1. Start with simple measures. 2. Make the measures visible and applicable. 3. Post the measures. 4. Change the measures over time if required.

Leading Change

Change is more likely to happen when leaders—in the form of sponsors and champions—support it. A sponsor advocates for the change, sees the value in the change, and commits resources to making the change happen. Often, an HR Scorecard has two sponsors. The *primary sponsor* is generally the head of HR. This individual calls for an HR Scorecard, assigns a task force to the initiative, ensures that the Scorecard aligns with business strategy, and allocates resources to the task force.

At GTE, executive VP for HR Randy MacDonald actively sought the buy-in of others and held them accountable for performance. He emphasized that the intent of the HR Scorecard was to develop highly effective processes in HR, rather than to identify poor performers. As the change leader, he modeled a commitment to deliver the best possible service to GTE employees, the customers of HR, as well as to increase the value of HR to the bottom line. MacDonald was able to use the HR Scorecard to drive the value proposition of HR within the business. He didn't just have a seat at the table; he had influence on strategic planning for the business. In this way, senior executive support of the performance measurement initiative was key to the successful rollout of GTE's HR Scorecard.

The *secondary sponsor* is often the head of the business or of a division. This person is highly focused on how the company can accomplish its business strategies and understands the important role that the HR architecture plays in strategy implementation. She or he knows that measuring a firm's HR architecture will improve the firm's chances of achieving its goals. Moreover, the secondary sponsor is concerned about the wise investment of HR resources. Given the scarcity of resources— in marketing, product design, or employee development—that many organizations face, a wise business leader uses the HR Scorecard to determine how much to invest in the HR architecture. This sponsor encourages the HR Scorecard initiative, uses the information collected to make decisions and public statements about the business, and holds other line managers accountable for delivering on the Scorecard.

The *champion* for the Scorecard has primary responsibility for making it happen. This person is generally a seasoned human resource professional with accountability for the development of HR. The champion often forms a team or task force to create the Scorecard. Sometimes the champion is responsible for other HR staff areas. For example, at General

Mills, the champion is also the head of compensation for the company. And at Prudential, the chief learning officer has taken the lead role in the company's creation of an HR Scorecard. At GTE, the champion is the director of HR Planning, Measurement, and Analysis. At other times, the champion is charged primarily with "HR for HR," applying HR lessons to the HR function, and is responsible for governance of HR as well as the Scorecard.

The champion likely dedicates at least 20 percent of his or her time to the creation of the Scorecard. He or she often assembles a team comprising HR professionals from corporate staff and business lines, business leaders, and finance or accounting staff groups. This team builds the business case for HR measurement, crafts the HR scorecard, and oversees its application. The champion requires the strategy performance competencies outlined in chapter 7. He or she reports frequently to the senior HR team about progress on the Scorecard, tracks early adopters to assess successes and failures, and adapts the Scorecard to unique business requirements.

Creating a Shared Need for Change

Change is more likely to happen when a clear reason for it exists. Moreover, the reason for the change has to carry more weight than any resistance to the change. The reason for a change may be related to danger ("we're in trouble if we don't change") or opportunity ("good things will happen if we do change"). Any change effort also offers both short- and long-term impact. It is important to share the reasons for change with those who will be affected.

Creating a shared need for an HR Scorecard requires understanding the importance of HR measures and how these metrics support the business's strategy implementation. Investing in HR measurement because other companies are doing it or because it is popular will not make the Scorecard sustainable. As we've discussed throughout this book, HR measurement must be linked to business results. The HR Scorecard champion should thus be able to articulate the potential outcomes of investment in the initiative. These outcomes might include better allocation of time and money spent on HR, a higher probability of implementing the firm's overall strategy, more productive and committed employees, a more competitive organization, and increased shareholder value. Sometimes, pointing to the need for an HR Scorecard means asking, "How do we know if we've done a good job in HR?" Without a Scorecard, this question often prompts vague answers based on respondents' personal experience and assumptions about what "good" means. An HR Scorecard gives context and concreteness to these assumptions and personal perceptions, and anchors them in hard data.

Garrett Walker notes that GTE's motivation to develop an HR Scorecard was primarily driven by accelerating changes in its business environment. Deregulation, the Telecom Act, emerging customer needs, global opportunities, price competition, and multinational reach were creating a new competitive landscape that highlighted a new emphasis on human capital and a new focus for HR. According to Walker,

> *The senior management team believed that the competitive ability of their workforce was a critical factor in determining their ability to compete effectively. In response to this situation, we developed a Human Capital Strategy that focused on matching employee capabilities with the needs of the business. The key elements of this strategy focused on talent, leadership, workforce development and customer service. We had a good mission statement and vision, an excellent strategy and no quantitative way of measuring how effective we were at executing on the strategy. Simply spending money and being busy were not part of the architecture of success for HR in our current business environment. We needed a way to focus on performance, clarify vision and reinforce business strategy while allowing for learning and change.*[9]

In clarifying the need to invest in an HR Scorecard, champions should avoid some common pitfalls that will create resistance to it. For example, if the Scorecard measures only part of HR's effectiveness, it may leave line managers with distorted views of how value is created in the organization. These distorted views can in turn prompt unwise decisions. One company built a Scorecard based primarily on employee productivity and efficiency indices (e.g., revenue/employee, labor costs/revenue, and headcount/margin). Managers in this sales organization thus focused on employee efficiency, not competence. Accordingly, they decided to reduce headcount in order to control labor costs. As it turned out, their lack of attention to the quality of the people on staff ultimately hurt the business.

Why? Because more seasoned and expensive employees would have produced more long-term revenue than the kinds of employees who survived the staff reductions. An HR Scorecard champion can avoid this sort of pitfall by using measures with a more effective focus.

Scorecard champions also face potential resistance from HR professionals themselves. As in any other function, some of these individuals don't want their performance measured. Being in HR without measurement can be a safe, nonthreatening career. With measurement comes accountability, and some of these employees may lack the confidence or competence to be accountable for the work they perform. A Scorecard champion can overcome their resistance through extensive training and investment to ensure that they have the competencies to deliver against higher expectations.

With the trend toward outsourcing many HR functions, measurement of effective HR becomes even more important. The short-term efficiencies that outsourcing may yield might not be sustainable as the longer-term costs—such as single-source suppliers, lack of parity in outsourced HR work, and lack of unique capabilities within the organization—kick in.

For all these reasons, HR Scorecard champions need to build a cogent business case for initiating and implementing the Scorecard. Skillfully crafted, this business rationale will inform line managers, help HR executives make smart choices, and guide and inspire HR professionals throughout the firm.

Shaping a Vision

Change is also more likely to happen when the outcome of the change is clearly understood, articulated, and shared in both aspirational and behavioral terms. Aspirations energize and excite those affected by the proposed initiative's outcome; definitions of behaviors communicate expected actions. Both become parts of a successful vision statement.

The vision for an HR Scorecard defines the desired outcomes of the Scorecard, states what will be measured, and describes the data-collection process. The desired outcomes are to make informed HR investment choices, identify high- versus low-impact HR practices, document relationships between the HR architecture and business results, and help implement strategy. These outcomes help line managers to accomplish business goals through HR, and human resource executives to govern the elements of the HR architecture.

At GTE, HR professionals responded to the imperatives of the New Economy by articulating a new vision for HR. The HR Scorecard developed by GTE's HR both communicates and reinforces that vision to all HR managers. Garrett Walker summarized this vision as follows:

> *We see talent as the emerging single sustainable competitive advantage in the future. To capitalize on this opportunity, HR must evolve from a Business Partner to a critical "asset manager" for human capital within the business. The HR Scorecard is designed to translate Business Strategy directly to HR objectives and actions. We communicate strategic intent while motivating and tracking performance against HR and business goals. This allows each HR employee to be aligned with business strategy and link everyday actions with business outcomes.*[10]

A well-designed HR Scorecard collects and monitors the information needed to achieve these outcomes. In chapter 3, we reviewed both the administrative and value-creating measures that might make up an HR Scorecard. The HR Scorecard team should begin by identifying the business strategy outlined by the organization. Then, by selecting key items from the choices available in chapter 3, the team may begin constructing the Scorecard. As we've seen, the Scorecard generally includes indicators for all three components of the HR architecture: employee behavior, HR system, and HR function. It should be able to pass a simple, but robust test. Simply ask yourself two questions: To what extent does this Scorecard link HR performance to firm performance? Would senior line managers draw the same conclusions?

Mobilizing Commitment

Change is more likely to happen when those affected by the change are committed to it. Commitment comes when these individuals have information about the change process, participate in shaping the process, and behave as if they are committed. Research on commitment suggests that when people behave as if they are committed to an initiative, in a public forum and by choice, they actually *become* more committed to the initiative.[11]

HR Scorecards require commitment from both line managers and HR professionals. Line managers' commitment intensifies when they see the alignment between the HR measures and the achievement of their own business goals. HR processes thus become early leading indicators of successful strategy implementation throughout the rest of the organization. Line managers' commitment to the HR Scorecard also strengthens when they are held accountable for the measures tracked. An organization in turn can encourage accountability by tying a portion of the manager's salary and/or bonus to the HR Scorecard. At Sears, employee attitudes, as measured by a commitment survey, accounted for 33 percent of managers' bonuses. For managers who had the potential to make six-figure bonuses, compensation linked to indicators in the HR architecture captured their attention and changed their behavior. As another example, one restaurant chain began to track average tenure of employees after noticing that front-line worker seniority seemed to correlate with the quality of service that customers received. Managers in this organization were held accountable for their restaurant results and began to hire people who would be more likely to stay. These managers also focused on building more positive relationships with employees and sharpening their retention strategies.

At times, merely making HR Scorecard data public builds commitment from line managers. One consumer-products firm was having trouble keeping future brand managers. The leadership team decided that each of the fifteen members of the executive committee would become sponsors of five newly hired potential brand managers per year for five years. Over time, each of the fifteen senior executives had twenty-five relatively new employees whom they mentored. This strategy entailed meeting regularly with the employees, providing them with career advice and counsel, and paying attention to them. Although the mentoring program was not incorporated into the fifteen executives' formal performance reviews, the managers provided annual reports on how many of their twenty-five charges left the firm each year. This informal pressure prompted each of the fifteen executives to reach out especially to those employees who would most likely leave the firm. These executives made a solid commitment to the HR Scorecard simply because its importance and visibility were crystal clear.

HR managers also must be committed to the Scorecard. If the items that it tracks are not central to the performance management of the HR professional, there is a problem with either the Scorecard or the performance management process. We tested this assumption with the head of

HR in a high-tech firm. We asked her, "When your CEO engages you in serious conversation, what issues is he most worried about?" She responded that the CEO wanted her to help attract thought leaders in the business, build the next generation of leadership for the firm, and hold leaders accountable for results. We then asked her to show us her HR Scorecard and personal performance metrics. They matched the three strategies that she had cited. Clearly, she was personally accountable for what the CEO wanted from her HR function. The alignment of the CEO's expectations, the HR Scorecard for her function, and her personal objectives ensured that her actions reflected and supported the firm's goals.

The commitment to the HR Scorecard accelerated at GTE as HR managers learned more about the business strategy, how it translated into HR strategy, and how it ultimately linked to business outcomes. Using strategy maps and leading and lagging indicators, they were able to help employees "connect the dots" and think across the organization and the business. By communicating business value chains where HR actions are simply part of the transformation process, HR managers were able to understand more than their functional silos. They could see the big picture.

In spite of this attention to change management issues, some resistance is inevitable. Garrett Walker notes the following:

Much of the early resistance from HR came from the release of information. Information is power and losing that power coupled with the possibility of "looking bad" was a real obstacle early on. However, each quarter that the Scorecard was in place more information was available. The Scorecard exposed HR managers as well as business leaders to workforce issues outside of their expertise and illustrated linkages to other parts of the business. Now, HR professionals and line managers discuss organizational and workforce issues outside their immediate responsibility. The HR Scorecard has created a distinction, a common language, for communicating critical human capital issues.

We rolled the entire HR Scorecard out at once; however, we communicated and published information in a phased approach. We began with senior HR leaders and business leaders, introducing them to the concepts and measurement model. The senior HR leaders then communicated to their organizations. To supplement high level staff briefings the HR Scorecard team provided on-site briefings to departments focusing on linkages between the departmental actions and business outcomes (cause and effect mappings). We also had "lunch and learn sessions" where informal Q&A from the HR Scorecard team was supplemented with success stories from HR practitioners who had used the Scorecard to positively impact the business.

The Scorecard was also immediately tied to incentive compensation at all levels of the HR organization. This was somewhat controversial at the time, but certainly kept the organization's eye on the ball. In hindsight, this action eliminated much of the resistance to the Scorecard.[12]

Commitment from both line managers and HR professionals increases when a firm frequently tracks the indicators on the HR Scorecard and shares the information openly. For instance, a bank created an HR report card to measure the firm's success at increasing its share of targeted customers. By sharing the report quarterly among all HR professionals and senior line managers, the firm ensured that the Scorecard influenced behavior.

Building Enabling Systems

Change is more likely to happen when a company makes the financial, technological, and HR investments required to support the change. The experience at Intel offers an apt example of financial support for the HR Scorecard. Patty Murray, the vice president of HR, invests in ongoing research to identify the key HR drivers of business success. She has an R&D function that is charged with identifying which HR practices are most critical to Intel's future success. For example, as Intel moved into the Internet business, Murray's R&D team identified the talents required for the firm to make this business transition. The team not only built a talent-acquisition strategy, but also designed measures for monitoring this strategy.

HR Scorecards also require technological investments to support the collection, tracking, and use of data. Cisco, for example, gathers employee attitude data through its intranet Web site. Organizations can also collect such data from a subset of employees monthly or quarterly and then quickly codify it to inform managers about employee commitment in subunits throughout the firm. Use of data-collection and analysis technology ensures that the Scorecard remains timely and accurate.

Building enabling systems also means that the results of the Score-card need to be communicated widely throughout the business. GTE has developed a wide range of integrated tools to communicate its HR Scorecard and to help managers make good decisions using the data. At the heart of this system is an intranet linked to a data warehouse. Previously, GTE had seventy-five different information systems, which were combined into a single system at the outset of this process. This system now places timely and relevant data on managers' desktops, which they can access using special software that enables them to set goals and track performance. GTE has also developed an interactive CD-ROM simulation that shows managers how to use the system to improve their decision making. Finally, GTE has prepared a wide range of reports and background material (available in hard copy or on the intranet) that employees can access at any time.

In the GTE HR Balanced Scorecard environment, there are different measures for major functions, such as staffing for each business unit, which are accessible via Internet technology. This makes the Balanced Scorecard a highly effective system for communicating strategic goals. HR leaders can view a virtual briefing book on their desktop computers that displays the performance results for the key peformance indicators they are most interested in. If they have a question about a measure or result, they can drill down by clicking on it to reveal more and more detail. Much of the detail comes from individual employees, who enter data and notes about what's happening on the front lines into an HR Scorecard system. These desktop briefing books also tell them how their performance matches their goals. According to Garrett Walker,

> *The HR Balanced Scorecard helps our HR professionals react more quickly as a whole, from the executive suites to the front lines. Even more important in a business environment of rapidly changing markets and accelerating technology advances, it helps management teams anticipate workforce issues so they can plan rather than react. In our previous business environment we often had weeks to make decisions. The HR Balanced Scorecard system allows us to rapidly adjust to changes affecting our business in real time.*[13]

In essence, GTE uses its Scorecard as a teaching tool and as a key mechanism for helping to implement its strategy. And the level of resources and visibility devoted to the project help to demonstrate the firm's commitment to the measurement project. The end result of these efforts is a much more effective HR measurement system and considerable visibility for the project—both inside and outside of the firm. At GTE, the Scorecard has helped to build internal and external credibility for both the HR function and the firm as a whole.

The HR Scorecard has also proved of considerable benefit in facilitating GTE and Bell Atlantic's recent merger into Verizon. The HR Balanced Scorecard is an evolving and highly valuable tool for both the HR management team as well as the business leaders. Its key value in merger integration was to pull together the formerly separate management teams of Bell Atlantic and GTE. GTE human resources relied on a centralized model, which delivered HR products and services by a strong central staff. Bell Atlantic, on the other hand, relied on a more decentralized approach. The differences in style and approach naturally gave rise to tug of wars after the merger.

In the early days following the merger, the HR Balanced Scorecard provided a process for the Verizon human resource leadership team (HRLT) to focus on common objectives and the future of the new business. The primary focus of the HR Balanced Scorecard forums was to translate business strategy into HR strategy and actions. The process allowed the HRLT to overcome their differences in management style and come together as a team. A shared sense of HR strategy and focus emerged from the early meetings. The Verizon HR Balanced Scorecard emphasizes a core common focus on the customer, especially the need to improve service, to attract and retain talent, and to increase value created for the business.

Building enabling systems also means helping to communicate the firm's strategy map and resulting HR Scorecard to the workforce. Like many firms, Sears found that many employees did not completely understand the company's strategy, business environment, or even key business processes. Sears responded by communicating its strategy to the workforce via "town hall" meetings and Learning Maps.[14] Learning Maps are large (forty-inch-by-sixty-inch) image-laden depictions of a firm's strategy or other key business processes. The figure in the center of the map is surrounded by a series of questions and learning objectives, on which employees work together in small groups in order to increase their understanding. Employees then go back into their work groups and repeat the process with a new group of employees. The authors of the Sears study describe the process as follows:

> *The goal of learning maps is economic and business literacy—but business literacy in the service of the larger goal of behavioral change. We want managers to change their behavior toward employees, to communicate the company's goals and vision more effectively, and to learn to make better customer-oriented decisions, because we cannot do well financially unless we do well in the eyes of the customer. We want frontline employees to change their behavior toward customers—to become more responsive, take more initiative, and provide better service.*[15]

Sears has developed several Learning Maps to date, with more on the way. The company has found them to be a highly effective way to communicate with the workforce. Sears's most recent map, "Ownership," describes their total performance indicators (TPIs) and shows employees how measurement can help them to create value. Using the metaphor of water running downstream, the "Ownership" map shows not only the key business processes around Work, Shop, and Invest, but also how the TPI metrics map on to these processes (see figure 8-2).

Finally, HR Scorecards require investments in human resource systems. Hiring HR employees with the competencies we suggested in chapter 7, communicating the Scorecard throughout the organization, and weaving HR results into reward and recognition systems all help to sustain the Scorecard. Such systems should ensure that HR measures change behavior in the right ways. For example, an HR Scorecard could collect data on the cost of turnover and thus show the importance of retention. But if these data are not used as part of a manager's performance review (in which questions such as, "What is the turnover rate of key people in your unit?" are asked), then the data is unlikely to change behavior. Or, if the data is collected but managers who have high turnover are consistently promoted to new positions, the HR Scorecard will lose credibility and impact. At Sears, fully one-third of a manager's bonus is linked to his or her ability to manage people. Prudential ties 20 percent of managerial compensation to its HR Scorecard. Many other firms are beginning to use the leading indicators embedded in their HR Scorecards as a component of managerial compensation.

Figure 8-2 Sears Total Performance Indicators

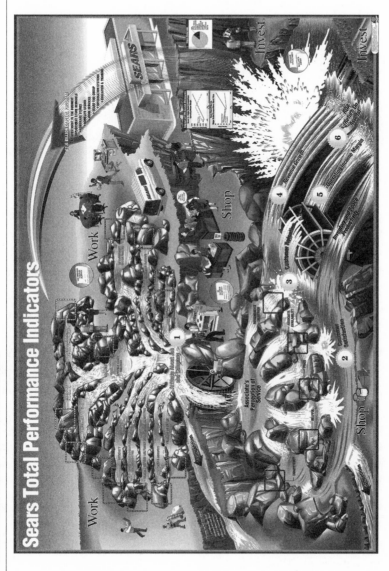

Source: Reprinted with permission of Sears and Root Learning, Inc.

Monitoring and Demonstrating Progress

Change is more likely to happen when a firm monitors progress toward the change. We thus recommend creating—and sticking to—a plan for implementing your HR Scorecard. Dividing the plan into milestones can help; for example:

- *Naming the champion.* This will be the person who will lead the effort, invest time and energy in it, and ultimately be held accountable for success.

- *Creating the Scorecard team.* The team will likely include HR professionals from both corporate and field, line managers who bring the business perspective, financial and/or strategy staff who ensure that the measures are consistent with corporate goals, and possibly external experts who draw on experiences from other companies.

- *Selecting targeted measures.* Based on the process described in chapter 3, the Scorecard team may choose appropriate measures for all elements of the HR architecture. These measures should be keyed to the firm's strategy implementation plan and reflect informed investment in HR practices.

- *Validating the measures.* Hypothesizing the right measures and testing their impact on business results require different skills. You can do some hypothesis testing retrospectively if historical measures of your firm's HR architecture and business results exist. For example, Sears's work showed relationships among employee commitment, customer loyalty, and firm performance, with twenty years of historical data collected at each store. This reservoir of data let managers test valid measures. Other validation may come from pilot tests, whereby you can collect data from limited sites to ensure that the selected measures will support desired business results.

- *Collecting data.* Once you validate your measures, you can collect the HR data you need to track key items. These data may come from employee surveys, existing corporate reports, or reports generated to track key indicators.

- *Monitoring and updating data.* As you collect data, you can track trends to create a longitudinal HR Scorecard that will highlight patterns and trends over time. With valid data, you can then assess the impact of HR and make decisions about which HR investments will help improve the firm's business results.

Data need to be updated in accordance with their level of actual variability. Relatively stable data can be updated annually—more variable (or urgent) attributes should be updated quarterly, monthly, or even weekly, as appropriate.

Monitoring your progress at each stage of creating and using the HR Scorecard ensures that the project unfolds as planned. Periodically revisiting the Scorecard itself also helps you assess how well it is helping you improve HR investment decisions and how well it is supporting the organization's strategy implementation efforts.

Making It Last

Change is more likely to happen when a change effort garners early success, builds in continuous learning about what is working and what is not, adapts to changing conditions, celebrates progress, and can be integrated with other work. To do all of this, you must make ongoing investments in your HR Scorecard. Here are some hints for making the scorecard last:

ENSURE EARLY SUCCESSES

Many companies face a dilemma: Should they invest in developing a complete, fully researched, and comprehensive HR Scorecard that takes months to develop? Or should they limit the effort to just those measures that let them evaluate critical capabilities right away, based on available data? We suggest choosing the option that lets you rack up some early successes, even if they're relatively small in scope. For some firms, this might mean running simultaneous experiments to identify which HR data exert the most impact on business results. It might also mean experimenting with various tracking methods (e.g., should you measure employee commitment by a pulse check, retention, or productivity?) and seeing which method best predicts business results. Having internal case studies that specifically demonstrate which HR data influence business success builds credibility for the entire Scorecard process.

Maintain Investment in the Scorecard

Once they establish the HR Scorecard, the initiative team should remain intact. As the company continues to use the Scorecard, these team members will need to continue to update and modify it. In addition, the firm should make regular investments, in the form of data collection, people, and money in order to ensure that the Scorecard remains robust, up to date, and relevant.

Integrate the Scorecard with Other Work

The Balanced Scorecard works because it measures all the dimensions relevant to a firm's success. Likewise, the HR Scorecard should be integrated with other measures of managerial success. To illustrate, a meeting in which participants examine the links among HR, customer, investor, and business process measures is far more valuable than one in which attendees focus only on HR measures. The more a company can integrate its HR Scorecard with existing and ongoing measurement efforts, the more sustainable the Scorecard will be.

Learn from Experience

With any change effort, you need to conduct periodic check-ups to examine what is and what is not working. Likewise, make a commitment to examine your HR Scorecard effort every six or twelve months. During these assessments, the Scorecard team should answer questions such as the following:

- What has worked in the HR Scorecard initiative to date?

- What hasn't worked? What explains any lack of success? Were data not available, not collected, not tied to results, not monitored, not part of existing management practices?

- What can we do differently, based on our experiences so far with this initiative?

As you address these questions on a regular basis, the HR Scorecard will become increasingly ingrained in the management process.

SUMMARY: DOING IT

HR Scorecards are not panaceas. They will not cure a poorly run HR function. However, they do provide a means by which you can collect rigorous, predictable, and regular data that will help direct your firm's attention to the most important elements of the HR architecture. Constructed thoughtfully, the HR Scorecard will help your organization deliver increased value to its employees, customers, and investors. By applying the seven steps we suggest in this chapter, you can integrate the thinking behind the HR Scorecard into every key aspect of your firm's management.

Our book has laid out the theory and tools for crafting an HR Scorecard. Using these ideas and tools will help HR professionals become full partners in their firms. While much of the work of an HR Scorecard is technical, the delivery of the Scorecard is personal. It requires that HR professionals desire to make a difference, *align* their work to business strategy, *apply* the science of research to the art of HR, and *commit* to learning from constant experimentation. When you create the HR Scorecard, using the approach we describe, you are actually *linking HR to firm performance*. But you will also develop a new perspective on your HR function, practices, and professional development. In measurement terms, the benefits will far outweigh the costs.

Appendix: Research and Results

THIS BOOK IS PREMISED ON the view that a firm's HR architecture has the potential to become a strategic asset with direct benefits for the bottom line. We argue that in addition to HR contribution to the overall quality of human capital, the basis of that strategic influence is through HR's alignment with the firm's strategy implementation process. Finally, we emphasize the importance of an appropriately focused measurement system to guide and evaluate this strategic HR role.

RESEARCH ON THE STRATEGIC IMPACT OF HR

Throughout the 1990s Mark Huselid and Brian Becker engaged in a program of research that had several defining features. First, it was premised on the importance of HR *systems* rather than individual HR practices. Second, it took as given that, for HR to be a strategic asset, those HR systems had to have a demonstrated influence on the measures that matter to CEOs, namely, firm profitability and shareholder value. By using measures of shareholder value, this research was also unique in that it focused on the level of the firm, as opposed to individual employees or work groups.

The foundation of this research effort has been an ongoing biannual survey of HR systems beginning in 1992 that targets a broad cross-section of publicly traded firms: firms with sales greater than $5 million and more than 100 employees. These data are then matched with publicly available information on financial performance. To date we have collected data on more than 2,800 respondents over the course of four surveys. While the response rate for these surveys was typical for such research, averaging nearly 20 percent, it's clear from table A-1 that our respondents were representative of the major industry groups in our target population.

As our understanding of the strategic influence of HR developed, so did the breadth and complexity of our measures of the HR system. The initial 1992 survey (focusing on the 1991 HR system) was limited to the fundamental elements of a professional, developed HR system designed to develop and maintain a high-performance workforce. These thirteen items measured the percentage of the workforce, both exempt and nonexempt, that was covered by such policies as validated selection procedures, promotion from within, annual performance appraisals, merit-based promotions, incentive pay plans, hours of training, and information sharing systems.[1]

This measure was broadened considerably for the 1994 and 1996 surveys, which were expanded to include the extent to which firms used different types of incentive compensation plans, the degree to which HR and business strategies were aligned, and how well the firm's strategy was communicated and understood throughout the firm. In addition, we collected indicators on other characteristics that might complement a High-Performance Work System (HPWS). These included the professional competencies within the HR function as reflected in their effectiveness across different functional activities, as well as senior leadership styles that emphasize motivation and vision, rather than command and control. Finally, in the 1998 survey, we focused on how two other systems that support strategy implementation

Table A-1 Industry Distribution of Firm Population and Research Sample

SIC Code	Short Industry Title	Weighted Average of Population	Weighted Average of Response
000–999	Agriculture, Forestry, Fishing	0.2	0.1
1000–1999	Mining and Construction	3.3	3.8
2000–2999	Mfg: Food, Tobacco, Chemicals, Printing	13.0	11.4
3000–3999	Mfg: Metal Industries, Industrial Equip., Elect., Transport	28.5	31.6
4000–4999	Transportation and Public Utilities	10.5	10.1
5000–5999	Wholesale and Retail Trade	12.5	10.6
6000–6999	Finance, Insurance, and Real Estate	18.0	19.0
7000–7999	Service Industries	8.9	8.3
8000–8999	Health, Legal, Social, and Engineering Services	5.3	5.2
9000–9999	Public Administration	0.0	0.0
Totals		100.0	100.0

(knowledge management and business performance measurement) might also leverage the influence of the HR strategy.

Each survey enabled us to construct an HPWS index that measures the extent to which a firm's HR system is consistent with the principles of a high-performance HR strategy. These indices are additive measures across the elements of the HR system. Thus, over the broad middle range of the index, a firm can increase its index value in any number of ways, depending on its circumstances. However, we have found evidence that the benefits of these systems increase as a firm improves its system across the board. This is consistent with the importance of internal fit within a systems framework. While changing survey formats have allowed us to explore variations in this index, the core elements supporting an HR strategy that emphasizes employee performance have remained constant. They also show a consistent relationship with other organizational outcomes and systems that would be part of a high-performance culture.

Consistent with our themes that systems matter and that successful strategy implementation requires the support of various intellectual capital systems, we find that firms scoring higher on our HPWS index are also rated higher on their usage of knowledge management systems and Balanced Scorecard–style business performance systems. Senior management in these high-performance firms likewise adopts a philosophy that supports this approach by viewing the organization's employees as a source of value creation. Finally, the firms in these two groups also differ on some objective benchmarks that we would anticipate to be related to the adoption of a High-Performance Work System. We find that firms in the high-performance group have much lower turnover rates and much lower levels of unionization. The average ratio of market to book value of equity is also more than twice as high in the group with High-Performance Work Systems.

Comprehensive Analysis of the Effects of HR on Firm Performance

Estimating the effects of HR systems on firm performance by comparing experiences across hundreds of firms is challenging for many of the same reasons it is difficult to measure these effects within a single firm. In both cases, it is difficult to isolate the independent effects of HR on the firm's financial performance given the multiple influences on firm performance at any point in time. In some respects, this is an easier task when comparing experiences across firms because, if one can measure those other influences, their impact on the HR-firm performance relationship can be controlled statistically. This is the approach we used in our research. We estimate the statistical relationship between a firm's HR system and firm performance, for firms of the same size and asset class, in the same industry, with the same historical growth rate, investment in R&D, unionization rate, and risk profile (beta).[2]

These estimates have been calculated over four different national samples through the 1990s. In each instance, we find very powerful support for a positive relationship between a High-Performance Work System and firm financial performance. Table A-2 provides a representative illustration of the magnitude of these effects across several outcome measures of interest. As an indicator of the *strategic* impact of HR, we believe the best reflection of this influence is the effect on shareholder value, or market-to-book value. The first two columns in table A-2 reflect different approaches to measuring such an effect. They indicate that if the average firm were to improve its HR system by 33 percent (one standard deviation), shareholder value would increase by approximately 20 percent. Though we believe the ultimate test of HR as a strategic asset is its relationship with shareholder value, it is also clear that these HR systems have beneficial effects on accounting profits, employee productivity, and turnover as well.

Table A-2   Effects of One Standard Deviation Increase in 24-Item HPWS Index[a]

	In Market Value	*In* Market Value/ Book Value	Gross Rate of Return on Assets	Sales per Employee	Turnover Rate
Percentage of effect of one standard deviation increase in the HR system index	24%***	17%***	25%**	4.8%*	−7.6%**

*** = p < .001, ** = p < .01, * = p < .05

[a]The model used to estimate these results includes as control variables: firm employment, percentage unionization, R&D expenses/sales, firm specific risk (beta), five-year percentage sales growth. When *In* Market Value or Gross Rate of Return is the dependent variable, *In* Book Value of the Plant and Equipment is an independent variable in the model.

Source: Brian E. Becker and Mark A. Huselid, "High Performance Work Systems and Firm Performance: A Synthesis of Research and Managerial Implications," in *Research in Personnel and Human Resources Management,* vol. 16 (Greenwich, CT: JAI Press, 1998), 53–101.

The Evolution of a High-Performance Strategy

While we have described HR systems as if they exist on a simple continuum, their character is obviously more complex. For example, do firms systematically emphasize certain elements of an HR system, and does this kind of emphasis have any effect on firm performance? In other words, if we believe that different HR systems will have different effects on firm performance, we ought to see some evidence that there are systematically different approaches to how firms structure their HR systems. If different HR systems are indeed present in our data, the next question is whether these different approaches have different effects on firm performance. Or, perhaps there are simply different approaches to the same objective, and no single High-Performance Work System really exists. These results are briefly summarized in chapter 1.

To examine this question, we compared our sample of firms on forty characteristics. Twenty-four of these characteristics focused specifically on the HR system (selection, appraisal, development, compensation, communication, etc.). Another sixteen measured other characteristics of the firm that would be expected to facilitate the implementation of a High-Performance Work System. These included the ability of HR professionals to effectively manage different elements of the HR system, the alignment between the HR system and larger firm strategy, the clarity and communication of the firm's mission, and the leadership style of the senior management. We describe these latter characteristics as *implementation alignment*.

Using a technique called cluster analysis, the firms in the sample were compared based on how they structured these forty characteristics into an overall HR strategy. This approach was appropriate, given our emphasis on the importance of systems. In effect, this type of analysis will indicate whether the firms in our sample can be categorized by the way in which they structure their HR architecture. We discovered four such systems, which are illustrated in figure A-1:

- *High-Performance Work Systems:* Firms in this group score well above average on both the HR system and implementation alignment dimensions.

- *Compensation-Based Systems:* Firms in this group score above average on the HR system index but below average on implementation alignment. We refer to this group as compensation-based because the only reason they score well on the HR system index is their very high ratings on the compensation dimensions.

- *Alignment Systems:* These are an unusual set of firms. They are slightly above average on implementation alignment, but they score among the lowest on the HR system. These firms approach strategic HR from the top down but don't finish the job. Senior managers say the right things, and HR is considered to be part of the strategic planning process, but managers have never made the investment in the infrastructure of a High-Performance Work System.

- *Personnel Systems:* These firms are characterized by scores that are well below average on both the HR system and implementation alignment dimensions. Such organizations approach their HR systems in a very traditional way and appear to make no effort to exploit HR as a strategic asset.

Does it matter which HR architecture a firm adopts? Are there any differences in firm performance among these firms? The data show very clearly that there are. Controlling for other firm and industry characteristics, a firm pursuing a High-Performance strategy had a 65 percent higher market value (for a given book value) than a firm using either the Personnel or Alignment strategy. Firms using only the Compensation

Figure A-1   Typologies of HR Architectures

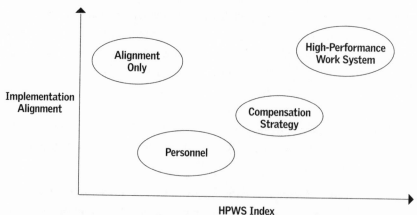

strategy had a 39 percent higher market value than similar firms using the Personnel strategy. There was no statistically significant difference between the experience of firms using the Alignment strategy and the Personnel strategies.

MORE RECENT RESEARCH ON
THE FINANCIAL IMPACT OF HRM

In this section, we highlight several key findings from the most recent survey by Mark Huselid and Brian Becker. These results are summarized in figure 2-5 in chapter 2 and describe a pattern of relationships among several intangible assets that are influenced by the HR architecture and strategically focused measurement systems.[3]

We can summarize the results of this study as follows:

- Strategy implementation is more important than strategy content. A 35 percent improvement in the quality of strategy implementation, for the average firm, was associated with a 30 percent improvement in shareholder value. A similar improvement in the suitability of the strategy itself had no effect on firm performance.

- Strategy implementation has three drivers: employee strategic focus, HR strategic alignment, and effective knowledge management. HR strategic alignment and the knowledge management system also drive employee strategic focus.

- A balanced performance management system affects firm performance through its impact on employee strategic focus, which in turn drives effective strategy implementation.

In addition to the effects that drive the strategy implementation process, Becker and Huselid have focused specifically on the relationship between the High-Performance Work System described in chapters 1 and 2 and shareholder value in earlier studies. Our results indicate that for the average firm, a 35 percent improvement in our high-performance HR index is associated with just over a 20 percent increase in shareholder value. These findings are part of a larger research literature demonstrating HR's impact on firm performance.[4]

We analyzed employee strategic focus as a response to three underlying management systems, looking specifically at the following relationships:

- the extent to which a firm has aligned its HR system with the demands of the *strategy implementation process*;

- the presence of a comprehensive *knowledge management system* that both generates and effectively distributes knowledge throughout the firm; and

- the presence of a *business performance measurement system* that reflects both the leading and lagging indicators of successful strategy implementation.

Our data show that each of the three systems would have to be improved by 50 percent to realize the gains from employee strategic focus described earlier. In short, there are ample economic rewards associated with superior human capital management, but there are no quick fixes. Developing such an approach requires a systematic method and commitment to the long-run development of people.

Notes

FOREWORD

1. Robert S. Kaplan and David P. Norton, "The Balanced Scorecard—Measures That Drive Performance," *Harvard Business Review* 70, no. 1 (January–February 1992): 71–79.

CHAPTER 1

1. Raphael Amit and Paul J. H. Shoemaker, "Strategic Assets and Organizational Rents," *Strategic Management Journal* 14 (1993): 33–46.
2. Steven P. Kirn, Anthony J. Rucci, Mark A. Huselid, and Brian E. Becker, "Strategic Human Resource Management at Sears," *Human Resource Management* 38, no. 4: 329–336; and Anthony J. Rucci, Steven P. Kirn, and Richard T. Quinn, "The Employee-Customer-Profit Chain at Sears," *Harvard Business Review* 76, no. 1 (January–February 1998): pp. 82–97.
3. Rucci, Kirn, and Quinn, "The Employee-Customer-Profit Chain at Sears," 89.
4. Robert McLean, *Performance Measures in the New Economy* (The Premier's Council of Ontario, Ontario Canada, 1995), 3.
5. Thomas Stewart, "Real Assets, Unreal Reporting," *Fortune*, 6 July 1998, 207.
6. Lawrence R. Whitman, GTE Corporation, from a transcript of an interview conducted by GTE employees for an article in *CFO* magazine, which was provided to the authors of this book.
7. J. R. Morris, W. F. Cascio, and C. E. Young. "Downsizing after All These Years: Questions and Answers about Who Did It, How Many Did It, and Who Benefited from It," *Organizational Dynamics* 27, no. 3 (Winter 1999): 78–87.
8. For further discussion of the concept of an HR Architecture, see Mark A. Huselid and Brian E. Becker, "The Strategic Impact of High Performance Work Systems," paper presented at the Academy of Management Annual Meeting, 1995; and Brian Becker and Mark Huselid, "High Performance Work Systems and Firm Performance: A Synthesis of Research and Managerial Implications,"

Research in Personnel and Human Resources Management, vol. 16 (Greenwich, CT: JAI Press, 1998), 53–101.

9. Mark A. Huselid, Susan E. Jackson, and Randall S. Schuler, "Technical and Strategic Human Resource Management Effectiveness as Determinants of Firm Performance," *Academy of Management Journal* 40, no. 1 (1997): 171–188.

10. The fifth wave of this study is being conducted as of this writing (Summer 2000).

11. Our entire research program is described in more detail in the appendix and in Becker and Huselid, "High Performance Work Systems and Firm Performance."

12. Robert S. Kaplan and David P. Norton, "Having Trouble with Your Strategy? Then Map It," *Harvard Business Review* 78, no. 5 (September–October 2000): 167–176.

13. Robert S. Kaplan and David P. Norton, *The Balanced Scorecard: Translating Strategy into Action* (Boston, MA: Harvard Business School Press, 1996).

14. Gary Hamel and C. K. Prahalad. *Competing for the Future* (Boston, MA: Harvard Business School Press, 1994), 11.

15. Kaplan and Norton, *The Balanced Scorecard*, 144–145.

CHAPTER 2

1. Anthony J. Rucci, Steven P. Kirn, and Richard T. Quinn, "The Employee-Customer-Profit Chain at Sears," *Harvard Business Review* 76, no. 1 (1998): 90.

2. Ibid., 91.

3. Robert S. Kaplan and David P. Norton, *The Balanced Scorecard: Translating Strategy into Action* (Boston, MA: Harvard Business School Press, 1996).

4. A more detailed description of the Quantum experience is available in Deborah Barber, Mark A. Huselid, and Brian E. Becker, "Strategic Human Resources Management at Quantum," *Human Resources Management* 38, no. 4 (Winter 1999): 321–328.

5. Robert S. Kaplan and Nicole Tempest, "Wells Fargo Online Financial Services (A)," Case 9-198-146 (Boston, MA: Harvard Business School, 1998, rev. 1999); and Robert S. Kaplan and Nicole Tempest, "Wells Fargo Online Financial Services (B)," Case 9-199-019 (Boston, MA: Harvard Business School, 1998).

6. These results are part of an ongoing research program by Mark Huselid and Brian Becker linking HR to firm performance.

7. This research also supports the fundamental premise of the new work by Robert Kaplan and David Norton, *The Strategy-Focused Organization* (Boston: Harvard Business School Press, 2000).

8. Michael E. Porter, *Competitive Advantage: Creating and Sustaining Superior Performance* (New York: The Free Press, 1985).

9. Robert S. Kaplan and David P. Norton, "Having Trouble with Your Strategy? Then Map It," *Harvard Business Review* 78, no. 5 (September–October 2000): 167–176.

10. Garrett Walker, HR director, GTE Corporation, interview by author (Brian Becker) August 2000; and George Donnelly, "Recruiting, Retention and Returns," *CFO* 16 (March 2000): 68–73.

CHAPTER 3

1. Jeffrey Pfeffer, *Competitive Advantage through People: Unleashing the Power of the Workforce* (Boston, MA: Harvard Business School Press, 1994).
2. For further work on efficiency and effectiveness metrics, see also Jac Fitz-enz, *How to Measure Human Resources Management* (New York: McGraw-Hill, 1995), and Dave Ulrich, "Measuring Human Resources: An Overview of Practice and a Prescription for Results," *Human Resource Management* 36, no. 4 (1997): 303–320.
3. Dave Ulrich and Dale Lake, *Organizational Capabilities* (New York: John Wiley & Sons, 1990).
4. See also Ulrich, *Measuring Human Resources*.
5. Dave Ulrich, *Human Resource Champions: The Next Agenda for Adding Value and Delivering Results* (Boston, MA: Harvard Business School Press, 1997).

CHAPTER 4

1. See Wayne F. Cascio, *Costing Human Resources: The Financial Impact of Behavior in Organizations*, 4th ed. (Boston, MA: PWS-Kent Publishing, 2000), for a series of detailed examples.
2. This question has received a considerable amount of attention in the field of utility analysis. For seminal contributions, see F. L. Schmidt, J. E. Hunter, and T. W. Muldrow, "Impact of Valid Selection Procedures on Work-Force Productivity," *Journal of Applied Psychology* 64 (1979): 609–626; and John Boudreau, "Utility Analysis in Human Resource Management Decisions," in *Handbook of Industrial and Organizational Psychology*, vol. 2, ed. M. D. Dunnette and L. M. Hough (Palo Alto, CA: Consulting Psychologists Press, 1991), 621–745.
3. Schmidt, Hunter, and Muldrow, "Impact of Valid Selection Procedures on Work-Force Productivity," and Boudreau, "Utility Analysis in Human Resource Management Decisions."
4. Thomas D. Cook and Donald T. Campbell, *Quasi-experimental Design and Analysis for Field Settings* (Boston, MA: Houghton-Mifflin, 1979).
5. A functionally equivalent procedure, known as the internal rate of return (IRR), discounts costs and benefits back into today's dollars, but solves for the *interest rate* yielded by the stream of cash flows less benefits. NPV analyses solve for the dollar value benefits of the investment.
6. See Cascio, *Costing Human Resources*.
7. Robert S. Kaplan and Robin Cooper, *Cost & Effect: Using Integrated Cost Systems to Drive Profitability and Performance* (Boston, MA: Harvard Business School Press, 1998).

CHAPTER 5

1. This famous quote is taken from Steve Kerr, "On the Folly of Rewarding A While Hoping for B," *Academy of Management Journal* 18 (December 1975): 769.
2. The relationships described in this analysis were based on more sophisticated and complex models than those included in our description. The purpose of these models was to rule out alternative explanations for the estimated effect of the Employee Engagement Index.
3. There are exceptions at the extremes. If product information availability and skills are very highly correlated, it becomes more difficult to isolate the separate effects of each.
4. Mark A. Huselid and Brian E. Becker, "An Interview with Mike Losey, Tony Rucci and Dave Ulrich: Three Experts Respond to HRMJ's Special Issue on HR Strategy in Five Leading Firms," *Human Resource Management* 38 (Winter 1999): 360.

CHAPTER 6

1. See also Jeffrey Pfeffer, *The Human Equation: Building Profits by Putting People First* (Boston: Harvard Business School Press, 1998), for a similar approach.
2. See R. N. Shepard, "Introduction," in *Multidimensional Scaling: Theory and Applications in the Behavioral Sciences*, vol. 1, ed. R. N. Shepard, A. Romney, and S. Nerlove (New York: Seminar Press, 1972), 1–20.
3. See J. Woelfel and E. Fink, *The Measurement of Communication Processes: Galileo Theory and Method* (New York: Academic Press, 1980); and J. Woelfel and J. E. Danes, "Multidimensional Scaling Models for Communications Research," in *Multivariate Techniques in Human Communications Research*, ed. P. R. Monge and J. N. Capella (New York: Academic Press, 1980), 333–364, for a discussion of the academic research surrounding Galileo. Perceptual maps have been widely used in marketing to understand consumer preferences and to guide advertising strategies (see J. Woelfel, *What's Wrong with This Picture? How to Spot a Bad Perceptual Map* [Amherst, NY: RAH Books, 1995]). We have adapted this technique to create perceptual maps of strategic alignment.
4. Woelfel, *What's Wrong with This Picture?*
5. See P. N. Johnson-Laird, *Mental Models: Towards a Cognitive Science of Language, Inference and Consciousness* (Cambridge, MA: Harvard University Press, 1983).
6. The strategic goals for this example are drawn from the experience of Mobil's North American Marketing and Refining Group. See Robert S. Kaplan, "Mobil USM&R (A): Linking the Balanced Scorecard," Case 9-197-025 (Boston, MA: Harvard Business School, 1996, rev. 1999), 16, exhibit 7.
7. The most complete description of the programs on which these figures are based is Joseph K. Woelfel, *Galileo CATPAC: User Manual and Tutorial* (Amherst, NY: The Galileo Company, 1990).

CHAPTER 7

1. A number of consulting firms have been instrumental in developing competence models for managerial behavior. In the 1930s, the Hay group worked to calculate how much to pay workers based on their demonstrated competence. Their model was built around know-how, accountability, and problem solving. Building on work by Dave McClelland, the McBer consulting firm has been instrumental in creating and propagating competency models. Much of this work is summarized in R. E. Boyatzis, *The Competent Manager* (New York: Wiley, 1982).

2. Arthur Yeung, Patricia Woolcock, and John Sullivan, "Identifying and Developing HR Competencies for the Future: Keys to Sustaining the Transformation of HR Functions," *Human Resource Planning* 19 (Spring 1996): 48–58.

3. IBM and Towers Perrin, *Priorities for Competitive Advantage* (New York: IBM and Towers Perrin, 1991).

4. Stephen C. Schoonover, *Competencies for the Year 2000: The Wake Up Call!* (Washington, D.C.: SHRM Foundation, 1998).

5. Dave Ulrich, Wayne Brockbank, Arthur Yeung, and Dale Lake, "Human Resource Competencies: An Empirical Assessment," *Human Resource Management* 34 (Winter 1995): 473–495.

6. Ibid.

7. Ibid.

8. Connie James worked as project manager for the third round of data collection. Her conceptual and project management work is acknowledged and much appreciated.

9. John P. Kotter and James L. Heskett, *Corporate Culture and Performance* (New York: Free Press, 1992).

10. Ulrich, Brockbank, Yeung, and Lake, "Human Resource Competencies."

11. Dave Ulrich and Robert Eichinger, "Delivering with an Attitude," *HR Magazine* 43 (June 1998): 154–160.

12. Todd D. Jick, "Mixing Qualitative and Quantitative Methods: Triangulation in Action," *Administrative Science Quarterly* 24, no. 4 (1979): 602–611.

13. Wayne Brockbank, Dave Ulrich, and Dick Beatty, "HR Professional Development: Creating the Future Creators at the University of Michigan Business School," *Human Resource Management* 38 (Summer 1999): 111–117.

CHAPTER 8

1. P. M. Senge, A. Kleiner, C. Roberts, R. Ross, G. Rother, and B. Smith, *The Dance of Change: The Challenges of Sustaining Momentum in Learning Organizations* (New York: Currency Doubleday, 1999).

2. Ron Ashkenas, "Beyond the Fads: How Leaders Drive Change with Results," *Human Resource Planning* 17, no. 2 (1994): 25–44.

3. James Champy, *Reengineering Management: The New Mandate for Leadership* (New York: Harper Business, 1995).

4. Jeffrey Pfeffer and Robert I. Sutton, *The Knowing-Doing Gap* (Boston: Harvard Business School Press, 2000).

5. See Douglas Smith, *Taking Charge of Change: Ten Principles for Managing People and Performance* (Reading, MA: Addison Wesley, 1996); John Kotter, *Leading Change* (Boston, MA: Harvard Business School Press, 1996); and Michael Beer, Russell Eisenstat, and Bert Spector, "Why Change Programs Don't Produce Change," *Harvard Business Review* 68, no. 6 (November–December 1990): 158–166.

6. Dave Ulrich, *Human Resource Champions* (Boston, MA: Harvard Business School Press, 1997).

7. This design team included Steve Kerr, Dave Ulrich, Craig Schneier, Jon Biel, Ron Gager, and Mary Anne Devanna (outsiders to GE) and Jacquie Vierling, Cathy Friarson, and Amy Howard (GE employees).

8. This material has been adapted from Ulrich, *Human Resource Champions*, chapter 6.

9. Garrett Walker, Director HR Strategic Performance Management, GTE, telephone interview with author (Mark Huselid), August 2000.

10. Ibid.

11. G.R. Salancik, "Commitment and the Control of Organizational Behavior and Belief," in *New Directions in Organizational Behavior*, ed. B. M. Staw and G. R. Salancik (Malabar, FL: Robert E. Drieger, 1977): 1–54; B. M. Staw and J. Ross, "Commitment to a Policy Decision: A Multi-Theoretical Perspective," *Administrative Science Quarterly* 23 (1978): 40–64; B. M. Staw and J. Ross, "Understanding Escalation Situations: Antecedents, Prototypes, and Solutions," in *Research in Organizational Behavior*, vol. 9, ed. B. M. Staw and L. L. Cummings (Greenwich, CT: JAI Press, 1987); B. M. Staw, "The Experimenting Organization," *Organizational Dynamics* 6 (1977): 2–18; B. M. Staw, "Knee-Deep in the Big Muddy: A Study of Escalating Commitment to a Chosen Course of Action," *Organizational Behavior and Human Performance* 16 (1976): 27–44.

12. Garrett Walker, interview by author.

13. Ibid.

14. Learning Map is a trademark of Root Learning, Inc. of Perrysburg, Ohio. Learning Map products are solely owned by Root Learning and cannot be reproduced or modified in any form without the company's express written permission.

15. Anthony J. Rucci, Steven P. Kirn, and Richard T. Quinn, "The Employee-Customer-Profit Chain at Sears," *Harvard Business Review* 76, 1 (January–February 1998): 95.

APPENDIX

1. Our entire research program is described in more detail in Brian Becker and Mark Huselid, "High Performance Work Systems and Firm Performance: A Synthesis of Research and Managerial Implications," in *Research in Personnel and Human Resources Management*, vol. 16, ed. Gerald R. Ferris (Greenwich,

CT: JAI Press, 1998), 53–101. See also Mark A. Huselid, "The Impact of Human Resource Management Practices on Turnover, Productivity, and Corporate Financial Performance," *Academy of Management Journal* 38 (1995): 635–672.

2. We have also tested several specific alternative explanations for our results. One possibility is reverse causation. For example it might be that more profitable firms were more likely to develop such policies because only these firms could afford to do so. Another possibility is that the results are due to the nature of the firms responding to our survey. Huselid (in "The Impact of Human Resource Management Practices") found no support for these hypotheses.

3. Firm performance is measured as the ratio of market value to book value of shareholder equity. These relationships are part of a broader model performance that includes industry, prior sales growth, size, investment in R&D, and unionization.

4. Over the past decade there has been a virtual explosion of interest in this topic, with scores of studies having been conducted in the United States, Canada, the United Kingdom, Germany, France, Hong Kong, Singapore, and Japan. Taken as a whole, the new body of research also supports the basic assertion that "HR matters." Interested readers can contact Mark Huselid for a bibliography.

Index

accounting systems
    role of, in cost-benefit analyses, 85
    in valuing tangible and intangible
        assets, 10–11
actionable value, 121
activity-based costing, 102
administrative costs, 104–105
Amaco, 177–178
Amazon.com, 8
Argyris, Chris, 159, 180
Ashkenas, Ron, 184
attribute measures, 112–113, 114
automotive industry, cost-benefit
        analysis in, 85

Balanced Scorecard. *See also* HR
    Scorecard
    of GTE, 44, 45–46, 48
    nature of, 21, 23–24, 204
Balanced Scorecard, The (Kaplan and
    Norton), 29
Barney, Jay B., 97
Beatty, Richard, 180
Becker, Brian E., 90, 207, 213
Beer, Michael, 185
behavior
    assessing HR management, 175–176.
        See also HR competency

strategic employee, 20. *See also*
        employee performance
Bell Atlantic, 199
benchmarking
    in analyzing HR management
        system, 96–97
    HR measurement principles of, 111,
        113–114
    in HR system misalignment, 138
    in measuring HR efficiency, 65–66
bonuses. *See* incentive programs
breakeven volume, 92
Brockbank, Wayne, 157, 180
business performance. *See* firm perform-
        ance; HR-firm performance
        measurement

causal flow, 28–29, 168
causal relationships
    estimating, 168–169
    measuring, 120–122
        GTE in, 122–123
        Sears in, 123–124
CEOs. *See* leadership; management (firm)
    champions
        defined, 190–191
        role of, in leading change, 189,
        191–193, 202

223

About the Authors

Brian Becker is Professor of Human Resources and Chairman of the Department of Organization and Human Resources in the School of Management at the State University of New York at Buffalo. Professor Becker has published widely on the financial effects of employment systems in both union and nonunion organizations. His current research and consulting interests focus on the relationships between human resources systems, strategy implementation, and firm performance.

Mark Huselid is Associate Professor of HR Strategy in the School of Management and Labor Relations (SMLR) at Rutgers University. His research focuses on the linkages between human resource management systems, corporate strategy, and firm performance, and has earned him numerous professional awards. Professor Huselid is Editor of the *Human Resources Management Journal* and consults widely in measurement and human resources strategy.

Dave Ulrich is Professor of Business at the University of Michigan. He has published numerous books and articles on human resource and organization issues. He consults widely with many firms on building leadership brand, creating organizational capability, ensuring speed, developing a shared mind-set, and shaping an HR agenda. He has received lifetime contribution awards from five professional associations and has served on a number of editorial boards.